MW00632618

A SENSE OF PLACE

"A good beginning makes a good ending."

I know you will enjoy this book as a Reference guide for your journey thru Scotland.

Merry Christmas!

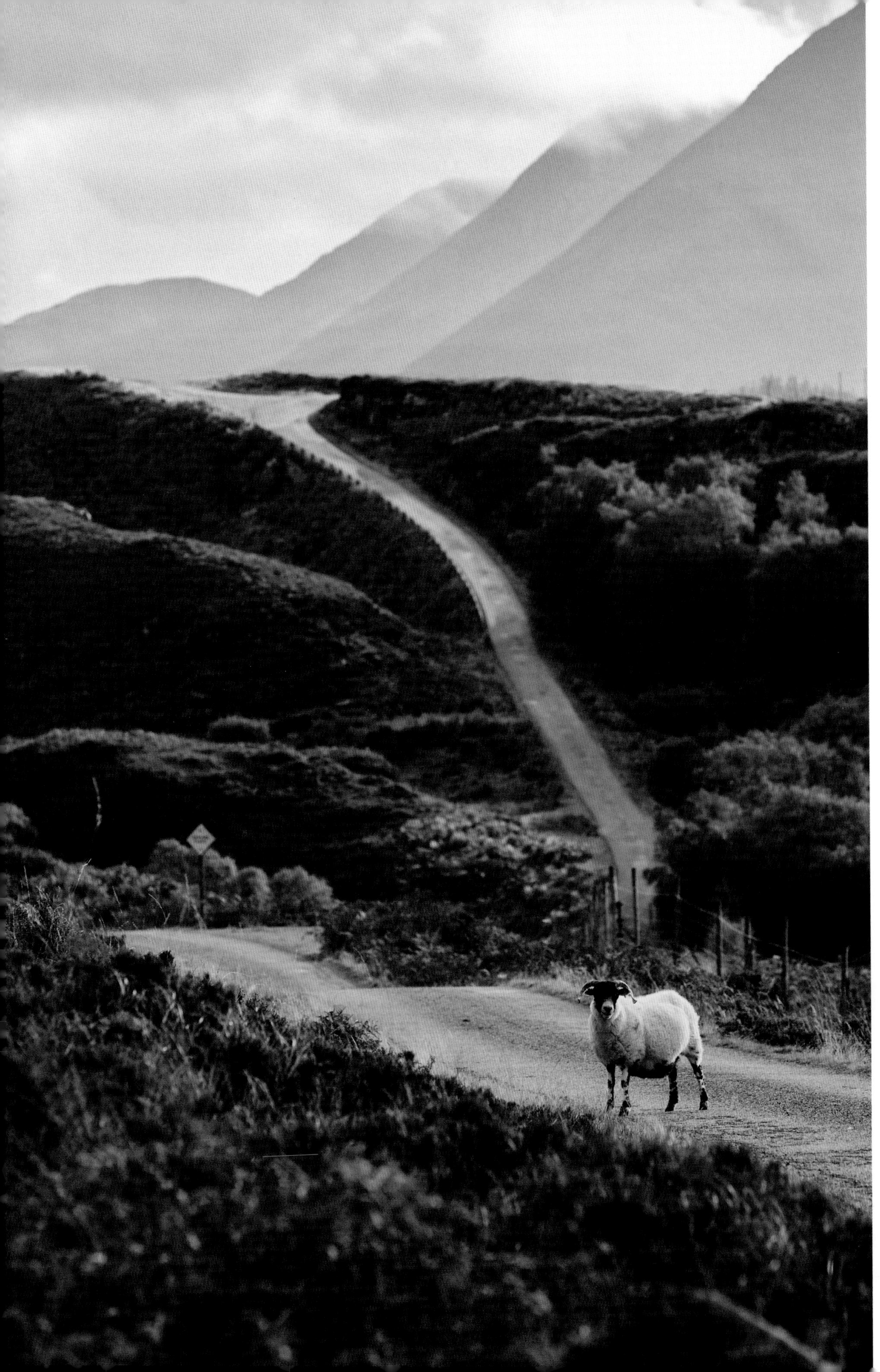

A SENSE OF PLACE

A journey around Scotland's whisky

Dave Broom

Photography by Christina Kernohan

Mitchell Beazley

First published in Great Britain in 2022
by Mitchell Beazley, an imprint of
Octopus Publishing Group Ltd
Carmelite House
50 Victoria Embankment
London EC4Y 0DZ
www.octopusbooks.co.uk
www.octopusbooksusa.com

An Hachette UK Company
www.hachette.co.uk

Distributed in the US by
Hachette Book Group
1290 Avenue of the Americas
4th and 5th Floors
New York, NY 10104

Distributed in Canada by
Canadian Manda Group
664 Annette St.
Toronto, Ontario, Canada M6S 2C8

ISBN 978-1-78472-671-3

A CIP catalogue record for this book is available from the British Library.

Printed and bound in China

10 9 8 7 6 5 4 3 2 1

Staff credits:
Group Publisher: Denise Bates
Art Director: Juliette Norsworthy
Senior Editor: Faye Robson
Copy Editor: Laura Gladwin
Senior Production Manager: Katherine Hockley

Design: Praline (Al Rodger, Max Casey, David Tanguy)

Dedication

Dedicated to the memory of Carl Reavey and the long conversations in which many of the seeds of this book were sown; and also to my old friend, sailing companion and partner in drams Charles MacLean MBE, who was the most convivial and generous host to this weary traveller during the long gestation of this project.

Introduction

Scotch whisky. A drink named after the country of its birth. The flavours of each of its distilleries are defined by location. This place, this flavour, this individuality. Place has always sat within whisky, but how deep does it go? Is the talk of it being important contrived, or is it real? What does location mean in terms of flavour, how does a distillery fit into a community, how does place impact on sustainability? With 140 distilleries operational in Scotland, will place become more significant? Where is whisky in the Anthropocene, how might it change and what role does place have in that transition?

These questions had been rattling around my brain for years. It was time to find the answers. There was only one way to do this: go on the road. Travel from north to south, go from the Neolithic past to the present...and peek into the future. Gauge the temperature.

At this point, it might be useful to say what this book isn't. It's not a guide to every distillery, nor is it a book of tasting notes. There are great titles out there that do that. This is less of a journey along that very busy main highway and more of a drive through the side roads that, hopefully, will give you a new and different view.

The distilleries were picked because they all showed different facets of this idea of place. They are large and small, old and new. There are many others that could have been included. Find them.

Whisky can be written about in many ways, but over the years the aspect that has intrigued me the most is seeing it as a cultural product. It can be a way of looking at a country: its history, people, stories and thinking. Scotch whisky is a distillation of these sensibilities and conditions and can only be made here.

Some of these thoughts became the film *The Amber Light,* which I made with Adam Park. This isn't the book of the film, but the idea of looking at Scotch as a reflection of culture is shared by both.

Making the film was the first time I met Christina Kernohan, who was doing the stills photography – while eight months pregnant. When the idea for this book came about, she was the only photographer I wanted to work with. Thankfully, she said yes. I'm in awe of her eye, her lunging ability, her ability to make people relax. She was the ideal travelling companion. This book is a joint enterprise.

It was also important to step back from the whisky world, so we met with craftspeople, farmers, a genealogist and a perfumer. Their stories and insights gave a deeper understanding of whisky's relationship to location and the way in which it is more than just a liquid in a bottle.

What did I find out? Read on...

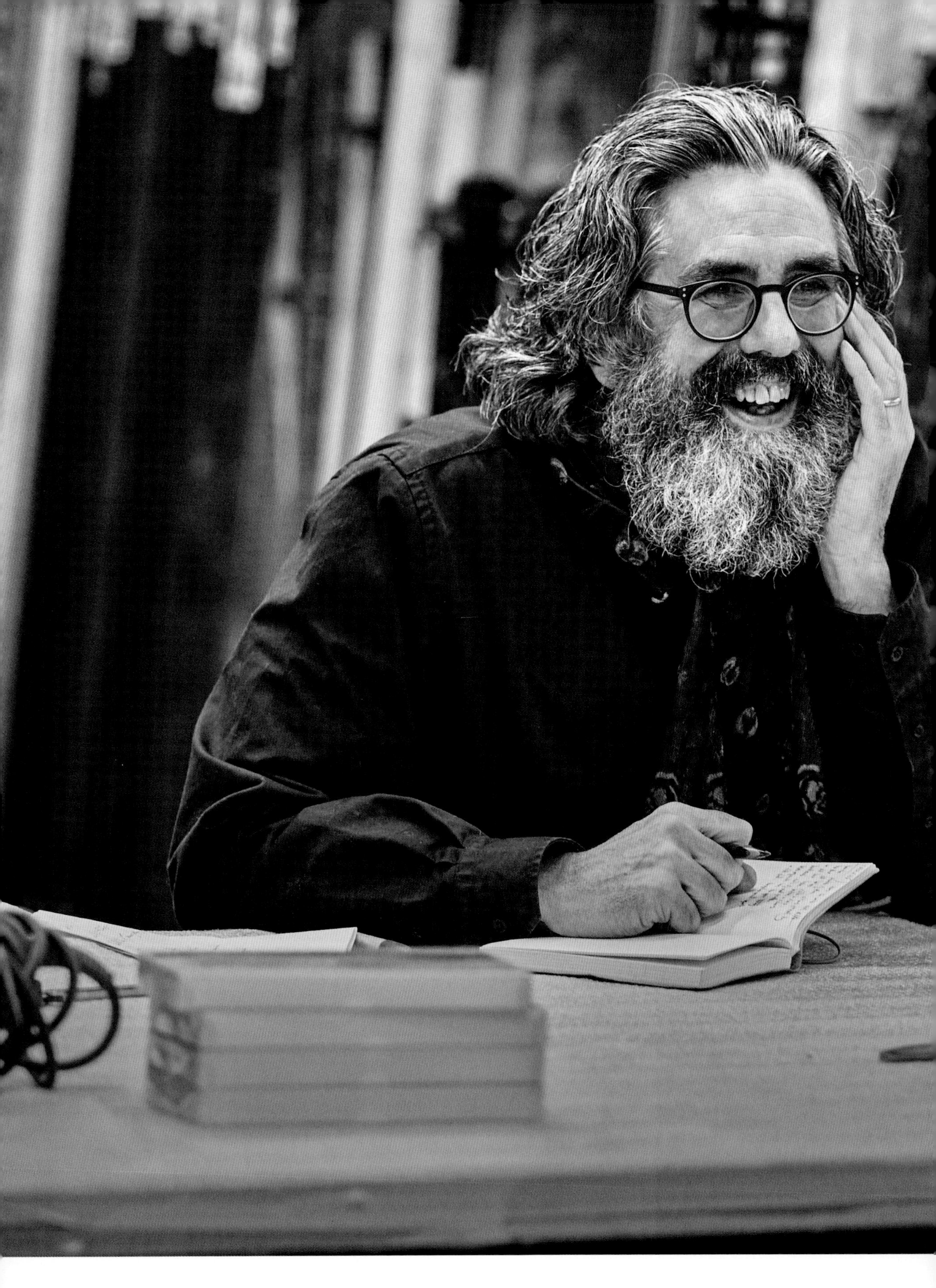

The author, snapped sneakily by the photographer without his knowledge (or permission)

ORKNEY

1

It has to start somewhere. Not only this journey, but the whole idea of taking a cereal, turning it into weak alcohol, then strengthening it through distillation to make it more than just a drink – by releasing an element within it that says: 'this is from here, this is from us, it is distillation of our sensibilities.' But we jump ahead.

The plane starts its descent through June clouds into Kirkwall airport. A flash of green, a wrecked ship, a beach, then we're down. This place of headlands and sea, of skies and low hills, thick stone walls and scant tree cover, a scattering of sandstone and fertile soil in the northern ocean, is a bulwark battered by the Pentland Firth, Atlantic and North Sea. All of this made Orkney the right starting point for this journey – the best way to establish conditions.

'The common conception of evolution is that of competing species running a sort of race through time on planet earth, all running on the same field...[but] if we look at this from the side of the "conditions" and their creative possibilities, we can see the multitudes of interactions through hundreds of other eyes,' the poet and essayist Gary Snyder wrote in his commentary on Dōgen's *Mountains and Waters Sutra*.

'We could say that a food brings a form into existence: huckleberries call for bear, the clouds of plankton call for salmon, and salmon call for orca and seal...Us? The whole of the earth calls us into existence. The condition dictates the response.'

Scotland's geology and climatic conditions called barley into

The Ness of Brodgar site has hugely complex archaeology

existence, and barley made people settle down and start farming. The barley gave bread, then beer and, finally, it called whisky into existence. Who were they, those first people?

...

Tyres and plastic cover parts of the trenches, visitors wander around. Archaeologists sit, squat, kneel, probe, write, gently clean, their trowels sifting through light soil. Heads down, they sit among neat, sandy-coloured dry-stone walls; not a single long-buried building, but an entire settlement, which they are reading, layer by layer.

We are on a thin neck of land that links the Stones of Stenness and the larger Ring of Brodgar. The brackish water of the Loch of Stenness is on one side, the fresh water of Loch of Harray on the other. A liminal place. Nick Card of the UHI Archaeology Institute, chair of the Ness of Brodgar Trust and director of the dig (see page 18), joins us, trowel in back pocket.

'You can sense its importance when you see its place in the landscape,' he says. 'We're in the middle of a large natural amphitheatre created by the distant hills, with the Ness as its focal point sandwiched between the two bodies of water. You feel central to the whole landscape. I think that's why the Neolithic people chose this place.'

The scale is hard to comprehend and, as Nick tells us, what has been uncovered so far accounts for less than ten per cent of the site. 'We are standing on top of 1.5 metres of archaeology,' he explains. 'At the top of the site it can be 4–5 metres, spanning the whole of the Neolithic, from 3500BCE to 2300BCE.

'We're trying to understand some of the most complex archaeology you will find anywhere. This is one of the most remarkable complexes of Neolithic buildings anywhere in north-west Europe. As they say about Orkney, when you scratch the surface, it bleeds archaeology.'

In 1999, the Heart of Neolithic Orkney was designated a UNESCO World Heritage Site, which led, in 2002, to a geophysics survey that revealed 2.5 hectares of possible settlement here, at the southern end of the Ness. When a large notched stone was uncovered in 2003 by a farmer ploughing, just scratching the surface, the first of a series of buildings was revealed. What was thought to be a natural mound was in fact a series of hidden structures and midden piles. 'The scale and complexity of what has been discovered has changed the perception of the site, the monuments and the whole of Neolithic Orkney,' Nick tells us. 'In its heyday, the Ness was one of the epicentres of Neolithic culture in the UK.'

 Bere in the breeze

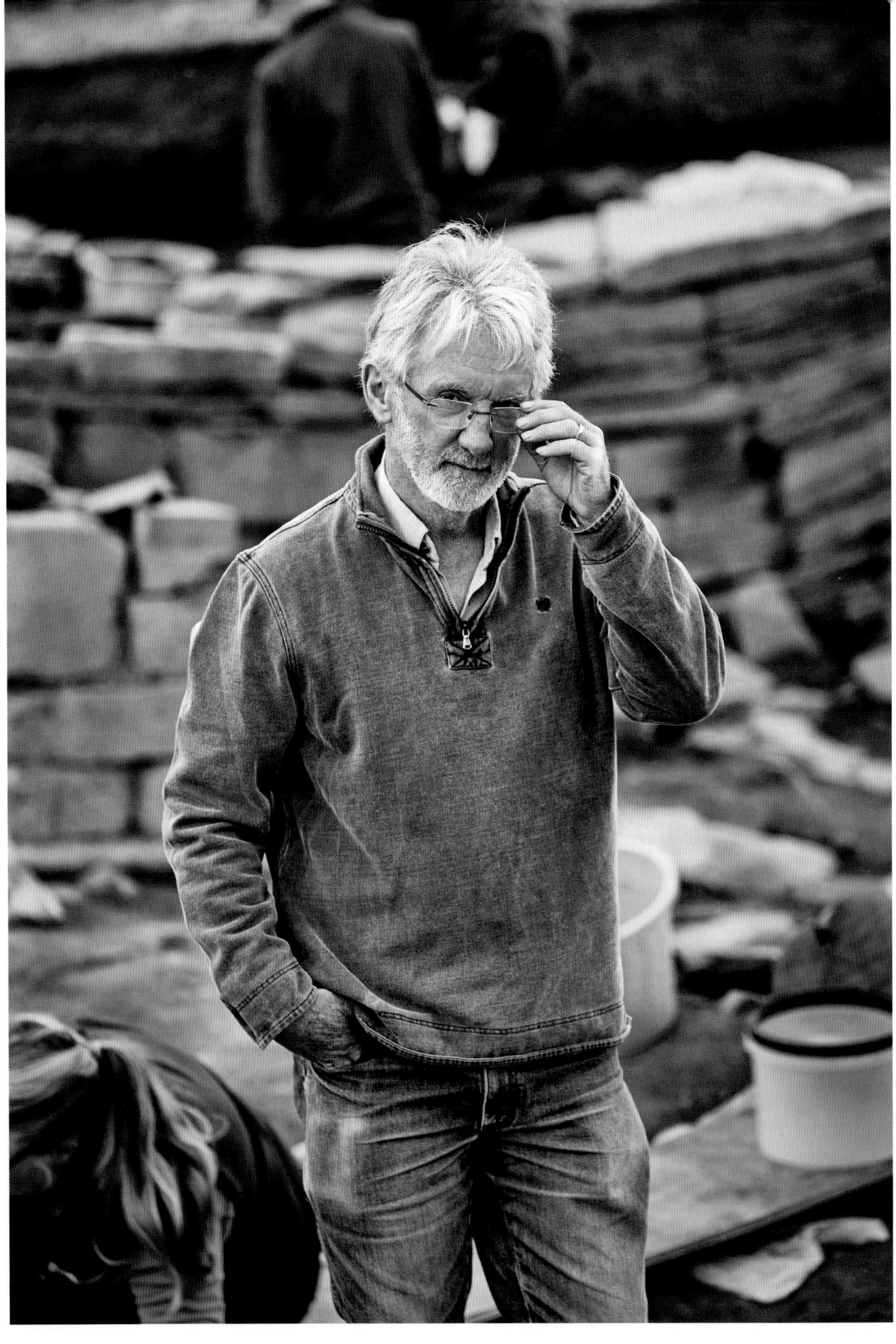

Nick Card, chair of the Ness of Brodgar Trust and director of the dig

It also gives a lie to the idea that these northern islands were only scantily populated. 'Thirty or forty years ago there were only three Neolithic settlements known in Orkney. Today, we have thirty settlement sites with more to be discovered, so we can estimate that the population was in many thousands – this land can support a sizeable population. Clearly there were enough people here to undertake building projects like this.'

The Neolithic age was when farming first began, and although it's still not known how it reached Britain and Ireland (or why it was considerably later than in Europe) it seems as if these proto-farmers arrived on Orcadian shores around 3700BCE.

Why here? 'It is down to the underlying geology,' Nick explains. 'Orkney has light, fertile soils, compared with Shetland. Here, it's relatively easy to cultivate crops and have animal husbandry. Red deer were probably brought here then. Imagine trying to navigate the Pentland Firth with deer or a cow on board!

'You'd be growing barley, probably a small amount of wheat, but still exploiting the wider natural landscape.'

Charred remains of naked and hulled barley, and of emmer, have been found at the Ness, but the scale of Orkney's ancient agriculture was only revealed fully with the discovery in 2006, at Ha'breck on the nearby island of Wyre, of a large, early Neolithic (3300–3000BCE) stone house. Inside were thick layers of tens of thousands of charred barley grains, the remnants of what was believed to have been a massive fire. The volume of debris suggests that this could have been a granary, conceivably for the adjacent islands.

We're looking into so-called Structure 10, its walls made from the flagstones of old red sandstone of the Orcadian bedrock, the blocks neatly shaped and aligned. This, the largest structure in the Ness, has further changed thinking about the life here at the time.

'Structure 10 is huge by any standards,' says Nick. 'When it was first built, it was probably the finest piece of Neolithic architecture in northern Europe. You can tell from the inside facing of the stones and the quality of the stonework with little imperfections being removed. They've been dressed, refined and in places decorated with incised and pecked art.

'The interior was a large central chamber and the walls were enhanced in different-coloured sandstone brought from quarries in Orphir – the same as you see in St Magnus Cathedral in Kirkwall. For the first time in British archaeology of this period, we've found the use of different pigments on the walls and pottery (some colours are derived from hematite found on Hoy). This monochrome image that you have of prehistory is transformed by thinking about these things in colour.'

The building and its decoration mark a shift from the simply functional to an underlying acknowledgment of permanence. The scale, the design, say: 'we are settled, we are here to stay'. They speak of a culture.

One of Nick's colleagues walks past, cradling a stone as if it were a child. It just looks like a large, flat, flagstone. 'It's that edge', he says, pointing. 'It seems worn, not natural. I was wondering if it might be for rubbing hides.' He makes the action. I wonder to myself if it could be for grinding barley, but wisely think better of saying anything. 'I suppose I must look a bit odd,' he smiles, clearly not caring that he does.

The evidence of the domestic humanizes these ancient people. While their stone circles remain enigmatic, here is the quotidian world – albeit one that existed 5,000 years ago. In a field nearby, cows start lowing, a tractor starts up. These Neolithic folk weren't that different from us. Orkney exists in a strange, constant present.

For 60 generations people ate, hunted and loved here. They clothed and raised children, traded, created, grew their crops. They started it all. Here's the bedrock.

As one building collapsed or was dismantled, its rubble was used as foundations or robbed to make the next structure. A layering of knowledge, a vertical passing on of information and understanding of not only how to survive, but also to prosper within a landscape.

The Ness is about the building of a community, the realization that, over time, we belong in this place, we eat what grows and lives here, we speak in this way, this is where we mark our presence. All of these are place, and where landscape and people interact, and art is made, culture arrives.

Like us, they would have talked and told stories, made music, drank, and feasted. Was there any evidence they also brewed? I ask tentatively, worried that Nick might think that everything I ask has whisky at its heart.

'There's no evidence of it yet,' he says, 'but with new technology we can look at the pottery and residues from the fabric of the pottery. We're about to enter a new project which is going to try and apply these new techniques. If that works, then we have a better chance of seeing how all of that is used. It would surprise me if they didn't brew beer...or take magic mushrooms. It's what we do as a species.'

Nick points to the exterior of Structure 10. 'There's a paved walkway running around it, and when the structure went out of use around 2350BCE, give or take a decade or two, there was this decommissioning event.

Evidence of a 5,000-year-old community

'In that outer passageway we came across hundreds of cattle bones. We recorded every one in 3D, and from that we found they were placed deliberately. In one part there were cattle skulls, covered in heaps of cattle tibia, and over the top of that were complete red deer carcasses. We found that 400–600 cattle had been killed at this time. It was a big gathering and celebration. The evidence for feasting, for mass consumption is quite incredible. Not just that big bone spread.

'In the next field are remnants of the largest midden mound, probably, in Neolithic Britain. Judging by the size, what they're trying to do is creating a monument out of this rubbish which is saying, "this is a reflection of what's happening here, this is what we can consume". It is a reflection of the Ness' status and significance.'

All of this, from everything we are standing among, to the dram in the glass, comes from someone, 5,000 years ago, deliberately planting a seed of barley here.

...

We're picked up at the Ness by John Strachan (see page 22), who rejoices in the title of Highland Park's 'senior visitor experience host'. He's a walking Viking: broad chested, long plaited beard, silver jewellery, a depth in his eyes. 'Jump in,' he says. 'Let's go to Stenness first.'

The Stones of Stenness form one of the UK's oldest stone circles. Four remain, the tallest six metres tall. Behind us is the dome of Maeshowe tomb; in front, the Ness dig and further on, the mighty Ring of Brodgar.

'My grandmother used to bring me here to tell me the old stories of the Norse gods,' says John as we wander towards the central hearth. 'She wanted to make sure that they didn't die with her. It's in the blood.'

He pauses, points at one tall stone and two smaller, round ones. 'Think this place might have something to do with fertility?' He laughs. 'In the last two censuses, Orkney was the most godless place in the UK. I think that's because we remember the old stories.

'I drive by these stones twice a day. We're aware of the importance of what society takes to be immutable, but we see things as impermanent. You build from your past, you're aware of it, how can you not be in this landscape, but we're not shackled to it.'

Back in the car, we drive west to the cliffs of Yesnaby. Their top is a 400 million-year-old seabed, now high above the Atlantic, the churns of ancient tides frozen in the stone, studded with the bulges of fossilized stromatolites. On the cliff face opposite are alternating strata of sandstone and flagstone: dun, beige, chocolate, ochre. Layer upon layer of time, each era a different shade.

The sun comes out, and the sea ignites into a deep azure. White waves curl around the skerries, whirl around the caves. 'Thor made these cliffs,' John says, as if the god of thunder was a neighbour. 'Carved them off with his hammer. Then he flung it into the sea. It's down there somewhere.'

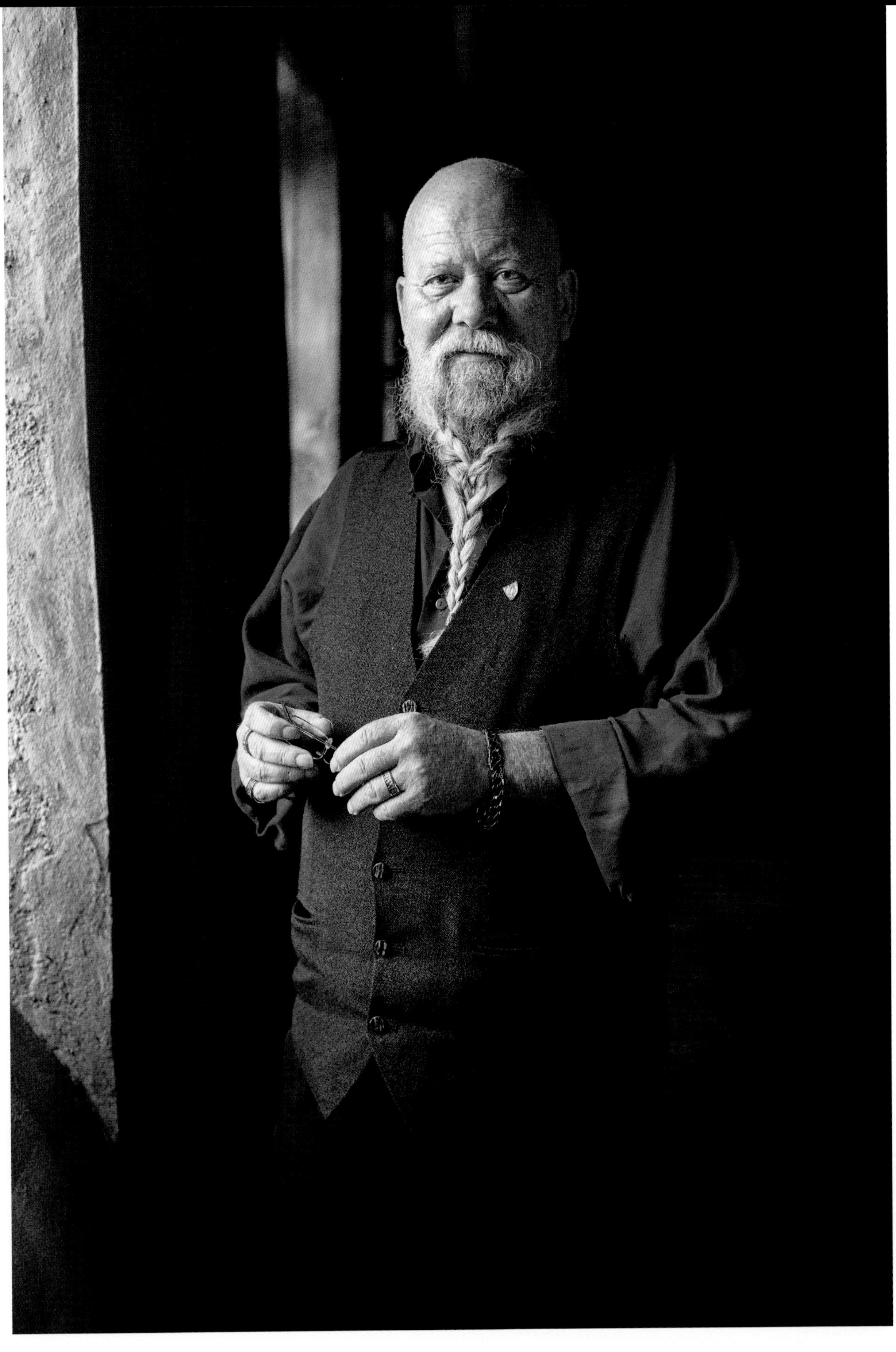

 John Strachan: guide, storyteller, Orcadian

That night, Christina and I, heads still spinning with time, go to Stromness to catch the light and try to find food.

A haar is lifting as we walk along the pier. The silvery light bounces off the sea, illuminating the low islands. Colours pop: blues, yellows and reds. A boat comes in, its skipper wrangling with a neon buoy. Gulls squabble with ducks, razorbills bob about. Opposite, a man stands under the red and yellow Scandinavian cross of the Orcadian flag, adding to the Nordic air.

Every house has its own pier, and both are made of stones the same colours we saw at Yesnaby, the same as those used to decorate the houses of the Ness.

The streets are silent, no sound but our footsteps and the skin slap of water. Orcadians don't appear to believe in pavements; the roads are a single surface of smooth flat slabs. Houses grow into each other, gable ends like prows of ships. A place that's thick with time.

At Login's Well, a plaque commemorates how Franklin, Cook and the Hudson's Bay Company all took on water and crew here. 'At its height, 75 per cent of the people working for the Hudson's Bay Company were Orcadian,' John had told us. Leif Eriksen started his voyage to America from here, as did Dr John Rae, the Orcadian doctor and great, but forgotten, Arctic explorer.

The strata of Yesnaby's cliffs

Orkney wasn't just a place to settle, but also one of transit, the fulcrum around which trade turned, be it Neolithic, Viking or later.

Scots are as guilty of parochialism as any nation, thinking Orkney and Shetland are the extent of the north, the upper limit. They aren't. Tromsø is almost 1,000 miles away, Svalbard another 400 further on.

Spin the map around, though, and Orkney sits at the heart of the northern world. Hub, haven and harbour. 'Orkney is different to the Western Isles,' John had said. 'There, people went abroad because they were kicked off their land. Orkney was never like that. You left to make your fortune, but then returned.' A place in the chain of trade and voyages, of beginnings and returns.

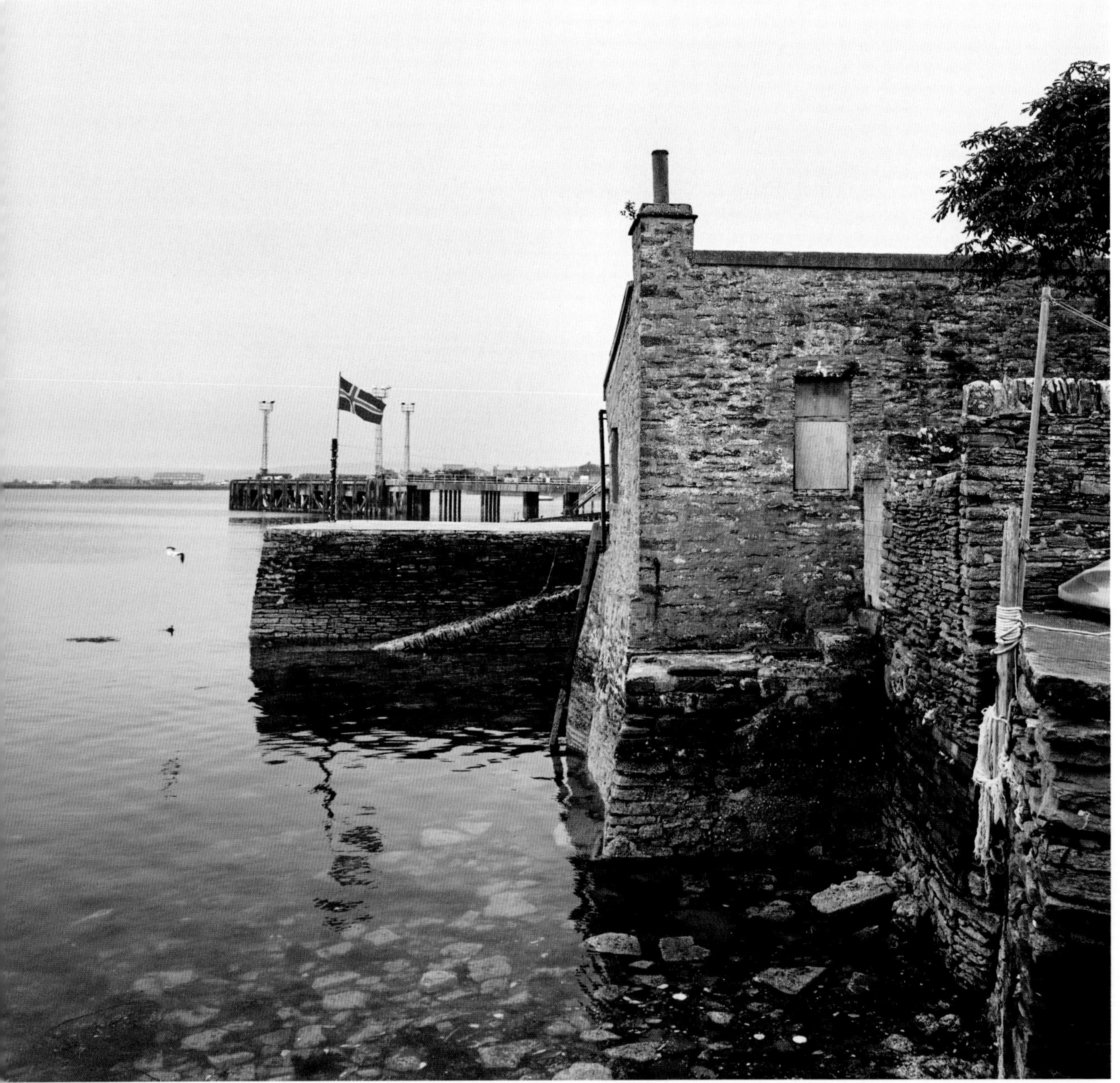

The Orcadian flag flies over Stromness harbour

FREE KIRK LANE

'It's like a pet.' He idly caresses the abrasive green awns (the bristles covering the grains) as he speaks. 'All the heads were up last week and it had this lovely silvery sheen when the sun hit it.' A wind blurs the field. The stalks are already almost at our waists. This is the green field we spotted from the plane. It belongs to the man speaking, John Wishart. The green is bere barley.

Barley has been the main cereal crop in the north since the Neolithic. Most of the early finds that Nick Card had mentioned have been of naked (i.e. hull-less) barley, with six-row, hulled barley such as bere becoming dominant in the Bronze Age. Bere is a landrace – a genetically diverse variety of a species (in this case barley), which over time has adapted to its environment and developed specific characteristics. Landraces are not the result of breeding but of natural processes. Along with small oat and Shetland cabbage, bere is one of the oldest agricultural plants growing in Scotland.

'We don't know how old bere is,' says Peter Martin, 'it's one of the ongoing research questions.' In the world of barley, Peter (see page 30) is Dr Bere. Director of UHI Orkney Agronomy Institute, he has been at the forefront of the preservation and the recent rise of interest in bere.

'There's a theory that it might have been brought here in Viking times, or been already in situ when they arrived – the Scottish strains of bere are different to those of Scandinavia.

'Another name for bere is "bigg", which is old Norse for barley, and six-row, hulled barley was the classical crop of Viking agriculture. Then again, if it was already here when the Vikings arrived they'd still have called it bigg! Most archaeologists think bere is probably older.'

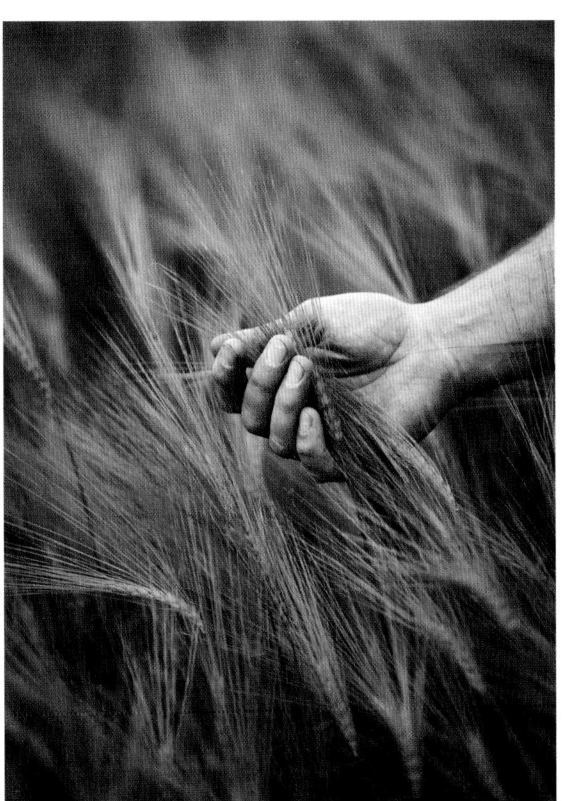

Why bere here? Conditions. It suited the acidic soil, became attuned to the climate. 'Compared to other British landraces, it came to maturity quicker. That's an adaptation to the very short, intense growing season we have here, and it's why it has a lower yield. Farmers plant oats first, then bere, but bere is the first to be harvested before the bad weather comes in. It fitted well into the traditional system.'

Opposite: Precious few drams up this way
Above: Bere barley: Scottish landrace

 Dr Peter Martin, aka Dr Bere

Across northern Scotland, oats were used for food, and bere for ale and, in time, whisky. The spirit's story starts with this cereal. Whisky was an agricultural product, which, in the north until the nineteenth century, was made by farmers.

This was the colour they would have seen, this the sound as it ripened. Bere helped them pay rent, raise spirits, inspire poetry and song, gave them their morning skailk. Bere kept them on the land.

Yet by the 1980s, fewer than 10 hectares were grown in Scotland – and most of that was on Orkney, where it was grown and milled at Barony Mill, Birsay. On any visit to Orkney, I'd buy a bag of flour and dutifully make the nutty, earthy-flavoured bannocks when I got home.

Bere wasn't suited to modern agricultural practices. It grows tall, gets knocked down by high winds and is hard to combine.

'It only survived here because we had a functioning mill, and local interest in keeping a few traditional products alive,' says Peter. 'In Shetland, where bere was still grown, there wasn't a commercial mill. Once you've used a hand-mill a few times the novelty wears off!'

The whisky industry had turned its back on bere by the end of the nineteenth century. New varieties, each one promising higher yields and easier harvesting, had begun appearing: Plumage Archer, Centurion, Golden Promise, Chariot, Oxbridge, Concerto, Sassy, a progression which continues to this day with exactly the same promises.

'When we started the Agronomy Institute in 2002, we drew up a list of crops we were interested in, and bere was at the top,' says Peter. 'What we aim to do is to develop cropping opportunities to help farmers and businesses, and we thought that bere had a lot of potential. Clearly there was also a heritage link with Orkney, and a connection between the Orcadian folk and bere, which gave it greater importance.

'In 2004, we managed to purchase some extra seed from the [Barony] mill and started to look for collaborators in the brewing and distilling industries – first Arran and then, more recently, Bruichladdich. When we started, we weren't aware of how important it had been to whisky.'

What started as a supply contract soon changed to growing for the Islay distillery and, 15 years in, 100 tons per year are being supplied. Orkney's Swannay brewery is also taking some, as is Sam Britton for his craft vinegar. The Barony Mill has also expanded its acreage.

New distillers, keen to have a point of difference – and also trying to find closer links to the land – are also beginning to look at bere again, but it does come with a higher price tag. 'Because you have lower yields you have to find end users who are willing to pay a premium,' says John Wishart. 'It wouldn't work with distillers who are trying to screw you down to the last penny. It suits someone who is willing to engage with the story and put it into a premium product.'

There is a deeper connection for him. 'Here, you'll have grown up with bere, you'll have had a bannock. It's part of being from here. To see on a big scale is satisfying, and to see it evolving into different areas shows there is merit to growing it. There's scope for farmers to grow more. As long as it is making money, they'd be happy to do it.' Bere is here because it is meant to be here, and as whisky begins to reconsider its past, so it re-emerges.

Modern varieties have been bred to give higher yields and are suited to the conditions of Scotland's east coast. They can struggle, however, in the west and north. Might bere offer an answer?

We drive south to the island of Burray, where UHI and the cereal research organization the James Hutton Institute have been running crop trials since 2017. Peter lets a handful of Burray's gritty grey soil run through his fingers. 'It's basically sand,' he says. 'It's deficient, principally in manganese, but is also low in copper and zinc. Many soils globally are manganese deficient, so if we can get varieties that are more tolerant to these conditions it becomes a more sustainable way of growing, because you don't need to worry about any extra inputs.'

There are 149 small plots on the site, with each replicate containing a mix of different strains of bere, modern barley strains, and rye. 'One year we just grew a selection of beres and modern varieties, which showed clearly there were beres with greater tolerance to these soil conditions. Even the beres that didn't grow so well did better than the modern varieties.'

Even with only half a day of getting the eye in, it was easy to spot which was which. The modern varieties were thin, mean hanks, the bere and rye tall, deep green and bruised violet, thriving.

'You get a bit of grief from the locals who keep telling us that our barley's looking terrible,' says John. 'We just say we're happy if it dies because that's a result.'

There are practical lessons being learned. 'All of these landraces have a tolerance to growing on nutrient-deficient soils where modern varieties won't grow,' says Peter. Could the solution be a cross between bere and a modern variety, giving tolerance to specific conditions but also a higher yield?

'That was one of the things the Hutton has done. One year they crossed some tolerant beres with Irena and Concerto, and we've then grown these crosses to see which lines have tolerance. They can then go on to further testing.' A solution emerges from the past.

If a modern variety can only grow with high levels of inputs, and then can only be harvested with an addition of glyphosate to finish ripening, then maybe the crop is saying, 'I don't belong here'. Instead, why not look at the conditions and adapt practices to suit them, rather than forcing something onto them.

Whisky is often viewed through the lens of inevitable, inexorable progress and improvement, as if the past is something to be admired, but in a patronizing way. Yet as Nick Card had told us, the Neolithic builders were better than the ones who came after. We can still learn practically from what has gone before, and use and adapt. Time viewed in this way, be it in barley, whisky or architecture, isn't linear. Instead, all time is present at every moment, and can be engaged with.

Opposite: Experimental plots on Burray

He laughs. Covers himself in glaur. 'Will this do?'

'It's probably a bit too much,' admits Christina. We're with Alan Eunson (opposite) at Hobbister Moor, where Highland Park gets its peat. Since peat 'grows' 1 millimetre per year and the bank is 2.5–3 metres deep, we're looking at 3,000 years. Its base is made up of the vegetation that the Ness' people walked on. There was peat laid down prior to that, the heather, moss and scrubby trees their ancestors had walked on, all the way back to the vegetation that existed before people arrived. Time compressed.

Peat is also here because of conditions. The land is waterlogged, meaning there's insufficient oxygen to feed the microbes that would normally break down organic material. So, every year for thousands of years, the plants and mosses have grown, died, rotted and been laid down in slowly thickening peat banks.

Tradition is often simply necessary practice repeated over time. The earliest distillers didn't use peat because they wanted to make smoky whisky. They used it because there was no alternative.

'We take three layers,' Alan explains. 'The top is the fogg – that gives the smoke; the next is the yarph. As there are still some roots it'll give you a little smoke, but also heat. Then there's what we call the moss, which is like coal. We'll use that for heat.'

Peat is a databank, filled with pollen records, fragments of vegetation, the decomposed detritus of life that can be analysed and give meaning to the past. The composition of the peat across Scotland will vary depending on what grew there in the past and because of that, the nature of the aromatics released are different. This treeless archipelago gives a fragrant smoke that calls to mind the heather that covers its moors.

A skylark starts to sing above us, a wee brown dot in the sky. The talk turns to people, place and community. 'When I was a lad every house had a peat fire,' says Alan. 'Everything smelled of peat, it's a nostalgic, comforting smell. It smells of place and home.' The smoke, like the bere, has an emotional connection.

Alan Eunson, Highland Park

THE HIGHLAND PARK VISITOR CENTRE
THE TASTING ROOM

The young team who have been working here are at the start of their whisky-making apprenticeship. 'Like a lot of boys, I started on the peat hill, then raffled about the distillery doing different things, then just gradually worked up until I got to the stills. Making whisky requires knowledge of the different conditions in each. You've got dynasties of families working.'

We drive back into Kirkwall, over the hill looking out at the Scapa Flow, the echo of water in the sky, and join up with John Strachan at the distillery, which sits like a tor on the hill above Kirkwall, a cluster of buildings with wings added as fortunes improved. Shades of grey, burnt umber and amber in the stonework, no pavements (naturally), slopes and slates. Whisky has been made on this site since 1818, though an earlier illicit still once stood higher up the hill.

It's silent season and the malt barns are empty; there's just the light playing off the swirling marks of the shiels and ploughs on the flagstones. It is one of only eight (out of one hundred and forty) Scottish distilleries to have retained the expensive and labour-intensive option of floor malting, which has been retained here because of that Orcadian peat and its specific aromas. The distillery's peated portion is blended with unpeated barley brought over from the Scottish mainland to produce the lightly smoked distillery character.

By the kiln someone's written 'swallows back', the date and a smiley face. Orkney as a place of comings and goings. Those who stayed, those who returned and those who drifted in.

Opposite: The old walls of Highland Park
Above: Malting floor

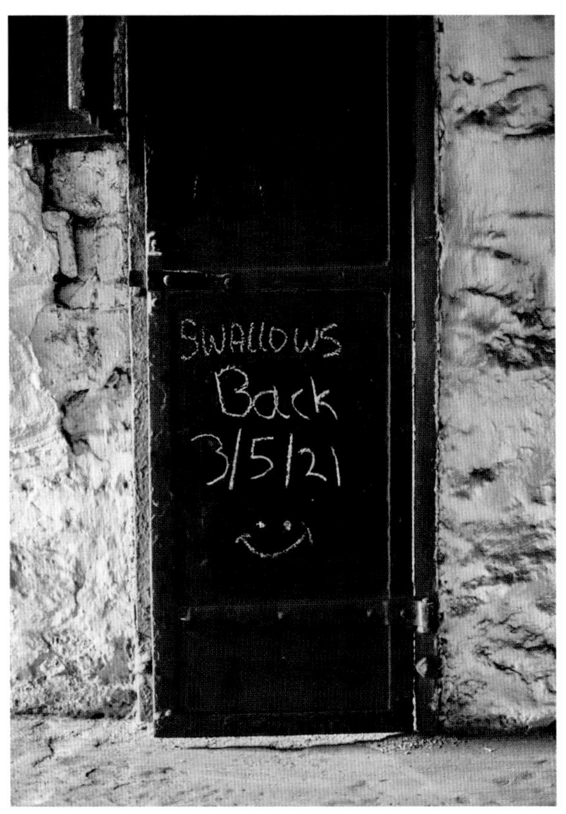

John was born in England to Orcadian parents. 'Orkney was poor in those days,' he says. 'They had to move to Little Scotland (Corby, Northamptonshire), then they moved steadily north. I've always been *from* here though.' That's a very Scottish thing to say. Where are you from means where are your roots, who are your family, not where are you living now. I live in Brighton, but I am from Glasgow.

'My uncle reckons the family's been here for 850 years.' He pauses. 'I'm not so sure about all his claims, but it's at least 300 or 400.' John eventually moved back. Grew his beard. Rejoined the community, started working here, told his sagas.

We walk through the distillery, the 12 washbacks, the varying lengths of ferment adding layers of flavour. 'It harks back to the traditional methods. This isn't a production line, it's a natural progression. We're now putting batch numbers on the label. We're not trying to make each one identical, but make the best of what's available. That's an immensely exciting change.'

We're in the cramped still-house with its quartet of stills. 'Science is good for predicting stuff,' says John, 'but this is alchemical – taking earth, wind, fire and water, raising them to crisis point, then transmuting them back into something else. The distillers are looking for the essence, the spirit. They should be wearing robes!'

So what is the essence? It's the peat, the approach, the maturing on site (most of which is in sherry-seasoned casks) and, now, a move away

Left: The seasons marked
Right: Washback detail

Still detail

from providing fillings for blends. Within three years, all of the distillery's production will be single malt.

We sit down to taste a range of bottlings for the distillery and its new Kirkwall shop. An 18-year-old distillery bottling adds a butterscotch edge to the smoke and a lingering fragrance to a palate that thickens into spices and barbecued pineapple.

A 14-year-old distillery exclusive is stronger and more rugged, the sweetness replaced by tobacco leaf, light smoke and bitter chocolate, with dark fruit richness on the back. It takes me back to the thick, citric, heathery old Highland Parks I first fell in love with many years ago, as does a 15-year-old made for the Kirkwall shop and aged in an ex-sherry puncheon – all resin, sweet leather, blood orange and tropical fruits.

Our walk through had barely touched on the production basics, the numbers and levels and cut points that are stock in trade at times like these. Our tasting was also more a chat, with Christina, John and I throwing around ideas, images and sensations.

Looking out to Rousay and Eynhallow from Gurness

There's an idea that whisky is all about the What: that as if by knowing facts and figures, a secret code can be cracked. Those details may be fascinating for the whisky geek (and I am one), but the Why is more interesting – the thinking that lies behind those decisions in terms of flavour and then, with whisky in glass, what does this do to you, where does it put you?

Highland Park is a distillation not just of barley, peat smoke and water, but the air and wind blowing against its pagodas, drawing the peat smoke upwards. It is about the people working their way up from the peat fields to distillery. It is their craft, an expression of what it is to live here.

At the Ness, Nick Card had taken us into a room filled with finds. He reached under the desk and pulled out a huge wedge of stone covered in bubble wrap. One face had a pattern incised into it, rows of linked triangles, each with patterns inside: 5,000 year old art. A response to the surface, or something else, a language of sorts.

The dressing and decorating of the stones, axe heads, carved balls and this mysterious piece all show attachment to location. They were

Art? Language? Another of the Ness of Brodgar's mysteries

made patiently, revealing the availability of time, a desire to care about quality. We're looking at the birth of an aesthetic.

I'm still hungry for meaning. Maybe, as with a glass of whisky, I should simply accept and engage. It is here. It exists. It is beautiful. Whisky too is art, a response to place.

...

Over the past two days, I'd noticed that everyone we'd spoken to had referred to the mainland as 'Scotland', defining Orkney as separate. 'We are different,' John had said. 'We have Norse roots, which separates us from the mainland. Gaelic's never been spoken here. Our society is built more on Nordic lines. There's no big landowners, just smaller farms.

'The farms next to the sea also own the shore and tidal area as far as you can wade at the lowest Spring ebb and then as far as you can throw a fish. That's ended up with one farmer getting rent for the oil pipeline that passed through his part of the sea bed.'

You can also fish in any river or loch, and as the swans aren't the Queen's property, presumably anyone can eat them. I start thinking about tonight's dinner.

Orkney became part of Scotland in 1468, when the cash-strapped Christian I, who ruled Denmark, Norway and Sweden, and James III of Scotland reached a marriage agreement over Christian's daughter Margaret.

In lieu of a dowry, Christian mortgaged the islands to the Scottish crown, redeemable for a payment of 50,000 florins. When, after a year, none of the money had been paid, the Scottish crown also obtained Shetland for a further 8,000.

Since any Udal (Norse) laws predating this exchange still supersede Scottish law, might it be possible that Denmark could pay the money back and bring Orkney and Shetland back into the Nordic fold?

That would seem to suit Highland Park, which has played the Viking angle heavily in recent years, with a seemingly endless stream of bottlings linking the whisky to sagas, warriors, gods and legends. There is so much more to Orkney, however. A need to create new stories lies at the marketing's heart, yet there is no need for invention or contrivance – the stories are out there in the landscape and the memories, they grow in the fields. Single malt is about creating flavours that are unique to a place. Understanding that place in a deeper way is, surely, also at its heart.

It chimes with something Nick Card had said about archaeology being a destructive process, and how important it was to log every detail to leave a permanent record for reassessment and reinterpretation. 'We use every method we can, to pass on this huge archive of material to the next generation,' he'd said. 'There is this evolution of thought and interpretation.'

That passing down of information, that understanding of a steady evolution also applies to stories, songs, legends and craft. Some ideas are lost, then rediscovered, reassessed and reinterpreted.

A whisky's style evolves as practices, techniques and preferences are laid down. It changes, is pushed this way and that through currents of expectation and the tidal flow of business, but it remains anchored. Sometimes it's important to take a step back.

'For 200 years we've been the distillery up the hill,' said John, 'Everyone knew the product, but we weren't involved.' This chimes with the oft-repeated tale that Orcadians' favourite dram wasn't Highland Park, but Scapa. Now, proactive work with hotels and B&Bs, free tours for locals in winter, working with artists, and the opening of a shop in Kirkwall High Street (also to capture the hordes of visitors from cruise ships) has resulted, he feels, in locals not only having pride in the whisky, but taking ownership of it as well.

Could this go even deeper? There's more bere being planted for whisky on Orkney, but all of it goes off the island to other distilleries. Couldn't there be a 100-per-cent Orkney whisky? Should there be? Could Stromness once again have a distillery, 94 years after its last one closed?

The northern whisky landscape has changed. There are distilleries in Shetland, the Faroes, Iceland, over in Denmark and Sweden, and all the way up the Norwegian coast as far as Tromsø. Orkney could once more be a hub, linked, if it cares to be, with the new Nordic whisky movement. The map spins.

...

Christina and I decide to go to South Ronaldsay to find a suitable end to the trip. The road thins, taking dramatic right-angled turns around old boundaries. There's a hay bale with boots sticking out of it and wearing a bra as if a couple were caught by the baler while at it, oblivious, wrapped in a confusion of straw. We end up at the cliffs at Windwick. Out there is Stavanger.

On the beach, a sea stack slowly emerges from the haar. We walk through meadowsweet and blood-red sandstone, the pebbles smoothed by endless turning, futtling, squeaking and coggling beneath our feet, and nibble seaweed that tastes of strawberries.

A flotilla of ducks guddle about, a bonxie cruises, a raven above, puffins skittering to safety. The only sound is a chuntering from white blobs on the cliffs. The more you look, the more there are. Fulmars, the northern albatross, wave skimmers, back from the ocean to nest. The call of home, Orkney's pull.

The haar starts to roll back in, the stack fades and the fulmars grey out. I pick up a stone. Black, it fits in the hand, its surface like silk, scribbled with a thin thread of quartz – a boundary, a Neolithic house, a road, an island's coast, waters, waves. Now we start to head south.

Beach at Windwick, South Ronaldsay

NORTH-EAST

Scotland's north-east coast, for all its apparent permanence – mountains, peat bog and moor, cliffs and sea – is a place of change.

Dunbeath's harbour is quiet. Just one tiny boat puttering in, a few creels on the back. Christina and I walk to the former ice house and see a verdigris mottled statue of a small boy bent almost double by the giant salmon he's hefted on to his back. This is Kenn, the protagonist of Neil M. Gunn's 1937 novel *Highland River*.

Dunbeath is the setting for his best-known work, *The Silver Darlings* (1941), which, along with *The Grey Coast* (1926) and *Butcher's Broom* (1934), make up a trilogy about the coastal community's history and how its people are indivisible from their environment. Gunn, the son of a fisherman, was born here. He became a gauger (excise officer), novelist, Zen adept and noted whisky lover. His book on the subject, *Whisky and Scotland* (1935), weaves, in typical fashion, myth, history, opinion and politics together. It is one of the strangest books on the subject and, for me, one of the best.

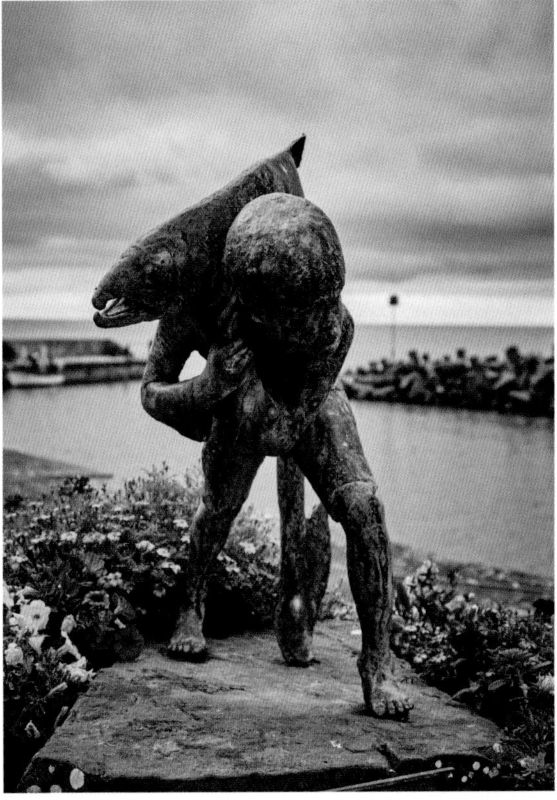

The herring fishing is long gone, but those creels we saw are still put to work. We wander over to the Tasty Toes food van for superb crab and lobster rolls and head to Gunn's river. The book is a journey along its length and through Kenn's life, a journey into self-awareness, but also one of an engagement with nature, heritage and place.

We follow the path past the old meal mill into the wood, filled with honeysuckle, the sweet smell of summer and the sweaty aroma of hot bracken. Clambering down through tree roots, we reach the bank. There's no surge of water, no peaty pool. Instead, it's an apocalyptic mess of pink and grey stone flags. This is more than the effects of a dry summer. The rivers are drying up.

We take the road south, 14.5 kilometres through the rollercoaster Berriedale Braes to a small lay-by. Parked up, we head through moor towards the sea. Hummocks of grass and bracken. There's an oppressive heaviness to the air. Midges cloud, the silence congeals.

We're surrounded by the ruins of the Badbea township, started in 1792 by people who had been forcibly removed from Berriedale and Kildonan as part of the Clearances to make way for sheep. Subsistence farmers put to the fishing, living on a cliff. The only supplement to their income was the making of their annual browst (distillation). Though by the late eighteenth century, small-scale private distillation such as this was illegal, the local innkeeper warned them of excise raids and the

Above: Statue of Kenn, Dunbeath
Opposite: Dunbeath harbour

CARINA
SCRABSTER

gauger even provided some of his crop to be turned into whisky.

The browst had long become part of Highland life. Things had moved on from the Neolithic brews. While bere was still used for ale, more commonly it was distilled, the crops ripening in the summer months when the cattle were moved to the high shielings.

The harvested grain would be put in a sack, immersed in a burn, then spread out on a barn floor to germinate. It was dried over a peat fire, ground, fermented using the house's barm, then distilled in a small copper still. There was skill to it.

The few early references to whisky as a social drink come mostly from Gaelic song and poetry, sometimes allusive, or comic, sometimes praising, occasionally condemning.

One of the first came around 1650 when the poet, An Ciaran Mabach (Archibald MacDonald) spoke of whisky in his lament about being exiled in Edinburgh with a broken leg (the 'dun fellow' is a deer).

My love the dun fellow
Who would sit at no board
Who would not seek to purchase
A pint of ale or beer.
A good double-distilled whisky [Uisge Beatha math dubailt]
You would not deign to drink.
You preferred the cress of the fountain
And the restless water of the burn.

Here is whisky existing within nature and also, for the scholar, an indication of how it was made. Double distillation would increase the strength, amplify the flavours and allow the distiller to select the ones he – or in pre-Clearance days, probably she – wanted.

Distilling was a beat in the year's rhythm, one of the annual ceremonies that exist in a multitude of forms in farming communities around the world.

It was also a collective enterprise. 'It is in general in the hands of poor illiterate farmers, six or eight of whom engage in a thirty- or forty-gallon still, merely for the sake of converting the produce of their farms and that of the neighbours' into a more saleable article', reported the compilers of *State of Facts, Relative to the Scotch Distillery* in 1798. Whisky had become an integral part of Highland life, and its making and drinking part of Gaelic culture.

The last gable end – Badbea Clearance village

A more detailed account can be found in Reverend Donald Sage's *Memorabilia Domestica*. Sage, who died in 1869, was one of the few ministers to write about the iniquities of the Clearances, and was also a family friend of John Sutherland (Iain Meadhonach). An angler and deer hunter, John, Sage writes, 'was also a smuggler and a first-rate brewer of malt whisky. My step-mother often employed him in making our annual brewst for family use. There, often during the process...have I sat with John, watching the process and hearing his tales.'

If you need evidence of how intertwined distilling was in community life, it is here. Sage's father, the minister of Kildonan, had no moral concerns at the start of the nineteenth century about hiring a smuggler to make illicit whisky for his family.

While tales of smuggling and the romance of moonshining provide a romantic undercurrent to many whisky books, it's rare that the wider historical context has been considered. Illegal distillation was used as a reason for forced removals, held up as proof of the apparent 'degeneracy' of the indigenous population.

Whisky – both legal and illicit – played a significant but little-discussed role in the Clearances, themselves a consequence of the agricultural 'Improvements' that had started in the early eighteenth century. They ushered in larger farms, better drainage, crop rotation, mechanization, changes in animal husbandry and, as a result, a dramatic change in population patterns.

Improvement also resulted in a shift in thinking on the part of landowners, who began to view their holdings as businesses that would help fund their increasingly lavish lifestyles.

In the northern Highlands, rents were raised, increasing whisky's economic significance. Farmers became illicit distillers not out of choice, but necessity. Moonshining was a way of staying on the land. In 1781, home distillation was banned and over the next four decades a series of laws was put in place. In 1785, Scotland was divided in two, with different legislation governing whisky production in the Lowlands and Highlands. In the latter, the minimum size of a still was raised to 40 gallons and export to the Lowlands was banned. With only one still permitted per parish, the small-scale distillation of the past was effectively banned.

Although these rules were scrapped in 1816, a simultaneous hike in the tax of malt and the removal of a subsidy for using bere raised the expense of legal distillation. It was cheaper to moonshine. In addition, the quality of the illicit stills was deemed better than the legally produced whisky from licensed distilleries – especially those in the Lowlands.

By this point, it was estimated that 300 small stills were in operation in eastern Sutherland, predominantly in Strathbrora and Kildonan. Because neither of the glens could grow the volume of barley required, grain was being imported.

In 1819, James Duncan of the Golspie Inn was found to have 240 gallons of illicit whisky in store, some of which was destined to be served at Dunrobin Castle. There's a bitter irony at work here, as the castle was the extravagant home of George Leveson-Gower, Marquis of Stafford (later Duke of Sutherland). He was Britain's wealthiest man, who, in 1785, married Elizabeth Gordon, Countess of Sutherland. Their joint holdings amounted to the largest landed property in Victorian Britain.

From the start of the nineteenth century, the Countess began what historian James Hunter calls 'the most extraordinary example of social engineering in nineteenth-century Britain.' It was overseen by two men, Patrick Sellar and James Loch.

The townships of the inland straths (valleys), where most of the people lived, were fertile, capable of supporting large numbers of people and cattle, and exporting surplus food. Despite this, houses were demolished and burned and, in Sellar's words, 'the people [were] brought down to the coast.' There they were 'placed in lotts under the size of three arable acres sufficient for the maintenance of an industrious family, but pinched enough to cause them to turn their attention to the fishing... surely a most benevolent action.' Their former farmlands were turned into sheep runs.

Sellar and Loch's reports to the Countess return regularly to illicit whisky as a major driver for the forced removals. Loch draws an equivalence between illicit production and a decline in moral condition, which, in Sellar's case, is entwined with racism. Moonshining, he wrote, was a practice that had 'nursed the people in every species of deceit, vice,

Looking down to Dunbeath

idleness and dissipation...debauchery and beggary.' This infected the children, who were 'trained in deceit, exceed their father in turpitude, and the virtue of a Scottish Highlander is exchanged for the vices of the Irish Peasantry.'

This is more than economics: there is a hatred and fear of Gaelic culture – the language, the attachment to land, the traditional practices – and the idea that the people were in some way uncivilized.

If, under the plans, Helmsdale was to become the main fishing port, Brora was to be the industrial centre. It had salt pans, coal, a brick works (and, in time, a weaving industry). In 1815, a brewery started operation and, in 1819, the Duke built a distillery on Clynelish farm. Typical for the time, it was managed by an incomer, but staffed by former moonshiners.

Though Sellar despised the illicit distillers, Hunter argues that they can be seen as exhibiting the attributes of free enterprise propounded by the very people who were kicking them off the land. Although solutions to the overpopulation of the times were needed, investing in the people and keeping as many on the land as it could have supported, as well as developing new industries, would still have ensured the estate could have functioned profitably.

Instead, as Hunter points out, the removal of cattle, the ending of mixed farming and introduction of large sheep flocks reduced the fertility of the straths, whose stock-carrying capacity was in decline by the 1880s. By the 1850s, most of the people had emigrated.

We stop at a layby so Christina can get shots of the sea. To the south, we can discern the statue of the Duke on Ben Bhraggie. Deep purple ragged clouds trail above him. We continue south, to Brora.

...

For much of the twentieth century, Brora's distillery, like every other across Scotland, was at the service of blends. By the 1960s, its Victorian equipment was creaking and in 1968, with blends booming in North America, it was replaced by a younger, slicker model, built a little further up the hill. Think of it as Scotch's mid-life crisis. The new distillery even took the old one's name: Clynelish.

Almost immediately, however, drought on Islay brought the old place back into production, as the blenders required a quick substitute to make heavily peated spirit. To avoid confusion, it was renamed Brora. Then, in 1983, as demand for Scotch crashed, like many other smaller, old-fashioned distilleries it was discarded once more. Its quiet life in service was over. Shuttered, its innards cannibalized, Brora sat silent.

By 2000, however, a cult had formed around it. Maybe because, like other silenced sites such as Ardbeg and Port Ellen, it was smoky, and therefore in line with the tastes of the new wave of malt lovers. It was they – foremost among them the French writer Serge Valentin – who preserved Brora's reputation, giving hope that one day it might reopen.

Maybe the fact it remained a physical entity allowed the question to be asked, 'what if?' Maybe it went even deeper. Could it be that Brora's outsider distillery character chimed with the personality of a certain type of iconoclastic whisky lover?

Let me explain 'outsider'. The world's most famous distilleries conform to an ideal standard of beauty. They are poised, sleek, elegant. Brora whisky is oily, waxy, oxidative. It doesn't play by the same rules, and it's this teetering on the edge of orthodoxy that makes it compelling.

But it was disappearing, sip by sip. Then, in 2017, news came that it was to be resurrected, which is why we're standing in smirry rain in front of its new gates, meeting brand-new home host Andy Flatt and manager Stewart Bowman (who has since left to become manager at Arran; see page 62). Both are fully tweeded up. Stewart's long beard is tied in a knot, Andy's neatly combed. Not for the first time, I feel underdressed and ill-groomed.

Any time I'd been to Clynelish, I'd sneaked down to the ruined site with its crumbling walls and moss-covered stones, peering through grimy windows at the stills and wondering. Now its pale limestone walls gleam, the gravel is raked, the lights are on, the distillery bell rings once more.

The reason the stills remained was nothing to do with secret plans. 'Without them the building would have fallen down,' says Stewart. 'To get them out they'd either have had to chop them up, or take the roof off, in which case the building would have collapsed.' It was dismantled stone by

Brora looking all spick and span

Brora has been impeccably restored

ESTD 1819

stone, foundations dug, a new steel frame put in place, then rebuilt. It is a remarkable achievement.

Stewart's father was the last excise officer in Sutherland. According to Stewart, an old weekly production ledger his father had put in the loft records that 'Brora distillery closed for an indefinite silent season, March 1983.' On 5 March 2021, Stewart started production once more.

We've been joined by Kevin Innes (see below), who started working at the distillery in 1977, aged 17. As the day progresses, it becomes clear how important his memories have been in making sense of the puzzle of how to recreate the idiosyncratic waxy and fruity Brora style.

It's easy to fixate on a single element as being key to a distillery's character, forgetting that distilling is a complex interplay between a multitude of different constituent parts. Here, clear wort from the mashtun is the first stage in creating Brora's DNA. This significantly reduces any nutty characters in the spirit. Then comes a 115-hour fermentation in wooden washbacks. Keeping the fermented wash in these after all the sugar has turned to alcohol triggers lactobacilli (LAB). Reacting with the higher acidity in the wash, they create fruity esters. The longer the ferment, the fruitier things become.

Stewart and I geek out over a recent paper, which showed that each distillery had its own individual colony of lactobacilli. 'Changing the plant or over-cleaning will hurt that colony,' he says. 'You have to have the right conditions. It's a living system.'

Kevin Innes

In the stillroom we're dwarfed by the pair of massive dull copper stills whose bellies seem to pin us back as they soar upwards, lie pipes running out to the worm tubs. Being Brora, there's another quirk. 'One washback gives us two wash-still runs, which then give 1.4 spirit-still runs,' says Stewart, not knowing that trying to explain maths to someone with dyscalculia is a tough gig.

'One week we'll do eight spirit-still runs, the week after we will do nine.' He grins, reading my bafflement, anticipating the next question. 'We don't really know what it does, but it's what they did back in the day, so we're fully committed to it.' He looks up. A slight sigh. 'Aye,' he says, 'they're bonny stills.'

'I found a rota book from 1966,' says Andy. 'In it, it said that on March 11 "the holy psalm book was produced and we sung a whole bunch of psalms, but the wash didn't come off any quicker." Imagine all the workers singing psalms around the wash still.'

Psalm-singing might be the secret ingredient to the waxy signatures of Clynelish and Brora. For me, the former's is more textural, like candlewax, while Brora's is thicker but oilier. Both are meant to result from the build up of a greasy deposit in the foreshots and feints receiver. Without this gunk, the waxiness goes.

'It's not just the gunk, though,' says Stewart. 'It's everything before that – clear wort, lower gravities, long ferments. A lot of analysis was done on the gunk to try and quantify where it's coming from, what the

Left: Brora's stills
Right: Inside the worm tub

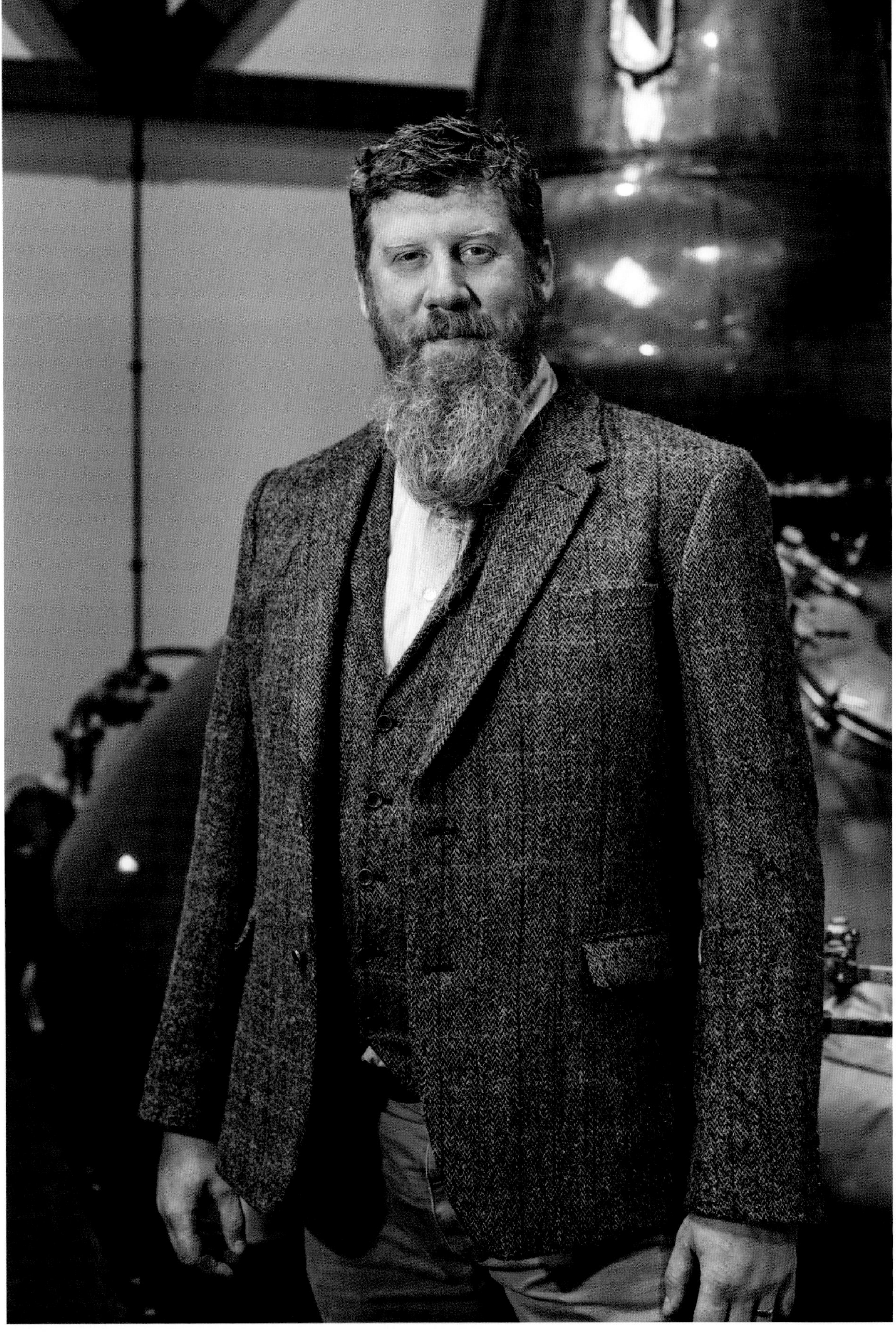

The magnificently bearded and be-tweeded Stewart Bowman

compounds are, but there are so many variables. That to me is where the artistic element comes in.

'The other thing is the terroir, which is something not defined and is a really interesting area. It's back to that LAB paper. There's an absolute link between location, water, environment and this waxy character. They tried it at Dailuaine, but it never reached the same intensity. Aberfeldy and Craigellachie were waxy, but they were different as well.'

I look to Kevin for help. He smiles. 'Can I tell you how it's done? No, but I can smell a washback and tell you it's there. It starts earlier than just in the still-house.'

To ensure the gunk sticks, they've scoured the inside of the new steel tanks. We look in, and there's stuff starting to form on the sides.

Later, when the others are having tea, Kevin winks at me. 'You ever seen the gunk at Clynelish? Come on.' We head up the hill where (with permission and gas monitor) we open one of the tanks. It's slathered with a thick grey black coating, soft as silk and weirdly beautiful.

We chat on the way back. Who taught you? 'All the old boys here,' he says, starting to list the names: Donald Cameron, Duncan Mathieson, Hoopy the cooper. 'They'd been working here all their lives, 40, 50 years.' He was learning from men who had worked at Brora since the late 1920s. Whisky is about continuity, passing knowledge on.

And the ways have changed? 'Stewart has the degrees. I have my nose and eyes. I can get you waxy, but I'll do it my way and it'll be different from the way they do it. I'm an awfa' tweaker. I can tell if it's no' right, and that can only come from time.'

The old guys he talked about would have said the same about their forebears. Naming the people is for me more of a link to the past than the beautiful restoration and the reception rooms for Brora's new high-net-worth clients.

Back inside, Andy brings out more ledgers. 'Brora was selling 90 per cent of its production privately at the end of the nineteenth century,' he explains. 'Remember that the railway arrived here in 1870. It brought in tourists, salmon could be sent overnight to London – and it helped distribute the whisky. The distillery is integral to the village's history, and the village is integral to the distillery's.'

What does its return mean to the community?

'It's huge,' says Kevin. 'Huge. Even when this was called Clynelish everybody called it "the Brora distillery". Having Clynelish is amazing, but not to lose the history of Brora is wonderful.'

'We need to open the gates and get the people in,' adds Stewart.

The distillery's plans – discovered in a bin bag

 Brora's dunnage warehouse

'Have community days, get in the old guys, my Dad, to tell folks the amazing stories. They helped so much.'

Was there much rivalry when both distilleries were operating? 'The old boys were loyal to here,' says Kevin. 'Going up the hill was seen as promotion but they stayed here. Clynelish was meant to be a replica, but they're not the same spirit.'

Given you worked at both, what are the differences?

'Brora was a better whisky!'

We're now in one of the old warehouses. Dunnage style, earth floors, low stacks of casks. The smell of damp, and heady fumes. 'The burn's running alongside, you see,' says Kevin. 'If you were working here, your feet would be in mud as thick as treacle. The dampness made for better whisky.'

Andy pours samples of the distillery-exclusive 39 year old. It's elegant, fruity, with touches of citrus, a mineral edge, stone fruit and foam bananas. All the way through is that weird oiliness which says 'Brora'.

Brora has been heavily smoked, lightly peaty or unpeated: variations on a theme. The oily pulse it gave to blends meant it was aged in multiple-use casks, with little flavour coming from the oak. After four decades, the air has had more influence, the oils have concentrated, the fruits drifted towards the tropics, dampness seeping in.

Flavours and textures are pushed beyond the safe and pretty into areas that bear no resemblance to what whisky 'should' taste like. The limits of language are revealed. What do these lists of words mean? Just give in to the sensation.

In *Highland River*, Kenn and his friend Beel become intoxicated by an 'inexplicable scent of honey in the fitful June air. They got it, they lost it...The scent was warmed by the sun; it had a rare entanglement.'

That 'entanglement' is an aspect of place. It is the magic in the glass. Words don't matter, the technical details fade away. It is just you, memory and the liquid. The response is visceral. It has you.

'Keep silent and still, and watch what happens,' Gunn wrote in his essay 'The Flash'. 'The real point of the experience is that one comes upon oneself...the experience is incredibly refreshing, cool as birch-scented air, and full of wonder.'

But although language falters, we still try to pin flavours down, just as Gunn did. 'I do not know the description of the taste of an Orange Pippin has ever been caught in a phrase,' he wrote in his autobiography *The Atom of Delight*, 'but we had our phrase for hazelnut...and it was "whisky taste".

'The crack...the mash, the mashing of the mash until with the help of a generous spittle the whole attains that degree of liquidity which frees to the full the ultimate flavours the quintessence of whisky taste.'

He's also linking 'whisky taste' with the nine hazel trees of Celtic legend, which surrounded the well of knowledge. When the nuts fell into the pool, the salmon of wisdom ate them. Discovering the pool, the hero

Fionn MacCaumhaill ate the salmon, thereby gaining wisdom and the knowledge of poetry. Whisky taste at the heart of it all.

Brora's taste speaks of all that, but also of people and that passing of things down, an old distiller learning through his senses, of Stewart and his father, and this idea of continuity. There is also the accepting of a challenge, the shades of these old men smiling, saying 'OK, you try and do what we did.' Finding the pieces, making assumptions, testing theories.

I think back to Nick Card on Orkney. Here, the pieces are hidden in lofts and people's minds, in tanks, casks and glasses. Brora is an exercise in memory, but it can't be in thrall to it, because you can only make today what you make today.

At the opening, Diageo's then master blender Jim Beveridge said, 'We will recreate the system, put everything back, and it will be what it will be, and it will be Brora.' It almost brought Stewart to tears.

There's a subtext here that, as with all distilleries, once things are set in motion, at some point flavours will warp and shift and the distillery will decide into what configuration they fall.

The Brora we think we know is only a tiny corner of the picture. We are assessing a distillery through ancient stock. Brora remains elusive because we don't know what it tasted like as new-make spirit, or as a young whisky. It's impossible to make a 39-year-old whisky, all you can do is set it up and hope. 'It will be Brora,' doesn't mean it will be the same as it was. It will be what it will become.

We're staying in an Airbnb that night, in a row of old railwaymen's cottages near to Lower Brora. We head past the small harbour, built for the coal boats, to the Sutherland Arms for a meal, but scarper, unable to cope with two drunken couples shouting at maximum volume about problematic childbirths. Thankfully, there's Sid's Spice, a truly great curry house (the leftover tamarind chicken went well with square slice and mushroom for breakfast).

We pour a couple of drams of Clynelish. Christina, smitten by Brora's weirdness, had earlier asked what the starting price was but, unsurprisingly, declined to make a purchase when Andy told her: £8,500.

The fact that Brora's currently a plaything for those who can throw a case into the boot of their Ferrari is an inevitability, given the rise of the luxury market and the low level of mature stock. This will, hopefully, change in a decade's time when the new whisky is available. In the interim, those wildcat gates should be opened to all who simply want to see this remarkable and praiseworthy resurrection. After all, it is 'the Brora distillery'. It belongs to the people.

The next morning, we drive through Strathbrora. It starts wooded, the road hugging the curves of the river. Aspen leaves flutter like wingbeats, older stands of pine above; then, as the woods fall away, we reach the first of the three lochs. It's surrounded by pasture land lying under the face of Carrol Rock, coppery sand in the river's meanders matching the late dawn sky in the east.

This was cleared land, but it's still evident how it could support people. Now there's some cows, a few sheep, the occasional large farmhouse and a country estate. How many here went to the mine, or the distillery? How many went to the fishing, how many stayed on that grey coast? How many got on board the ships that carried them away?

The narrowing road rises behind Struan Lodge, which can be rented out for shooting and stalking parties. It's part of the Gordonbush estate, built at the end of the nineteenth century. According to *Ainmean-Àite na h-Alba* (Gaelic Placenames), the Gordon family 'called it by the English name of Gordonbush [as] Gaelic was then well out of fashion among the land proprietors. By older Gaelic speakers [it] is sometimes called Bealaidh, "broom".' A change of name speaks of change of land use, that switch from Gaelic to English signalling the end of a culture.

We move from the plains towards the moor and what would have been the summer shielings. There's a flash of bright green down the slope towards the river. We look at each other. Barley? There's a tiny touch of smugness when we go down to the fenced-off plot and see our hunch is correct. 'Looks bere like to me,' says Christina with confidence.

We look over this strange field in the middle of this landscape, both so out of place and yet so natural. Caught between the moor and the shore. This should be here. It was always thus.

There was something of Patrick Geddes' Valley Section here. Geddes (1854–1932) was what Scots call 'a lad o'pairts': biologist, geographer,

Above: Heading up Strathbrora
Opposite: Struan Lodge

 Brodie Nairn, master of glass

ecologist, arts activist, town planner, internationalist and educator who coined the phrase 'think global, act local.'

'Community', he wrote, 'can be defined by place, work and folk, but also from the sharing of knowledge, value and norms with the other people who live there.' In Geddes' world, culture and environment were inextricably intertwined.

The Valley Section diagram was his way of demonstrating this. It shows a river valley flowing from mountain to sea, with the occupations of the people in each part: hunters, foresters, shepherds in the uplands, farmers in the lowlands, market gardens and fishermen by the coast. It shows how interdependent it all is, how its evolution generates history, culture and belonging.

Geddes' Valley Section is Gunn's river; it is every river. It shows how land, people and culture are entwined. It is a model of what could have been – or maybe could still be – in these straths. What could have happened had the Improving been considered and empathic? The distillery would still have been there, as would the mines and industries, but the glens would have continued to support life and a living culture.

The road curves over the hill through Rogart, presumably no longer 'entirely packed and crammed with smugglers,' as Sellar wrote, recommending that its people 'should be put into Brora'. Back on the A9, we drive south, towards Tain.

...

The rain starts as we walk past the church, down the hill behind the grand, pale sandstone buildings of the main street. A narrow road, with a few small houses, the sort of place where you imagine, in the past, artisans of various descriptions would have set up workshops. A wheelwright maybe, perhaps a blacksmith's forge, but not the roaring furnaces of Glasstorm, the studio glass-works owned by husband and wife Brodie Nairn (see opposite) and Nichola Burns.

Both Scottish born, after art school they spent a decade working and training in studio glass-works around the world. 'Nicky started at the top, I took a more winding road,' as Brodie puts it. In 2005, after teaching at North Lands Creative in Lybster, 80 kilometres north, they set up Glasstorm.

'We realized that we couldn't sell £2,000 pieces from the start, so we went back to our roots,' he says. From that came the Glasstorm range. There is now a separate art glass collection, North Coast. 'Then the drinks industry heard of us, which is when we started to dance with the devil in the pale moonlight.' He laughs. Glasstorm is now the go-to for luxury Scotch bottles. 'It's saved the business, he says, 'both through the recession, and now Covid.'

We're looking at a range of bottles he made for top-end Bowmore bottlings. 'Bowmore came to us and asked us to do something that looks great, can hold our whisky, and be artistic. They really pushed boundaries with us, going to an extreme craft level.

'We went to Islay and explored. They wanted the rocks, the crashing waves, the rockpools, so we found new techniques and did it all at 1,120 °C.' He picks up the bottle for a 54-year-old whisky, distilled in 1957. A textured glass wave surrounds its base, breaking over one side. 'Bowmore's Japanese-owned, so I thought about Hokusai's great wave crashing against No.1 Vault. Then we put platinum inside the wave.' He laughs again. 'I mean, no-one's done that before.'

How did you get it in? 'With my magic!' I lift it up and the metal flickers, like sunlight through spume on a wave's crest.

He hands me a thick column of dark, textured glass. 'Look into the end.' I hold it close to my eye. The effect is trippy, like being hurtled into space at light speed. Dots and streaks of light through blackness. 'Doesn't it feel fluid, like a river? It was cast, colours put in, polished, then we used this technique called battuto to give it this ripple. Want to have a shot?'

It's not what I was expecting, but when will I get another chance? He talks me through what will happen, what to do, what the tools are. Patient, clear instructions. The furnace roars a vivid orange, yellow and white.

'It's important to be able to feel the flow. Glassmaking is an art form.' He points at the furnace. 'This phones me at night, tells me it's too hot, or cold, or needs help. That's modern technology. These...' he points to the instruments of torture arranged in front of me, 'would have been the same 2,000 years ago. The Romans developed techniques we're using today, and some we're still struggling to work out.' I can't help thinking of Stewart trying to workout the mysteries of Brora.

'Ready?' I'm not, but I nod.

A blob of molten glass is gathered on the pole that's then placed on the edge of the bench. 'Keep rolling it, feel it, watch how it flows.' It's glowing, pulling itself toward the floor. 'Keep rolling. Now, blow.' A bubble forms.

More glass, 'Keep your hand left of mine. Roll it. Pick up the jacks [long tweezers], cut a groove, light.'

More glass, form the shape in a wooden block, another blow. 'Keep rolling. Hand left of mine.'

I begin to feel through the jacks what was liquid becoming more granular. Then use a taglio knife to shape the base, add the pontil (metal rod). Go inside with the jacks to open it up. 'Close the blades, pull out. There you go. That's you made your first-ever glass.'

A few weeks later I got a parcel.

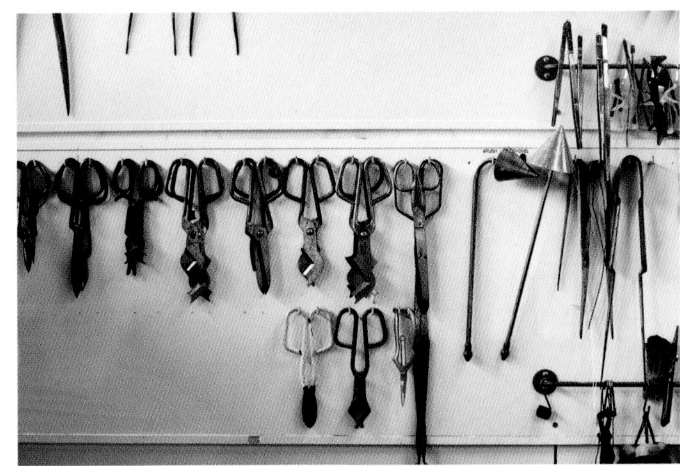

Glassmakers' tools

The glass is more of a weapon than a fine piece of crystal, but it's mine.

We continue the tour, look at drawers full of diamond-dusted wheels, each angled into different profiles for specific projects.

'That wheel is made from the stuff they use to polish the nose cones of rockets. Madness!' Each department has another pair of hands, another set of eyes seeing blemishes invisible to anyone else. Passing information along. 'Each bottle takes four days. We care…we have to. It will pass through ten sets of hands.'

He'd talked earlier about the differences between Venetian (thin glass, adding colours) and Scandinavian (thicker glass, all about refraction) techniques. Is there a Scottish style?

'We're mixing things up. That column you held? It's Italian technique, added to Scandinavian. The nuts and bolts have been worked out, but mixing it up is where it gets fun. When people say it can't be done, I say, "Really? I think you'll find it can. Then I find out how to do it!"

Top: Heating the glass
Bottom: Moulding

We chat on, about photography, the birth of the studio glass movement in the 1960s, kids. 'I love making these series for the whisky firms,' he says, apropos of nothing, 'but what I really love to see in any piece is the hand of the maker, the evidence that there's some element which shows it's made by someone, that it's not identical.'

That morning, I'd watched an interview with the musician Aidan O'Rourke about his soundtrack to the film *Iorram*, in which he spoke of a piece based around an archive recording of the song 'Fhir a'Bhàta'.

'We spent time trying to accompany it, but the pitch wavers,' he'd said. 'It wavers so beautifully. I'm so into music that breathes. Being stuck to a strict metre I find difficult, and all these archive songs, even the rhythmic ones, the way the time moves within them is interesting. It made us listen.'

We respond emotionally to the waver, the hand of the maker. Things that are identikit take you away from that impulse, reduce the item to a product. Great music, great art like Brodie and Nicky's, is the opposite of that. So are the great whiskies. There is a signature flavour, but the finest examples play with it. They waver.

...

The next morning, we're walking through Dornoch's medieval-looking streets, down the side of the Castle Hotel to the town's tiny, former fire station. Smells of ferment and new make, tanks, pipes, two small Hoga alembics and, in the rafters, wooden fermenters. 'Pardon the mess,' says Phil Thompson (see page 79), who, with his brother Simon, owns this, one of Scotland's new wave of distilleries.

The Thompson brothers (also the name of their exemplary independent bottling arm) also own the hotel's whisky bar and are part of a group of young single-malt lovers who collected, and more importantly drank and shared, old bottlings, comparing their greater physicality and richness to the modern equivalents. The whiskies that is. From that came decided views on what whisky should be. These old whiskies weren't just different, they argued. They were better.

'Simon and I had discussed building a distillery, and doing it properly. We had our old-style whisky hats on, and no-one in those days, bar Springbank, was making it the way we thought it should be made.' He laughs. 'It's our personal philosophy, but it's one based on old records and information from older distillers.' In 2016, with help from a crowdfunding campaign, the Dornoch distillery opened.

Polishing wheels, Glasstorm

He looks around the clutter. 'Simon, Jacob – he points to a grinning, baseball-capped distiller lurking behind one of the tanks – and I just figured stuff out for ourselves. What worked, what didn't. We had no choice.'

Distillers Jacob Crisp and Euan Christie (see page 80), who emerges from the shadows, are both graduates from Heriot-Watt's school of brewing and distilling, although both point out that, in their day, distilling was dispensed with quickly. They too have learned on the job.

What's the biggest lesson?

'Having vessels that empty themselves,' says Jacob with resigned amusement. 'The amount of time we've wasted over super-stupid things like that.' Not that they seem to be in any rush at all. The ferments are long. Very long.

'Seven days,' he says laconically. (That's four or five days longer than the standard.) 'When things are happy, the ferment is done by the end of day two, then everything just sits fizzing away with all the lactobacteria and funk going on. In winter it ticks along and you get cleaner spirit, when it's warmer in summer you get things that are nice and funky.'

They use heritage strains of barley like Plumage Archer and Maris Otter, with trials of Scotch Annat, Scotch Common (also heritage strains) and Orkney bere, all malted by Fife's Crafty Maltsters, underway.

Dornoch is deliberately taking a different path to the rest of the industry, which chooses its barley from an approved list, made up of

Dornoch distillery is in an old fire station

strains bred for yield. If you are willing to take a hit on that, the counter-argument goes, then heritage varieties and landraces come into play, and with them come different flavours. We're back to Peter Martin (Dr Bere)'s argument.

'Barley and yeast are the focus here,' says Phil. 'After two years of propagating and selecting our own yeasts, the bulk is now coming from Cromarty brewery. We're just moving back into propagating our own, so we can now cycle in some of the best with the brewer's yeast.'

It's a further break from the standard approach. Ask most Scottish distillers about yeast and they'll claim it has no impact on their distillery character – mainly because distiller's yeast is there for efficiency, not specific flavours.

'It's so strange,' says Jacob. 'In beer you'll find the same recipe using different strains getting huge flavour differences. Brewers will talk for days about yeast! The whisky industry just pretends to.'

'I can see the need for efficiency from the perspective of the big distillers,' says Phil. 'They'll be looking at their portfolio of distilleries and thinking, let's homogenize these elements and keep costs down. We're different. We're only concentrating on flavour and we're so small that our choices only add £1.50 per litre to the price. That's nothing if you have a product with more character.'

This seems a step back from the fundamentalist arguments of a few years back. Are you saying there's room for both approaches? After all, Diageo has to be able to make 18 million cases of Johnnie Walker every year (not to mention all its other blends and malts). This model might be a tricky fit.

'I've huge respect for the big guys,' he says. 'I might not like every single one of the products, but what they do for Scotch whisky is amazing. We're buying stock from them for our bottlings, and they do an incredible job in liquid consistency. If I was a blender I'd want to ensure that everything I got every year was the same. I totally get that and have huge respect for it. It's just not what we're about.' It's the waver, it's Brodie and Nicky creating their individuality through a mixing of techniques.

There are also sound commercial reasons for this, he explains. 'We have to make sure that in five to ten years time, we're bottling something interesting and not just a bunch of first-fill Bourbon barrels from the same barley variety.

Phil Thompson, Dornoch distillery

Jacob Crisp (left) and Euan Christie (right), Dornoch's distillers

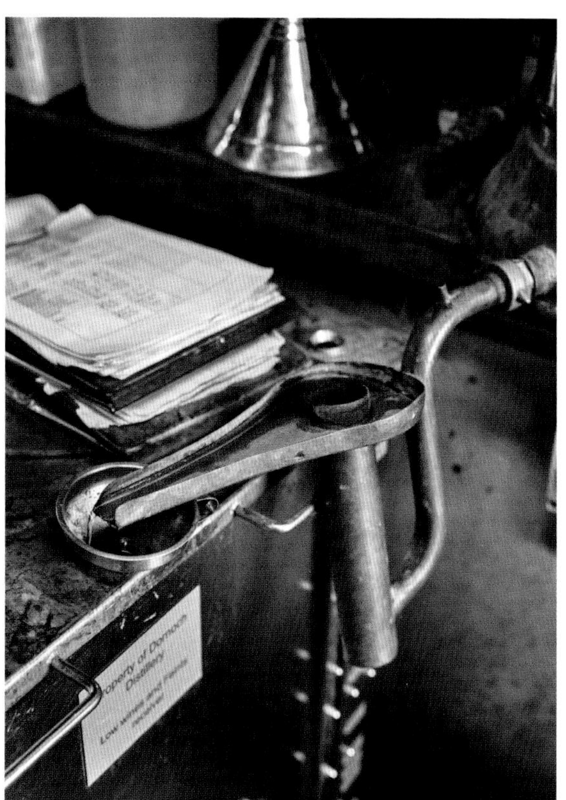

'From a small distillery perspective, there's no point in making something which is made the same way, with the same raw materials as the big guys, but which is 15 per cent more expensive.'

All the way through our chat he keeps repeating, 'we're just fumbling our way through', but I don't buy that. There's always been a clarity to the brothers' intent, which also goes deeper than simply making whisky.

'We feel a degree of commitment to Dornoch because of the bar,' he says. 'It's good to bring distilling into the heart of this community. We want to give young people something to stay here for.'

...

The dawn hits the the hills over Bonar Bridge. From the balcony of the Dornoch Links Hotel, I can see across the firth to Glenmorangie's soon-to-open Lighthouse distillery, which is also taking an experimental approach: yeasts, barley strains, everything surrounding whisky being questioned.

In *Whisky and Scotland*, Neil M. Gunn describes the whiskies from this area as being filled with the same 'rugged individuality' as the landscape. That individuality is there in the thinking as well.

It might seem perverse to try and compare the new, luxurious, Brora with Dornoch's guddle, but there are parallels. Both are asking: what are we, where have we come from, what can we learn?

Brora has picked a point in time, and is trying to return there. Initially, Dornoch appears to be doing the same, but the manner of their application is moving whisky forward. Dornoch has to be new. Brora, on the other hand, has to be about the past, a reclamation, an atonement in some ways.

It is the North-East coming to terms with the past, journeying like Kenn from the sea to the source, in a process of self discovery, becoming embedded once again in a community.

BALVENIE
BALVENIE

SPEY VALLEY

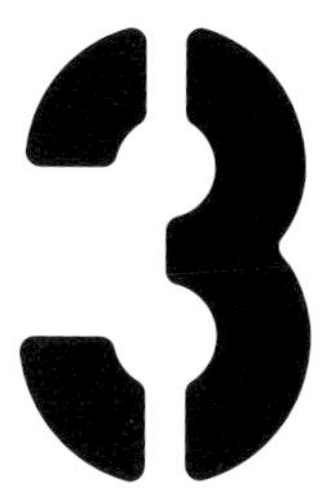

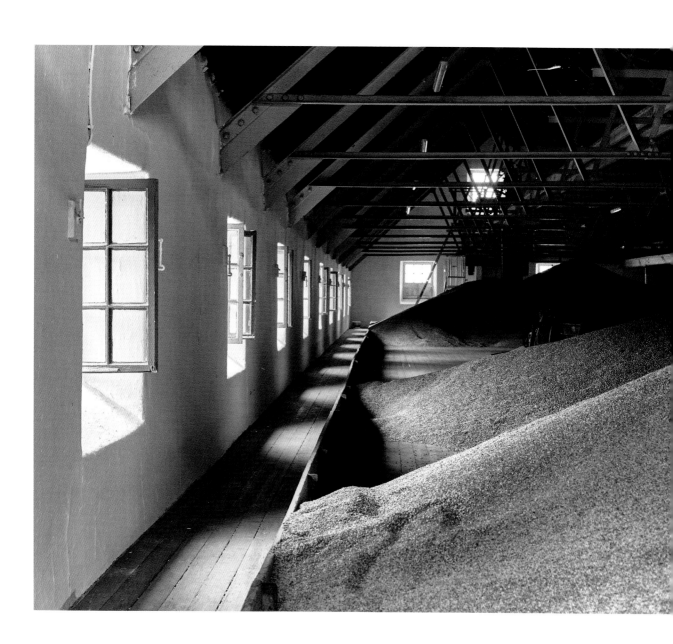

We are the only two cars on the road across the softly lit high plain. There are no houses, bar the occasional isolated farm; the gate at Auchmair's reads: 'The Slough Of Despond. May The Lord Be Praised.' Slightly disconcerted, we press on, startling a young roe deer, which panics, runs along the fence line, then leaps to safety. Steadily, the conical shape of the Buck rises.

I climbed it as a kid while staying at my adoptive auntie's croft in Lumsden, on the Aberdeenshire side. Baffled by my first hearing of Doric, but happy with a bowl of cream to dip my porridge into, comb honey to be spread on white bread, and browsing in the Toll of Mossat shop ('we sell everything from a needle to an anchor', both items prominently displayed to prove the point).

There's a sense of space here in the Cabrach, a 16 by 13-kilometre area known as 'Scotland's Siberia'. It's a forgotten part of the country whose bareness has been accentuated over the years as, one by one, the lights of its farms went out.

The road ends at a white-painted house. We step into silence. Only the wind, hissing in the grass. Crows caught by the gusts, ragged feathered, seek refuge in the small stand of pines. 'Welcome to Reekimlane,' says Grant Gordon (see page 107).

Grant's great-great grandfather Charles was the schoolmaster here in the late nineteenth century. In 1897, he married Isabella, daughter of William Grant of Glenfiddich, and a dynasty was formed. The firm

The Buck from Reekimlane

remains family owned, as is Reekimlane, and you can tell from the way Grant speaks as he takes us around the house that this is where he feels most at home. Our tour ends in a large, high-ceilinged lounge – a converted threshing shed. 'A dram?' Generous Glenfiddichs are poured and and we sit and talk.

Space is what attracts people to Scotland, yet much of its emptiness is engineered. In the early nineteenth century, 800 people lived here in the Cabrach, an area famed for the quality of its illicit whisky. Distillation was a communal exercise, as it had been for generations, a glue for the community.

In their paper on local distilling in the first half of the nineteenth century, Kieran German and Gregor Adamson estimate that, each year between 1800 and 1820, up to 80 people were distilling in the Upper Cabrach, producing at least 4,800 gallons (nearly 22,000 litres) of whisky annually, part of an estimated 400 unlicensed stills scattered throughout the Cabrach, Glenrinnes and Glenlivet, where the main form of agriculture was raising cattle rather than arable farming. Distillation was a way to supplement income. With demand rising, the fact it was illegal was immaterial.

Later, I catch up with Alan Winchester. The former master distiller at The Glenlivet, Alan doesn't just know the history, but also the names of the people, their family lines. He knows fields' names. He gives perspective. One of his retirement projects is uncovering lost bothies (sites of illicit stills).

'It's fascinating. It's part of a wider story. We haven't uncovered them all yet – there's more than we thought.'

So, you're getting your eye in?

'Oh aye...absolutely. We keep finding them in the wrong places.'

But what's the relevance?

'To give perspective on the present-day picture. Our marketers [he still speaks of The Glenlivet as his] are looking to use information for their story, but there's so much more.'

...

Our route back from Reekimlane to Dufftown follows that of many of those distiller-farmers. Built in 1817 by James Duff, fourth Earl of Fife, to provide accommodation and employment after the Napoleonic wars, it sits uphill from the original settlement of Mortlach.

By the late eighteenth century, Mortlach's minister was concerned about his flock. In the *Statistical Account of Scotland,* published in the 1790s, he reported that 'the mode of living is much altered here, and not to the better...the drinking of whisky instead of good ale is a miserable change, and so likewise is the very general use of tea. These put together have been exceedingly hurtful both to health and morals.' It's unlikely that the new town's arrival dampened down demand for either liquid.

Dufftown joined a number of other planned new towns: New Keith (1750), Grantown-on-Spey (1765), Rothes (1766) and Aberlour (1812), all built by landowners as part of the Improvement movement. An infrastructure developed as former subsistence farmers became weavers, wheelwrights, blacksmiths, tanners, innkeepers and labourers on the new larger farms. In time, distilling would become part of the mix. It all fits rather neatly into Geddes' Valley Section and stands in contrast to the ravages of the mismanaged estates of Sutherland and the west.

Dufftown was ideally placed, almost symbolically so. To the south, the Cabrach, to the south-west Glen Rinnes and Glenlivet, all smuggling lands, with their bothies. To the north and east were fertile lands. The seam of limestone in which Dufftown sits was quarried to provide lime for fertilizing the improved lands (it also gave the young William Grant his first job).

The illicit era was ending. In 1823, the Excise Act imposed greater control on legal distilling, with detailed regulations on capacity, pipework, operation, even buildings. Just as subsistence farming had been replaced by larger units, so distilling ceased to be small-scale and communal. Distilling was not only now commercial, but expensive. Whisky was a business. The first to appear in Dufftown was Mortlach.

It's widely believed that the new licences were taken out by old moonshiners. In reality, few made the jump. The new distillers tended to be hand-picked tenant farmers on the larger farms.

Dufftown sat at the fracture between the past and the future. By 1850, like many of the earliest legal stills, the three distilleries that started up in the Cabrach had failed. German and Adamson report that in 1827, at least 80 Cabrach men had emigrated with their families (10 per cent of the population). The exodus continued between 1861 and 1961, the Cabrach losing 75 per cent of its population.

Whisky can be used as a measure for the impact of Improvements and effects of Clearances. The new stills are next to roads, rivers and, from the 1860s, railway lines. The hinterland is virtually abandoned as distilling moves into towns. Whisky's story isn't just about where the distilleries are, but also about where they aren't. The gaps speak. Whisky isn't at the periphery of Improvements, but at the heart.

...

By 1958, Dufftown was a capital of whisky-making, with six distilleries. If you weren't working in one of them it's likely you'd be employed at a cooperage, a coppersmiths, or in transport. It was that year that the 16-year-old Dennis McBain was nervously waiting one Saturday night for Gordon MacDonald, Glenfiddich's brewer, to come back from the cinema, part of his weekly routine.

Dennis (see page 91) was born half a mile from the distillery; his great-uncle had been at Glenfiddich from the 1920s; his father was

Door detail, Balvenie distillery

at Grants's second still, Balvenie, as were his brothers. It took him three tries before he plucked up the courage to cross the road.

'I asked, "I wonder if there is a job at the distillery, brewer?" Everyone called him that. He asked my name and said if anything turned up he'd let me know.' Soon after, Dennis was walking into Balvenie's malt barns to start work. 'My first impression? There were four of them sitting on a wooden bench. I thought, "Jesus Christ, they're ancient! What am I doing working with these auld mannies?"'

Dennis officially retired from the firm in 2008, but is still always around, 'doing odd jobs', when he's not playing golf or fishing. I've met up with him to catch up and have a wander around.

The maltings are still operational. They only make up to 120 tons per year, some from the firm's own farm, accounting for 10 per cent in every mash, but they're part of the distillery's character, part of its story. Today, the malt floor is quiet. I imagine the 'auld mannies' at work, the scrape of the shiels and the barley falling like golden rain as it was turned.

'They showed me the ropes,' says Dennis. 'Ensured I knew the ethics of the company.' It's not the only time he uses the phrase in our chat. 'What I learned in those nine months has stood me in good stead for the rest of my career, but, oh, it was a dusty job.'

He joined at an important point in the firm's development. Seven years previously, Charles (Charlie) and Alexander (Sandy) Gordon,

Malt barns, Balvenie distillery

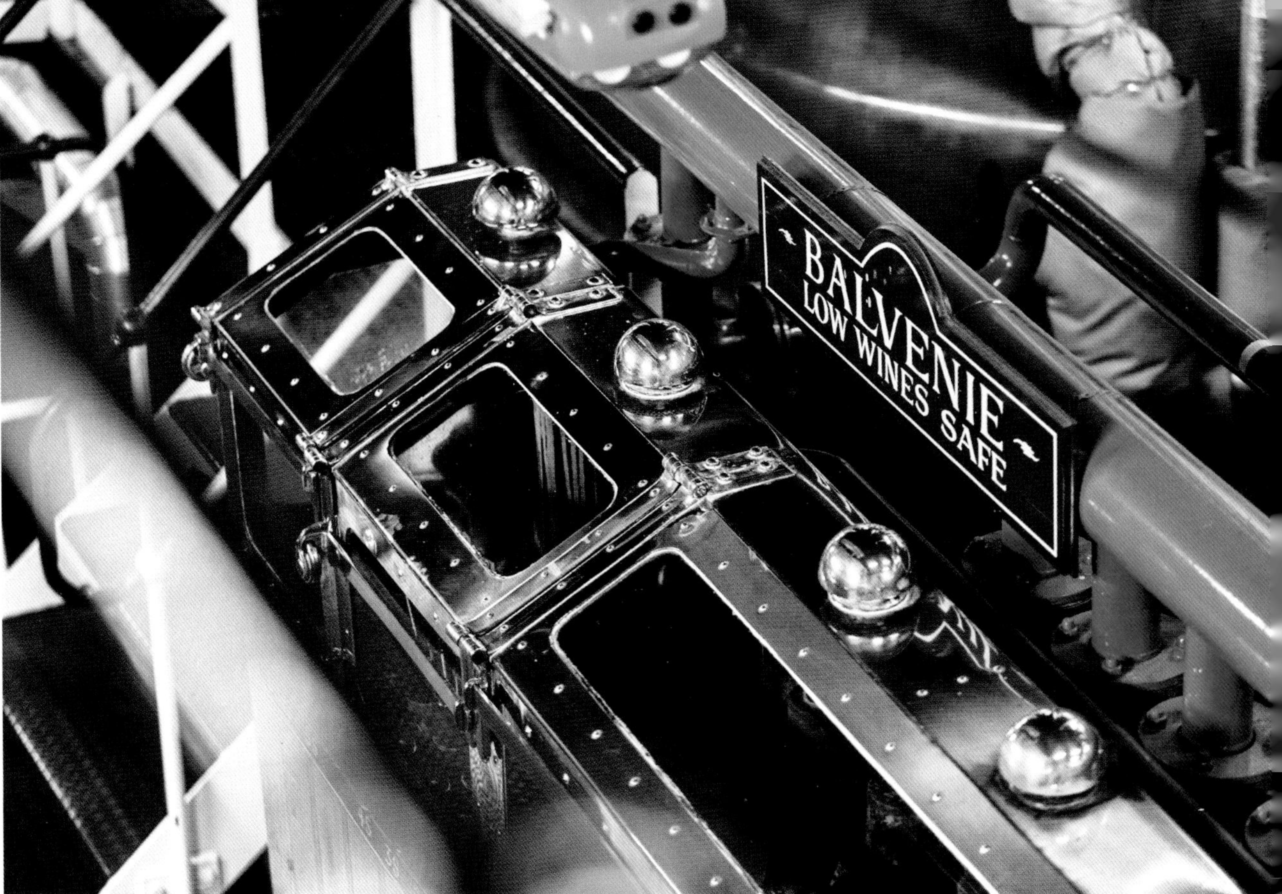

Charles Gordon's grandsons, had been appointed as directors. They had taken over a firm much changed from 1886, when their great-grandfather William had left his job as Mortlach's manager to start his own distillery, building it by hand with his family, buying the old stills from Cardhu.

Charlie and Sandy took over as the market was shifting. America was booming. It was time for expansion. Young Dennis finished his stint at the malt barns and was sent to the site's coppersmiths, where he would remain for the next 50 years.

'The coppersmith was a man called Willie MacLaughlin, who Charlie had poached from the local smiths,' he recalls. 'It was Willie who convinced Charlie that we could make our own stills.'

But why? No distillery had a coppersmith. 'We were determined to prove that we could do as good a job as Forsyth's in Rothes, or Grant's [no relation] up the road, and do it cheaper. It gave us control and that was a thing with Charlie Gordon. If he got people and material that he could control they weren't going to muck it up.' Those were Grant's ethics – to do it properly, take responsibility.

We're in the still-house, its six dull gold stills, with distinctive boil balls sitting above the polished brass spirit safes. It's warm, surprisingly narrow, filled with pipe work and a tiny wooden office for the stillman. It's one of those places where you can hear and almost feel the spirit being made.

Taste that new make, and Balvenie's signature honey and light maltiness is already present, qualities that carry through for decades,

Balvenie's spirit safe

picking up nuances and complexities from cask and time, but never losing its supreme balance.

I'm imagining the noise of the smithy – the shine and sheen of the sheets of copper, rolled, planished, beaten, shaped and welded. A trade, a craft, art? Dennis looks at the stills. 'A bit of all of them. It's art because you can manipulate it in whatever way you want, if you are careful.'

In what way? 'Well...look at the swan neck there.' Eyes move to the elegant curve at the top of the neck. 'To do that out of a flat piece of metal is the most difficult part. It and the boil ball are the two focal points, because you'd notice an imperfection. Getting the head and the swan neck in an ever-decreasing diameter, getting that curve, that narrowing, that's the art.'

What about this story that if you make a new still you had to replicate every dent? He looks at me, serious for once. 'Dave, do you honestly think I'd spend that amount of time making something so beautiful and then put a bloody dent in it?' Fair point.

We've reached the coppersmiths. Time for his portrait. Without being directed, he dons the top half of a pink boiler suit, picks up a hammer and immediately strikes a pose, eyes straight down the lens. 'You've done this before,' says Christina. A smile. 'Aye, a few times.'

Looking at him, I think of the McBains, the Grants and Gordons, and all of the other families across the area, their stories interweaving through the history of this area. Not brands, not marketing or PR, but people's tales.

 Balvenie's stills were made by...

…Dennis McBain, 50 years a coppersmith

Andy Fairgrieve, keeper of the William Grant & Sons' archive

‘Smell this! Smell that history!’ Andy Fairgrieve (see opposite), black clad, bearded, waist-length dreads, is holding an old book. We’re in the firm’s archive, which is housed in two cottages, rooms stuffed with racks, books, bottles and advertising. In one, a wall is taken up with the extensive and, let’s face it, utterly confusing Grant and Gordon family forest.

Andy arrived here 20 years ago to research his dissertation on the gendering of whisky and was taken on as an archivist. A deep-voiced east coaster, his academic background is never far from the surface. He hands me the book, and I inhale the intoxicating, slightly foxed aroma of old paper. It’s the barley book from 1887, the writing is William Grant’s. It shows the first deliveries to the new distillery – farmer, tonnage, amount paid – and shows that bere as well as barley was being used.

With the largest concentration of distilleries in Scotland, writing about Speyside was always going to be a challenge, so I figured it best to explore it from the heart, Dufftown, then the heart of the heart – the site containing Glenfiddich, Balvenie and Kininvie – and so, hopefully, tell the area’s story through the work of one family whose lives and decisions have been moulded by, and which have in turn moulded, the modern industry.

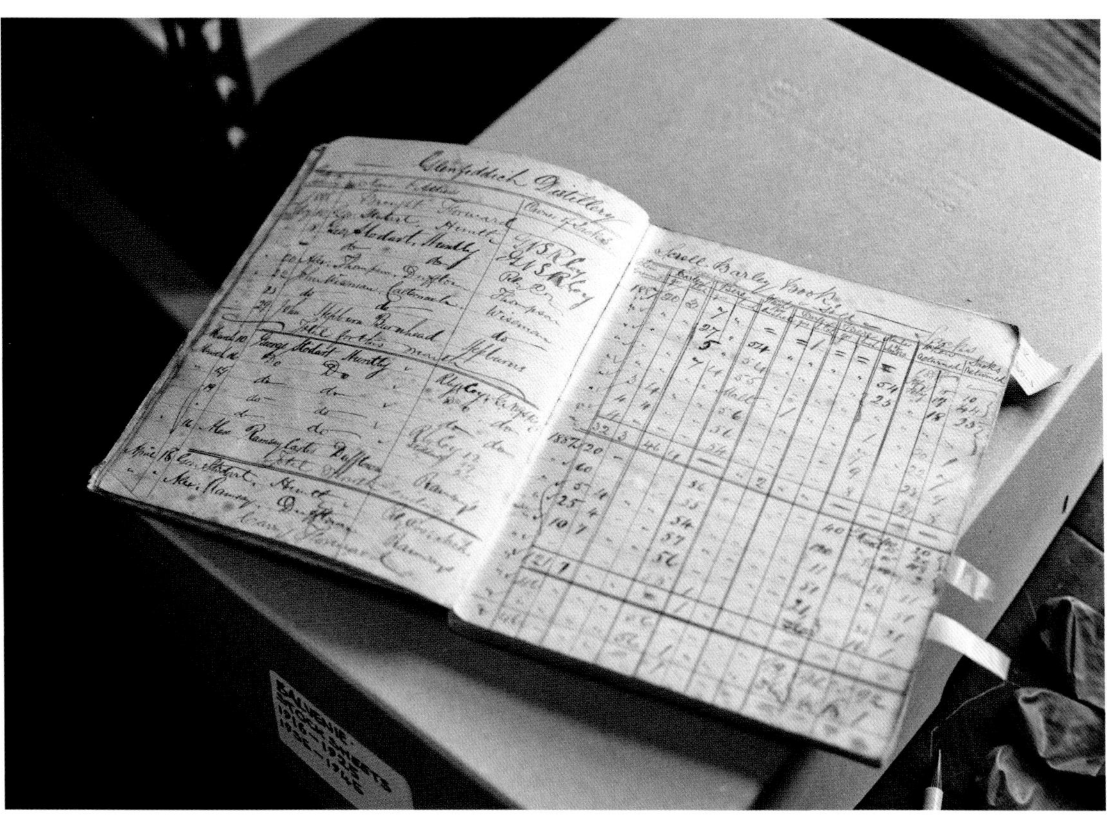

Glenfiddich’s first barley book

Dennis's tale is one element, and more is to be found in these book stacks and marbled indexes. 'We have this unique position of having been owned by the same family who never threw anything away,' says Andy. 'That's a north-east trait: "aye, it might come in handy".

Women drinking whisky? In the 1950s!

'You think an archive gives you answers. It gives you questions. An answer might appear, but only with more questions tacked on.' I recall Nick Card in his room at the Ness of Brodgar, speaking of seeing links, creating narratives, testing theories, Alan Winchester with his bothy hunt. Whisky as archaeology.

Here are the hard data of ledgers and accounts, but Andy is also undertaking an oral history project. 'It humanizes the spirit,' he says, leaning against a set of shelves, 'because whisky is a cultural thing. I can't think of anything else that is made in the past, but is contemporary when you enjoy it.'

In particular, it has helped him reveal the significance of that generational shift when Charlie and Sandy took control. 'A lot of people got upset by Charlie, and some of his thoughts were wild and crazy, but a lot were right. He was a driven man, always talking about how quality was important.

'Sandy was very much test, research, decide. My opinion was when they took over, the equipment hadn't changed much since the 1920s. The business was there, the question was how to expand it. When Charlie and Sandy had their feet under the table they were more able to push harder for things.'

From that came the decision to market Glenfiddich as a single malt and the triangular bottle, and on 5 July 1969 it became the first distillery to open to the public. We went there as a family from Lumsden. I barely remember the visit, but recall my dad was very happy on the way home. By opening the distillery doors, by showing hospitality, the world of whisky was changed.

...

The previous night, we'd arrived at Torrin, one of the firm's guest houses. There was a shout of hello and Kirsten Grant Meikle (see page 96) appeared, laughing, 'Dump your bags. We've got wine and way too much food!' She's to be our host and guide. She is currently in a procurement role – 'but I've had several different jobs since I joined'. More importantly, she is a member of the family. Wine is poured, overstuffed fridges examined and the chat begins. In recollection, it barely stopped.

Archival tomes

Kirsten Grant Meikle, family member and one of the 'cousin consortium' that runs the firm

When did you become aware of all this?

'I spent some time in my early years in the summers at my Granny Jean and Grandpa Gray Grant's house near Alford. From time to time, Grandpa would take us off to visit our "other family" in Dufftown.' The complex family tree comes into play here. Kirsten is the great-granddaughter of Captain Charles Grant, who left the firm in 1920 to buy Glendronach. There was, it appears, a schism.

'No-one from my branch of the family had worked in the business since then, but for some reason my uncle Charlie (by then Life President) asked me if I would like to join the business. I spent a good three years learning something new from him every day.'

Charlie's generation were retiring. Another shift was under way, and a new market to address. It was an eye-opening time, she says. 'The cousins really didn't know each other that well and to keep a business like this going, you have to know and understand each other. If we didn't, this would be gone.' Today, the firm is governed by a 'cousin consortium', in her words, with Charlie's son Glenn as the executive chairman.

Does family ownership come with extra responsibility? The answer is immediate. 'It's huge. It is everything that you do, because you cannot get away from it, and part of it is because you don't want to get away from it. It sounds clichéd to say "we are custodians of the brand", but that is exactly how we feel and it is not going to fail on our watch. We're not going to be the ones who bring it down. What really matters is the

Distilling at scale: part of the new Glenfiddich still-house

people, the place, the heritage. Anyone who works here understands how important this heritage is because they have a closer relationship to the family. We're here in our pyjamas!'

The next morning, Kirsten, Christina and I walk to the new Glenfiddich still-house, which has made it the largest malt whisky distillery in Scotland, capable of making 23 million litres of pure alcohol per year, the biggest of three mega-distilleries (Macallan, the Glenlivet and Roseisle) that have appeared in Speyside in recent years.

We walk down the seemingly endless ranks of copper stills, look over a field of washbacks, admire the girth of the mashtun. The idea that malt whisky is intimate, carrying a vestigial memory of the bothy days, has long gone. This is what a global single-malt brand looks like. Deal with it.

I think back to Phil and the team in their Dornoch fire station. Without distilleries like this creating this thing called 'single malt' would distilleries like theirs exist? Maybe not. It needed another two guys in a changing world to make that leap.

Can place exist in here? Is there a point when you get so big, that the intimacy of that concept is impossible to comprehend? No matter how impressive the new still-house is, you feel something slipping away, because scale creates distance. Provenance, heritage and place are vital elements for single malt, yet large distilleries with their computers can seem oddly detached, rootless places.

...

It all changes when we open the doors of Warehouse 8. Inside is a deep reserve of old casks and mysterious black marrying tuns where all of Glenfiddich's whiskies are brought together to rest and mingle. There are the Solera vats, where different combinations are measured and married. The vats are never fully emptied, the whisky's richness deepening as the old stock mix exerts its subtle influence on the young. A metaphor rears its head.

We're joined by Ian MacDonald (see page 100), Glenfiddich's former head cooper, who started here in 1969. He used to haunt the town's two other cooperages as a kid, then started here after school. Five years of apprenticeship. Learning a trade. 'I was taught by Don Ramsay [his predecessor as head cooper], so that's 100 years of experience between us.'

The cooperage has been retained. Of course it has. 'There's no way there would have been one if we weren't family owned,' he says. 'If we did it ourselves we didn't have to worry about a'body else, we control our own destiny.'

It seems to be the Grants' way. 'The biggest thing I learned from Charlie was don't compromise,' says Kirsten. 'If you do it, do it properly or not at all because you have to keep that integrity, can't lose control.'

 Opposite: Secrets lurk within

NEW OAK
BULK LTRS 2112
ROTATION No
TUN No 6012

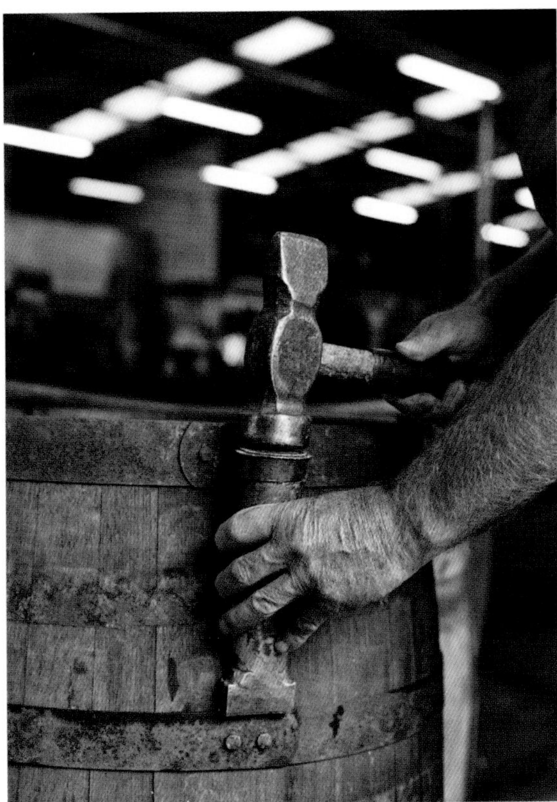

Your brand integrity is also a personal integrity?

'It's sheer bloody-mindedness! We're stubborn, and we're control freaks and that means we've got to know everything to control the process.'

We stop beside a cask. Ian looks at the chime. 'That's one of mine. See the mark?' Each cooper applies his own stamp when the cask is finished.' Hand of the maker. You get the feeling that he knows every one. His own map. 'It's sight and feel, Dave,' he says. Just like Dennis with his curves.

If I think of Glenfiddich, I think of the people and how they have guided a single malt, which can be fresh and apple-laden when young but then – guided by time, cask, air and skill – picks up layers of fruit, chocolate and sophistication.

For me, it's here in Warehouse 8 that this attention to detail becomes apparent. You don't have to marry whisky before bottling, but they do and at scale because it adds a layer of complexity. It is part of its identity, and is about care, depth and being rooted.

The story of the Grants of Glenfiddich and Balvenie is also the story of Speyside – the move to towns, the adaptation to new ways, the years at the service of blends, the rise of single malt, the tourists, the retention of crafts – all here in one place.

The framework exists, albeit in different forms, across the area, from Gordon & MacPhail's warehouses, to the handed-down mysteries

Left: Ian MacDonald, head cooper
Right: Ian at work

of Mortlach's distillation, the family roots of the Grants of Glenfarclas and so many more. You have to dig deep to find Speyside.

...

The concentration of distilleries here has resulted in the area being self-sufficient in whisky's other skills: coppersmithing (Forsyth's of Rothes and Speyside Copper Works in Elgin) and the building of washbacks (Joseph Brown Vats of Dufftown) and cooperages, one of which, Speyside Cooperage, is in Craigellachie, 6.4 kilometres from Dufftown.

It was started 75 years ago by the Taylor family, part of the outsourcing of skills as distilleries geared up for expansion. With a new site in the central belt and two in the US supplying the bourbon industry, it's now part of Tonnellerie François Frères Group.

'We're employing over 100 people for the first time,' says general manager, Andrew Russell. 'It's a sign of whisky's rise. Every distillery is increasing capacity. We're busy.' Quite how busy becomes apparent when we get on to the shop floor. The echoing blatter of hammer against wood and metal, the shriek from the machine as hoops are tightened around the bilge of the cask. Oil and water on the floor, bundles of reeds (to seal the cask) and a blur of glaur-streaked, red-shirted men.

Croze, plucker, chiv, flincher, driver, punch, brace, adze, plane. Strange names, tools unchanged for hundreds of years. Creating a

Inserting a reed to seal the cask

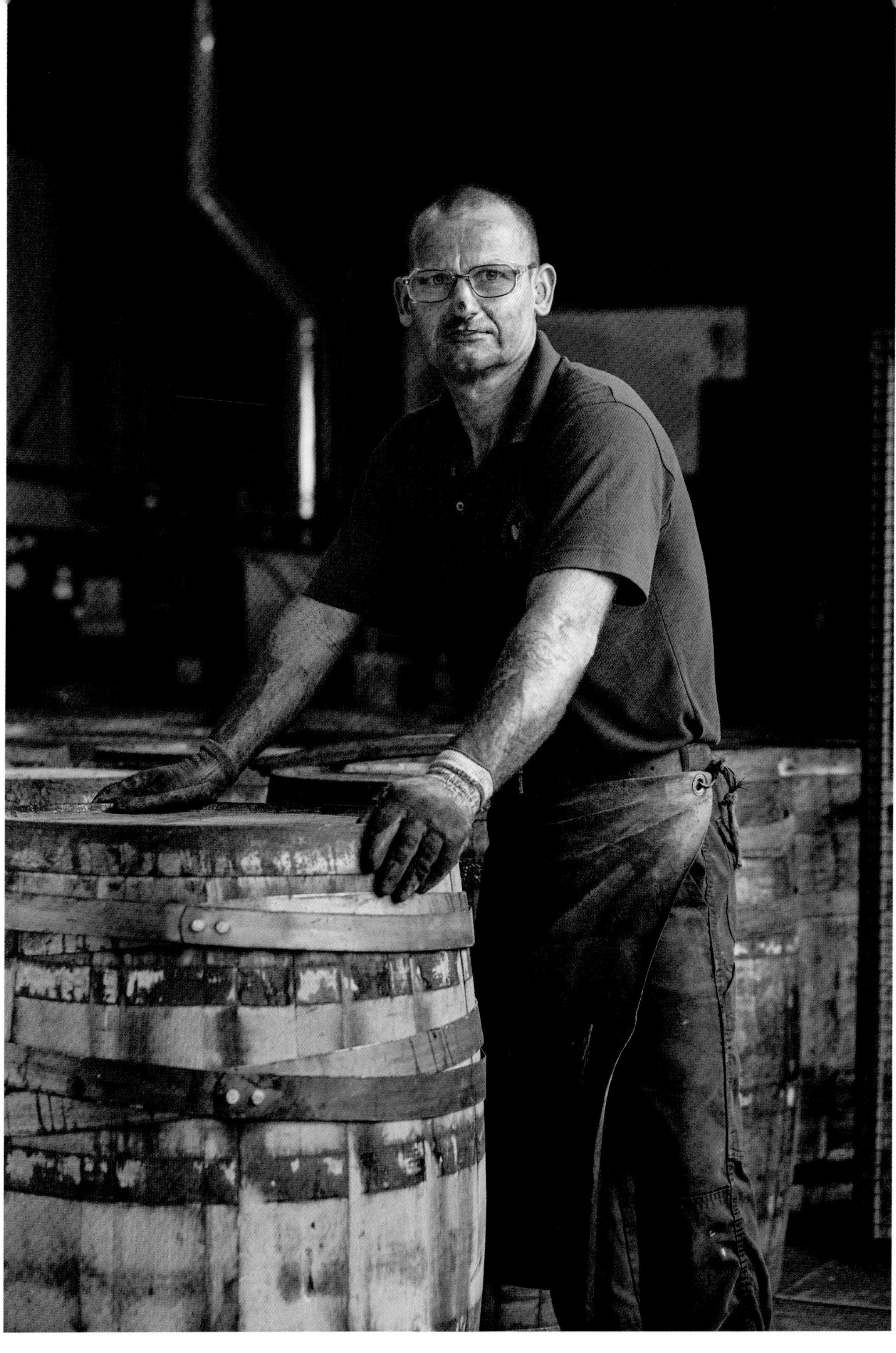

 Cooper, Speyside Cooperage

container out of oak is an ancient craft. Making something that is liquid-tight, but can breathe, made without glue or nails; something that can be rolled with one hand despite weighing a ton.

We find a space and watch this strange choreography, whose percussion reverberates in the air and in the head. Details emerge. What seems to be wild aggression is tempered by delicacy, an understanding of stresses and fits, qualities assessed with a glance. Perpetual motion, with Christina dancing around them, finding her own angles. Somehow she manages to get one cooper to stop for a second to pose.

We walk to the back shop to see a cask being recharred. Ends off, charcoal flailed off, then put over a gas burner. A few sparks, then it ignites, scarlet and gold flames rearing. Although it appears that this would destroy the wood, the heat is both toasting the fresh oak, transforming the lignins and tannins into complex flavour compounds that add themselves to the spirit. The new char helps to remove sulphur and aggression from the new spirit.

Without this alchemy the cask would be an inert container. Refill it too often and all that flavour is stripped out, leaving it inert once more – hence the re-charring.

Once filled and in the warehouse, a flavour dance begins between oak, spirit and air, taking the distillery character and shifting it, sometimes gently and slowly – in a refill cask – sometimes giving a rapid impact, as in that recharred cask we've just seen made.

It seems timeless, but innovation is at the heart of the process. 'Our sister company, Demptos, has developed a design-a-barrel programme with 2,000 different combinations: oak type, grain, toasting levels, degrees of char,' explains Andrew. 'Every element produces a different effect.' After the clang and clatter of the shop floor, this talk of subtle shifts in temperature seems paradoxical.

'We're doing lot of speciality and hybrid casks at the moment,' he continues. 'There's 50 or 60 different varieties of oak, and they all have a different flavour. Chinquapin has recently popped its head up because it is vastly different. The rise in small distilleries has been a positive for us because they pay a lot of attention to their wood and are extremely willing to experiment.'

It's also led to a long-term project involving six different casks being filled with the same spirit. 'It might take 25 years to get the final conclusions, but along the way we can tell distillers that this is what to expect at 3, 5, 9 years. It's a shop window that's particularly useful for new distillers who don't have decades of stock to learn from.'

Learning is also key. We're back in the din of the shop floor. On one side, the apprentices (some of the 25 the firm now employs) are building small casks. 'We're still the only cooperage in Scotland that raises new casks,' Andrew says, with a hint of pride. 'An apprenticeship here gives them skills that no others get.' Generations passing skills on in the same way as they are in coppersmiths, tun builders, distilleries and farms.

'You need that skill at the end of the day,' says Andrew. 'Every cask is different, because it is made from a living thing, and each living thing is different. We're always told we're all different. Trees are the same.'

...

Further down the hill is Craigellachie distillery with its weird waxy floral oiliness. In the distance is the triangular shape of Ben Rinnes. From its summit, you can look at the glitter of the river, sun glinting off distillery pagodas, steam rising, farmland, moor and quiet towns. To the south, the blue foothills of the Cairngorms; to the north, flatlands green with barley, then the Moray Firth and, on a clear day, the coast at Brora.

A series of river systems, watersheds, drainage and geology; a web of people and occupations. Only from this height can you see the spread and complexity of the area. There is more to the Spey's 3,000-square-kilometre catchment and 36,500 kilometres of rivers and tributaries than whisky. It's home to Atlantic salmon, otters, freshwater pearl mussels. There's wetlands and moors, hydro power, forestry, agriculture, baking, weaving and fishing. Then there's whisky, with its ancillary industries: transport, coppersmithing, coopering. It's a complex web.

'German and Adamson opened my eyes with their research,' Alan Winchester had said. 'All of a sudden I realized I'd never looked at how well connected the Cabrach was at the time. If you stand at the top of there, on the Ben, or Carn Mor at Braeval, you can see how it was linked.'

He was talking about smuggling routes, but the connections remain – threads of water, iron, tarmac, contours, the lines of ploughs, lineages of people and cattle, lines of knowledge being passed along. Speyside became what it is because everything it needed was here. Still, though, a worry nags away.

'What is Speyside?' I asked George Grant of Glenfarclas once. He'd given me a slightly old-fashioned look. 'I don't know. We don't call ourselves that. It's a new term.' That's the sort of perspective that six generations of ownership gives.

He is, of course, right. He often is. 'Speyside' is a modern construct. Prior to the term's arrival, whiskies from the area would have been known as Strathspey, maybe North Country. Before that, the shorthand for the area was Glenlivet, a catch-all term that had nothing to do with geography.

'We use Speyside to position ourselves,' Alan had said. 'It's a more modern term. We'll break it down into different areas, but Speyside is useful for explaining to folks we're half way between Aberdeen and Inverness.'

The Scotch Whisky Regulations 2009 define Speyside as 'the wards of Buckie, Elgin City North, Elgin City South, Fochabers, Lhanbryde, Forres, Heldon and Laich, Keith and Cullen and Speyside Glenlivet of the Moray Council as those wards are constituted in the Moray (Electoral Arrangements) Order 2006(b); and the Badenoch and Strathspey ward of the Highland Council as that ward is constituted in the Highland (Electoral Arrangements) Order 2006(c).'

Odd that something that purports to be a geographical region is defined by political boundaries rather than natural features such as, say, the Spey watershed, although since that would remove the whisky towns of Elgin, Forres and Keith from the definition, problems would undoubtedly ensue.

The other issue lies in the assumption that the drawing of a whisky region's boundaries also fixes its flavour. There is no single Speyside style. It's as elusive as one of the river's salmon. The joy of exploring the whiskies from the Spey Valley and surrounding catchments (I see why a catchier title is needed) lies in their diversity, not their uniformity.

They can be rich and meaty (Mortlach, Benrinnes, Glenfarclas, Balmenach), or waxy (Craigellachie). There's plump fruits in Benriach, nuts in Glenrothes and Knockando; there's the freshness of Glen Grant and Linkwood, the smoke that drifts through Benromach. The new makes from William Grant's three distilleries are completely different. If there isn't even a single Dufftown style, then how can you say there is one that stretches across the region?

If distillery character supplants region, can we even speak about place? I'd argue it is the only way. Place is what lies beneath the branding.

Here, it's about the rivers and the landscape, what made people settle here, how conditions dictated what could be grown where, how the railway allowed easy communication with the Lowland markets, resulting in distilling becoming a specialization.

Speyside's public face is about branding and talk about 'the region', but there is a private one, known to the people who live and work here, held in stories, music, dialect and those handed-down skills. How all of this weaves together with place are the truths that distillers can use. Place is the 'I am from here', and it is this diversity that is to be celebrated.

...

We head back to Torrin for a quick change. By the time I get downstairs, George Grant has arrived, clutching a magnum of Pol Roger. Seems rude to refuse. And so starts, as evenings in Speyside often do, a whirl of people, gossip, friendly banter. Older drams are brought out, things become more serious for a while, then a joke is cracked and we're off again before spiralling back to the whisky. Drinking as it should be.

At one point, the talk turns to the importance of community in whisky. 'Take Dennis,' says Kirsten. 'All he has known is us. If we don't hear from him for a few days, someone will go up to his house to check on him. To me this is normal, but it isn't, is it? Getting Dennis along to meet you both is fascinating insight for you – but it also allows me to check he is OK'.

Andy Fairgrieve had touched on the same thing the previous day. 'You're writing about community, aren't you? Well, why should a community be restricted to the present day? Why can't it involve people who lived 130 years ago – especially when they have left stuff like this? They can still contribute to our lived experience today. You holding that book is you connecting with the hand that wrote it – and that was Willie Grant.'

A distillery isn't just a building, a whisky isn't just a liquid or a bottle. Its essence, its tangibility, lies in these stories being shared by this circle of friends, and those with the ability to tell those stories, about whatever brand, can take them around the world and bring more people into that circle, make them share in the idea of this being from a place. This is the magic in the glass.

Whisky, however, is in danger of losing all of this as it starts to play in areas where surface is more important than depth, where the bottle is fetishized and the people forgotten. It's not as reductive as saying it's too expensive. It is about losing the resonances that tie the liquid to the people who made it. Forgetting the stories.

...

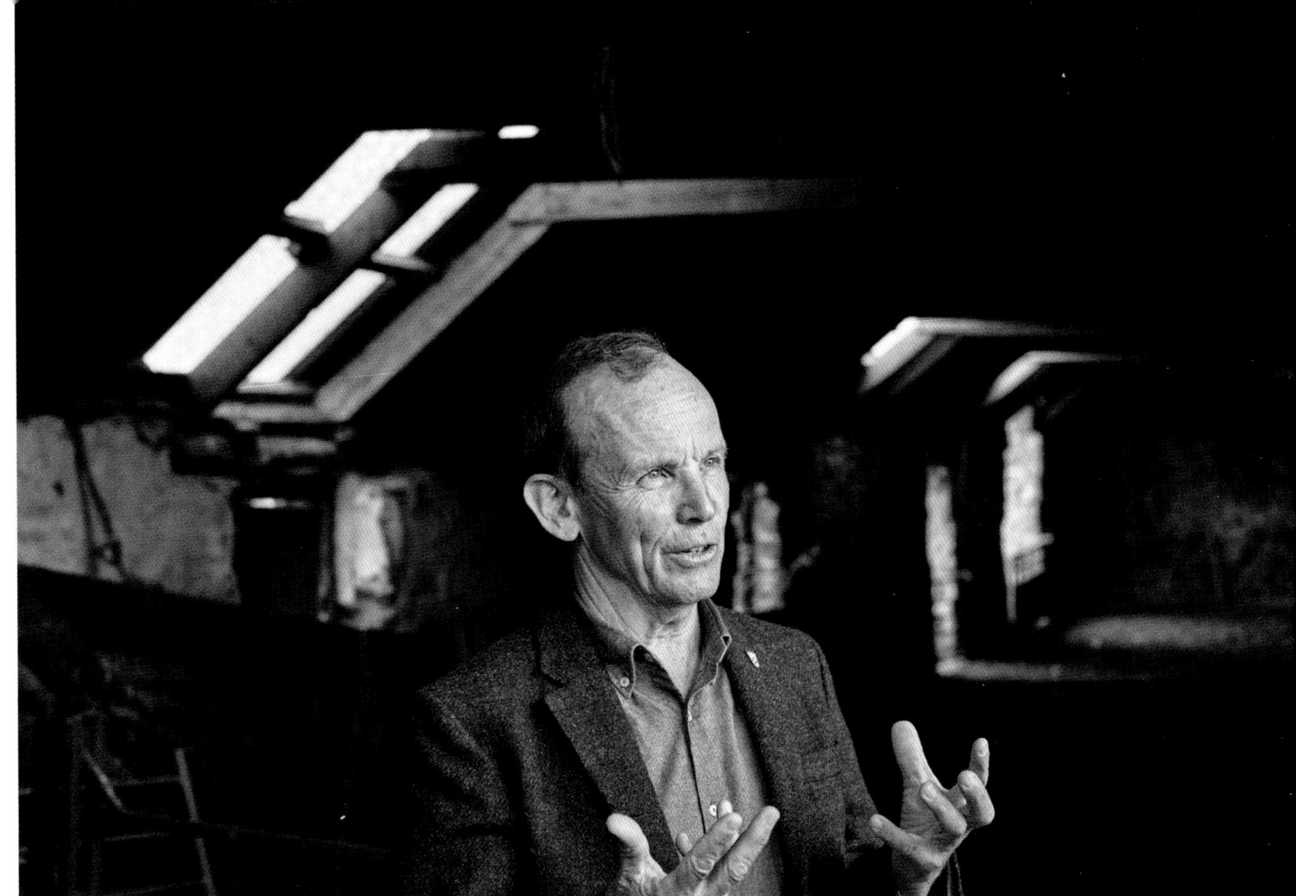

If lost, can these links be re-established? Grant Gordon (see above) believes they can. In the Cabrach, at the meeting of the Deveron and Blackwater, there's an eighteenth-century farm that sits at the heart of an effort to regenerate the area by The Cabrach Trust. Established 11 years ago, it has purchased a 175-acre site, including Inverharroch House, and the farm.

'It was a once-in-a-lifetime chance,' Grant, who is a Trustee, had said as we went into the farm's abandoned buildings. 'At its heart was the idea of bringing a community back to the Cabrach. It has to involve building affordable houses of different types. We spent six years working out where the new opportunities could be. The priority had to be economic regeneration and sustainable jobs, so the first thing is building a distillery here.'

The earth-floored, thick-walled steading buildings are long empty, but as he talks, so the empty space becomes filled with equipment and people. His eyes gleam as he describes the heritage centre telling the Cabrach's story, points to where the power comes in, where the mash tun will sit, the wooden washbacks, the stills. An old sheep shed will become a malting floor, using barley grown locally.

'If we want to make spirit in today's quality terms, we have to use one type of equipment,' he explains, then grins. 'We then thought, how can we talk history if we don't make whisky the old way? We had funded archaeological excavations of the old Blackmiddens distillery, which

Grant Gordon – philanthropist, social entrepreneur and Trustee of the Cabrach Trust

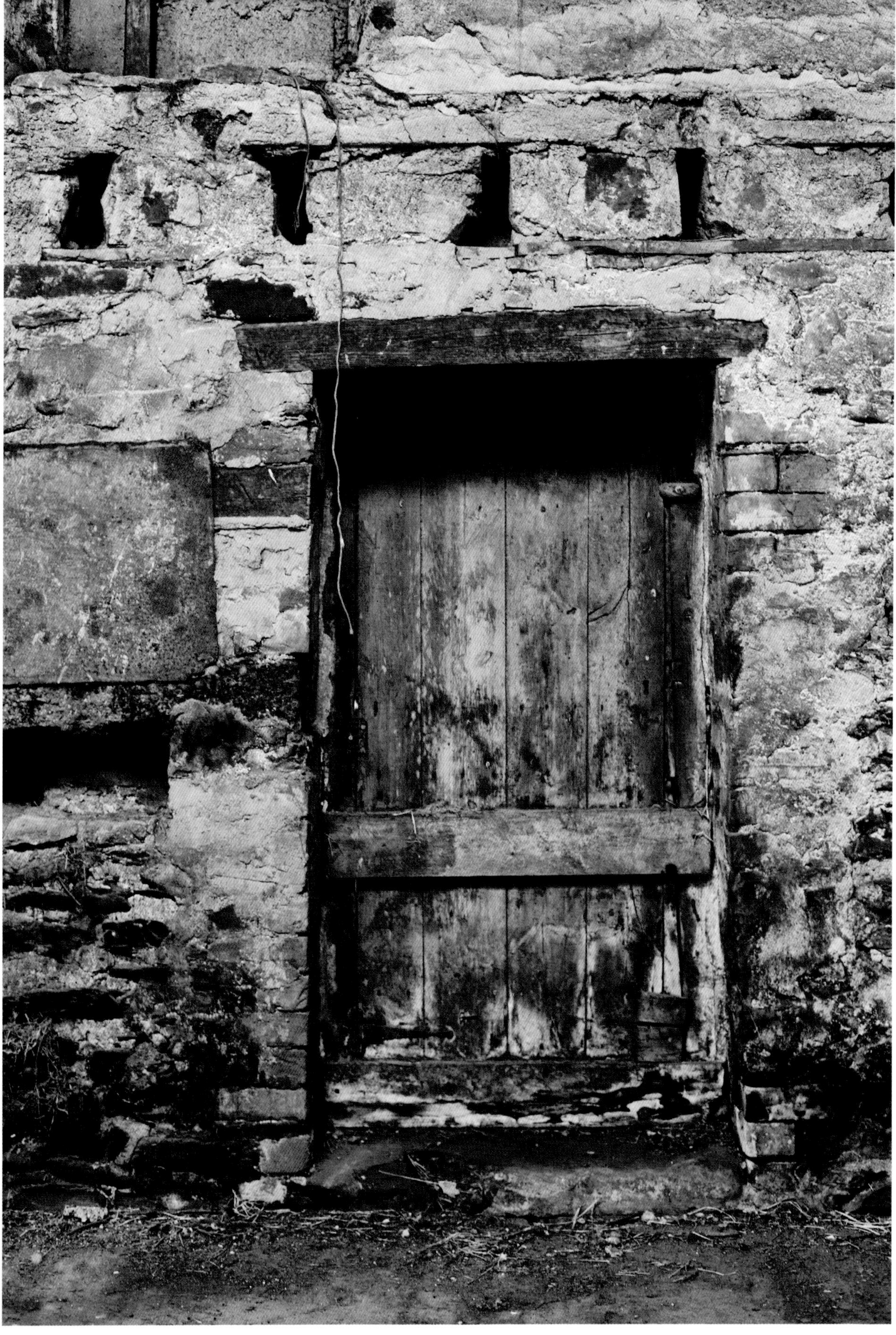

 Interior of what will be the Cabrach's new distillery

closed in the 1850s, so why not use that information to have another distillery here?' With one still, direct fired, it will be called the Buck, another old Cabrach name.

'The Cabrach's story is at risk of being lost,' he continues. 'This is our chance to tell the authentic story of whisky and of it being the beating heart of a community.' A loop is closed and, in a way, the true story of this elusive thing called Speyside may finally be told. Will it work? Think of who Grant's ancestors are.

...

The following day starts with rain stotting off the slabs. Undaunted, Christina and I head to the heritage railway for some final shots. This story has been about movement, of people, of knowledge and also, physically, of whisky. Speyside as we know it was built by the railway.

A young roe deer stands in the middle of the track. Looks our way, uncaring. Wild raspberries, rosebay, sticky willies (cleavers), dripping pines and oaks next to the rusting solidity of the trains, beside the steam and smells of the distillery. A complex co-existence.

We're both heading home. A question niggles as I sit in Inverness's excellent The Malt Room, refuelling before the train south. What will happen to Speyside as malt whisky moves into this new phase where place becomes more important? Embrace it, or move down a route that is more Napa Valley than Spey?

If whisky is about flavour, and regions seem sidelined, what are the different ways to read place, location and whisky? Maybe it will become clear in the west. For the moment, there's a dram to be drunk.

10

PENINSULAS

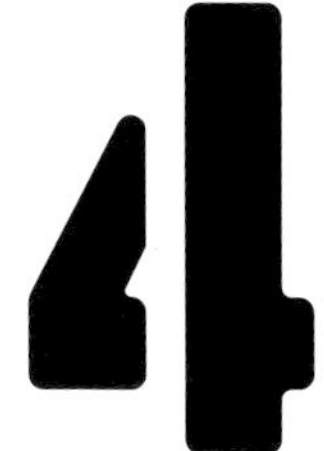

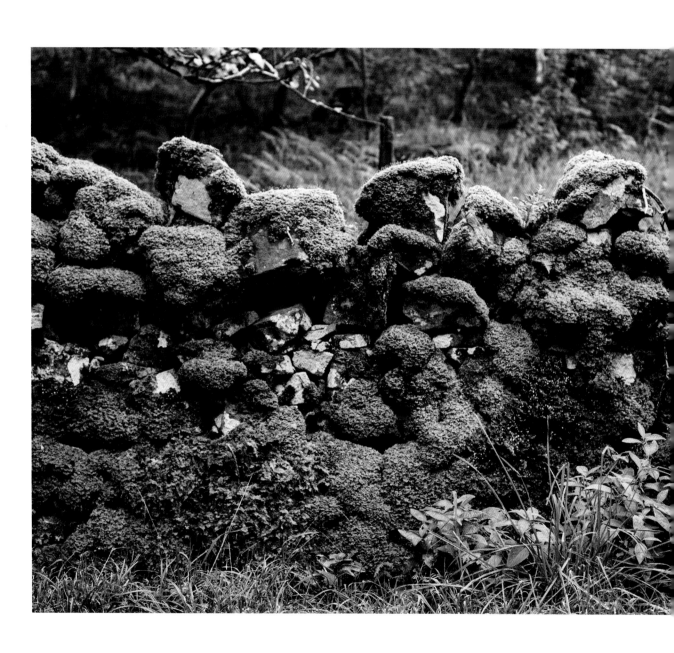

Westwards we go. Dunblane, Doune, Crianlarich. Past hotels that only exist for bus tours, then the stretch towards Tyndrum, where the road splits and the choice is made: either straight on to Taynuilt and Oban, or north-west. We're taking the latter. Christina is on holiday, following later, so this is a Broom family trip. Jo driving, Rosie again consigned to the back seat.

The road climbs up Glen Orchy, towards the triangular bulk of Ben Dorain, sides riven by streams, haunt of deer, setting for the great poem by Donnchadh Bàn Mac an t-Saoir (Duncan Ban MacIntyre, 1724–1812).

What's this thing about Gaelic poetry, you ask? For me, it's a way in to discover the links, old and new, between place and the drink, the relationship between landscape, people and culture, and how they help to create this thing called Scotch.

'Moladh Beinn Dóbhrain', published in 1768, is a 500-line description of the mountain, an account of the ways (and hunting) of its deer, its trees, herbs and flowers, arranged in the form of a pibroch: themes, variations, improvisations. It is a poem with a profound awareness of land and biodiversity.

Gaelic nature poetry has clarity and crystalline directness. Its lack of emotion and ecological awareness aligns it with poetry from China or Japan. The contemporary popularity of the eighteenth century's bards among the Gaelic-speaking population also demonstrates a shared mindset. Get to grips with that, and a different way of looking emerges.

Ben Dorain

As John Murray writes in *Literature of the Gaelic Landscape*, 'The land is often perceived through a prism of animism...landscape is frequently described in anthropomorphic and biomorphic terms.' It's accurate, forensic, metaphor-free and clustered with jewel-like detail. The quiver of a cleg-bitten flank or a tiny flower, is more important than the vastness of the landscape.

Whisky appears in the poems of this period. It is there in Iain MacAilein's fantastical tale from the early eighteenth century of the mystical, magical Tuatha Dé Danann transforming themselves into whiskies from Glasgow and Tiree in order to disguise themselves from the invading Milesians.

It's there in 'The Royal Bottle Song' by another great nature poet, Alasdair Mac Mhaighstir Alasdair: 'delightful on a spring day to hear the clucking, the whispering, the flask makes to the bowl...Sweeter than the cascade thou makest going into the cup...Sweeter than the music of the woodcock as he sings on the hillock is the murmuring of the bottle to the glass.'

Duncan Ban MacIntyre's 'Oran do Chaora' (Song to a Ewe) is also a poem of place, this time Glen Etive, an account of how he went 'thigging' (asking for wool) because his sheep had died and he needed a coat. It is a weave of place and people.

In Gleann Ceitlein he 'gets a fill of the scallop shell from the daughter of Grey Donald of the dram'; at Guala Chuilinn, whisky is

'fetched down to try and see if it will shake the sadness off me.' Whisky-fuelled, he is singing the glen into life.

He liked a dram. His wife, Mairi, was the daughter of the innkeeper at Inveroran, which we're just passing. Once married, they moved to Edinburgh where he joined the City Guard, while she ran a shebeen in the Lawnmarket.

MacIntyre's contemporary was the poet Robert Fergusson, the first to write in Scots about whisky. Imagine the session if their paths had crossed in Mairi's howff. Their linked tales speak of emigration to the city, the emergence of the big Highland policeman, and the start of a change in thinking about the Highlands – and whisky, which up until then had been passed over in preference for brandy or rum by the Lowland population.

Fergusson's poems mark the start of whisky becoming Scotland's national drink, because the idea of Scotland itself was changing. The 1823 Excise Act, which fundamentally changed the nature of whisky (see page 86), was one element in this tectonic shift, the results of which would ultimately benefit this new industry and take it worldwide.

The Highland Line, which a previous Act had imposed for legislative purposes, roughly followed a geological fault separating Lowlands from Highlands. This was also a cultural divide, whose existence was co-opted into the wider ramifications of the Improvements project – the strategy to 'civilize' the post-Jacobite Highlands. Literature played its part in this.

In the 1760s, James MacPherson published two works that he claimed were the rediscovered works of a bard called Ossian. They became a worldwide phenomenon, and although the existence of Ossian was debunked quickly in Scotland, the reframing of the Highlands as misty, sad and haunted was established.

Ossian, in turn, is linked to Edmund Burke's 1757 *Philosophical Enquiry,* which outlined the concept of the Sublime, and led to the Europe-wide Romantic movement of the late eighteenth and early nineteenth century. 'The passion caused by the Great and the Sublime in nature, when those causes operate most powerfully, is Astonishment,' Burke wrote, 'and Astonishment is that state of the soul, in which all its motions are suspended, with some degree of horror.'

 Glencoe in the sun

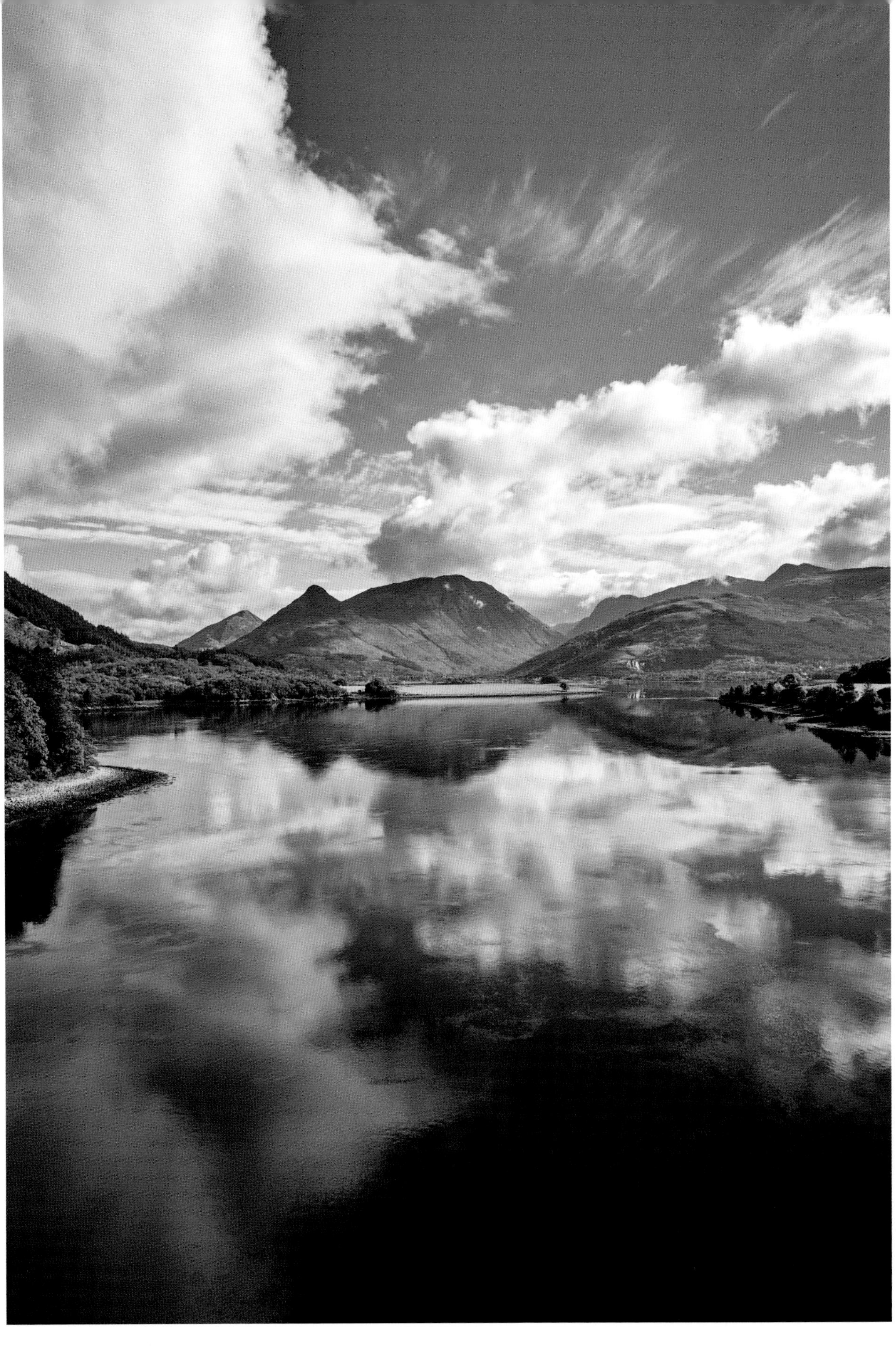

Mountains and crags? Dark waters? Tempestuous weather? Tick, tick, tick. Scotland's landscape provided the perfect mix of awe and terror to thrill the Romantic soul. The castles were ruined, the land empty. The threat of noble savages sweeping down from the glens was gone. They could be civilized, or moved. Scotland was safe, a blank slate on to which a new national myth could be written.

Into this landscape wandered the Romantic poets: Keats, Southey, Coleridge, and William and Dorothy Wordsworth. Their Scotlands are always steep and rugged, filled with chasms and foaming streams, gloom, mists and lonely maids singing. William and Dorothy stayed at the Inveroran Inn. Their take on the Highlands was very different from that of Duncan Ban MacIntyre.

As historian James Hunter writes in *On The Other Side of Sorrow*, 'The Highlands which the generality of people both wanted to visit and read about was a place whose primary purpose was to gratify the wider world's conceptions of what the Highlands *ought to be* [my emphasis]. Wordsworth's natural world is to be experienced emotionally much more than it is to be methodically observed...Duncan Ban's verse is never introspective...it is strictly naturalistic.' The Romantics observed and commented, at one remove. The Gaelic poet inhabited the landscape.

Whisky has been, dare I say at the risk of being pretentious, Romantic in its approach to using place. My own thinking about whisky has also shifted from that of an onlooker, a noter of facts, volumes and flavours, to one who attempts, with varying degrees of success, to inhabit the sensation of the liquid, and feel it bringing me into a web of connections.

...

The road rises and starts its curve to the west. We're on the fringes of Rannoch Moor, lochans the colour of lapis lazuli, low russet peat hags, lone, wind-mangled pines. Then, ahead, the land drops away and the road plunges into Glencoe. As ever, there's a piper in the lay-by at the top, crowds of tourists, phones out, snapping this Instagram-perfect Scottish moment. Behind him the bulk of Buachaille Etive Mor and Beag. Memories return of the last trip here, climbing the latter in a snowstorm simply to open a bottle of whisky at the top. With Lauren MacColl's 'Landskein' playing, we drive down the glen, hemmed in by mountains, over the bridge at Ballachulish, then across Loch Linnhe at Corran ferry, with its first smell of the sea. We are feeling the pull of the west coast.

On to the Corran ferry

We're now in Morvern, the most southerly of Lochaber's three peninsulas: 518 square kilometres of hill, moor, shore and woods. Its northern border is Loch Sunart, its eastern Loch Linnhe, and south-west the Sound of Mull.

The road, ever narrowing, switchbacks through moor, then downhill to Lochaline, before a right turn along the Sound of Mull. The road now has grass in the middle of it and no sign of a distillery. Not for the first time, Jo is beginning to wonder about my skill with directions. Then a sign saying 'Almost There'. The world turns green as we enter winding, twisting, moss-festooned woodland. Round the corner and, beneath us, blond stone buildings. Nc'nean.

...

An open square, rough harled walls, the stills framed in a picture window, with what seem to be tomatoes growing inside. The sky bright blue, sunlight casting a diamanté sheen on the sound of Mull. Across the water is Tobermory. We're met by Amy Stammers and her dog.

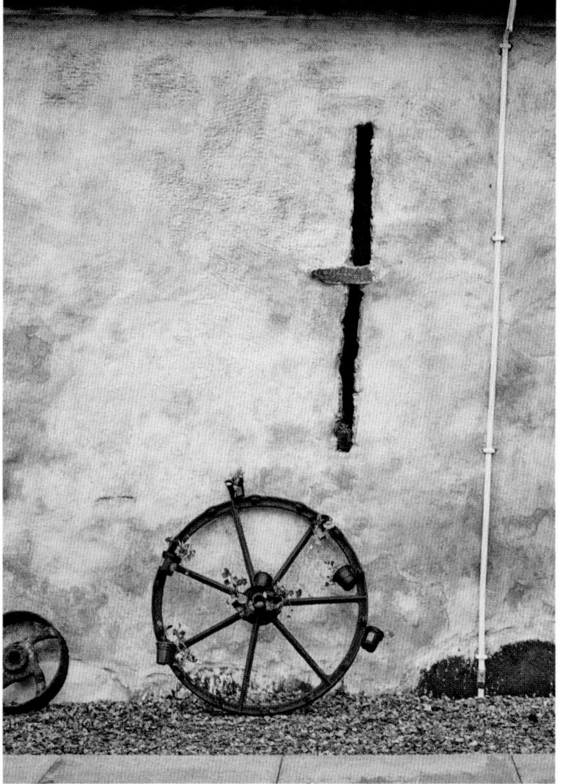

'This is dug,' she says.

'He's lovely. What's his name?'

'Dug' she replies. 'Like Douglas.'

'You have a dug called Doug?'

'I know...' Amy, who has a background in environmental law and hospitality, moved here from Norfolk (where people have dogs), via Glasgow (where they have dugs).

'My only aim in getting a job was that it had to be in Scotland, because it's more environmentally aware than England,' she says. 'I found Nc'nean after working in hospitality in Ardnamurchan. Organic... and whisky? Perfect!'

That's Nc'nean in a sentence. Its founder, Annabel Thomas (see opposite) had no whisky background, but did have a vision of a distillery that was organic and sustainable. The reason why it's here is because her parents purchased the Drimnin Estate in 2002, and started a project to make it self-sufficient and earn its keep.

'This was the tail end of that,' Amy explains. 'In 2013, there was a debate whether the buildings should be holiday lets, or a distillery. They wanted to create year-round employment, and build a sense of community. A distillery meant people moving here and staying. Apart from Gordon (Wood, the manager; see page 124), none of us had any experience in

Old steading walls, Nc'nean

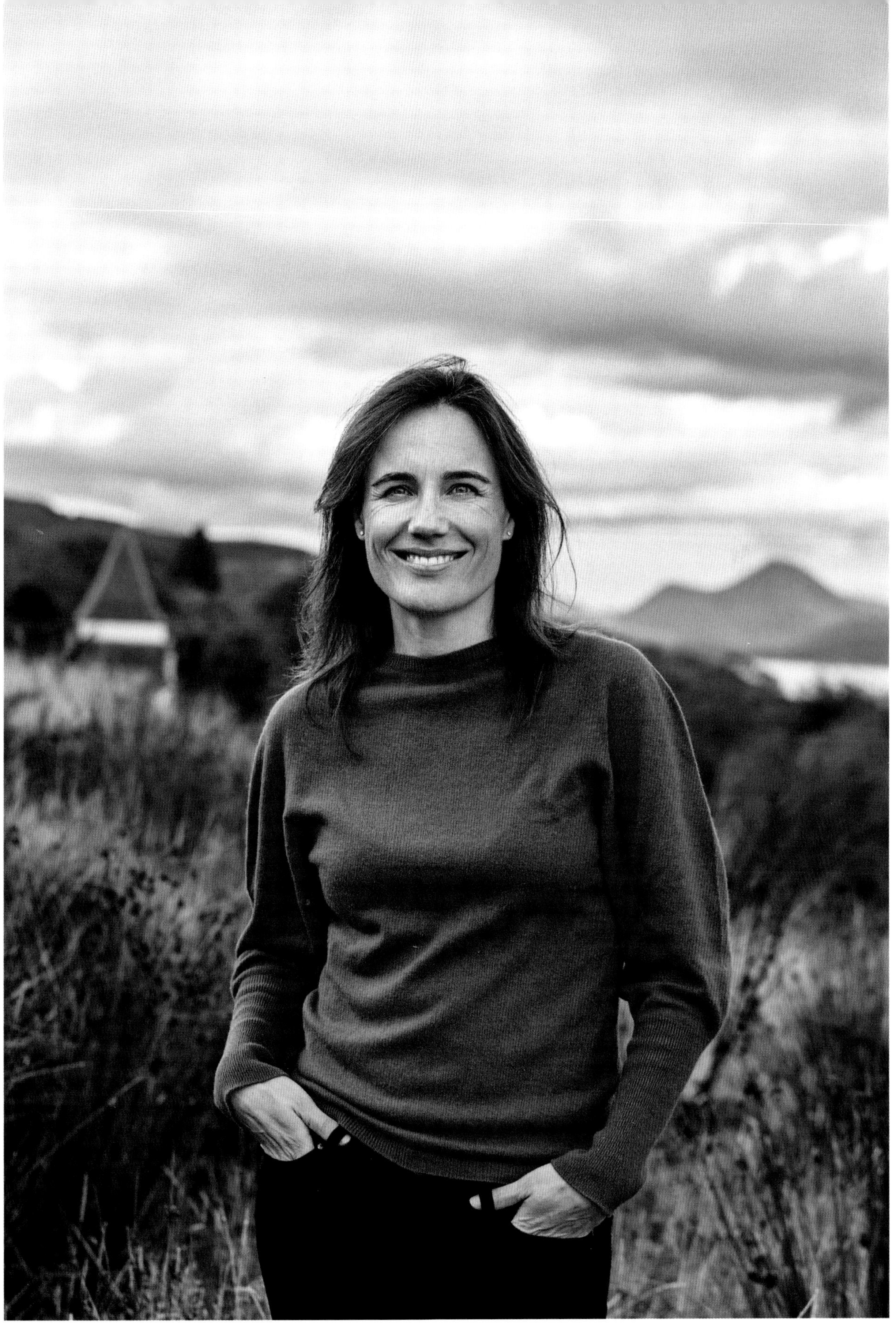

Annabel Thomas, CEO of Nc'nean, Scotland's first organic whisky distillery

Manager Gordon Wood, with some of the distillery's fuel

whisky. Lorna (one of the distillers) arrived here with her husband, who manages the farm. Cindy (office manager) relocated from Devon with her husband, who also works on the estate. Then her brother-in-law and wife moved up. Simon' – she points at a chap feeding a wood-chipper – 'was a chef. We've all brought something different to the mix.'

Building a distillery is an expensive process, necessitating deep pockets, and investors who understand that they won't see a return for many years. By law, Scotch whisky must be aged, in Scotland, for a minimum of 3 years in oak casks of no more than 700 litres. That means a constant outlay in wood, barley, warehousing and energy, even before the first bottle is filled. The costs run into millions.

One way around this, which has been adopted by newer distillers, has been to make a gin. Without any ageing requirements, this can be released as soon as it's made, generating cashflow. Gin is a neutral spirit redistilled with botanicals, which (legally) must have a predominant flavour of juniper. When it opened in 2017, Nc'nean took a different tack, and released a botanical spirit. Five of these (heather, thyme, sorrel, bog myrtle, angelica) are sourced locally, with juniper (at low levels, so it's not legally gin), coriander and grapefruit brought in. In doing so, they tapped into whisky's oldest manifestation: as a medicine.

There is strong argument that the first distillers in Scotland were a family called the Beatons, who had arrived from Ireland in the fourteenth century. They were doctors, translators of medical texts, including those on distillation, from Latin into Gaelic. Queen's College, Dublin holds an early-fifteenth-century text in Irish from a similar medical kindred, the O'Leighins, which gives a recipe for 'usquebaugh' (water of life), the name that would be given to 'botanical' whisky from Scotland and Ireland until the nineteenth century. Contemporaneous Beaton texts in Gaelic are being studied at the National Library of Scotland.

A central character in Neil M. Gunn's novel *Butcher's Broom* is an old woman, Dark Mairi, the keeper of the ancient ways that are disappearing as the Clearances begin, 'the human mother carrying on her ancient solitary business with the earth, talking good and familiar sense with boulder and flower and rock.'

The novel starts with her, a basket on her back, collecting ingredients for medicines: dulse, linarich (samphire), slake (laver), as well as spirewort, which, when packed into a limpet shell that was fastened to the thigh 'in order to raise a big blister', was a cure for sciatica.

Usquebaugh (and by extension whisky) started as a curative and, as the knowledge of distillation spread into the community, it, like brewing, would have been women's work. That female power runs through Nc'nean, which is named after Neachneohain, who was (depending on your source) either a Gaelic goddess or a witch (aka a wise woman).

'We want to bring in a new generation of whisky drinkers, who are into mixing cocktails,' says Amy. 'Gin taps into that, and the botanical spirit was a bridge, which also tells the older story of whisky.'

Nc'nean is the first 100-per-cent organic distillery in Scotland. Was the decision taken for marketing purposes? 'Not at all,' says Amy. 'We want to make a whisky that has as little impact on its environment as possible, and for us that means it had to be organic. We're losing insect populations, pollinators, and soils are so degraded they can only be productive due to fertilizers.

'Ninety per cent of the barley grown in Scotland is used in whisky, so the industry is a huge part of that issue. Whisky is linked to farming. There's a responsibility there.'

Gordon has appeared. He was an operator at Oban distillery before coming to Morvern. 'There's more to do here,' he says. 'It's more hands on. OK, it's remote and you have to get your head around that, but it's been fantastic going from Oban's ways to this – different barleys, yeast trials, organics and the boiler. It's nice to have all of those different tweaks that you can apply to create flavour. That's the beauty of being new.'

You don't often start a distillery walkthrough by spending time beside its boiler, but this is where Nc'nean's drive for sustainability begins. Boilers usually run off LPG or heavy oil. Here it's woodchips. It's a huge beast, the size of a tank. 'It took some learning,' says Gordon looking at it with a sense of pride. 'The size of the woodchips, how to feed, the right pressure and temperature.' It devours between eight and fifteen tons of wood a week, all coming from the estate, which is now running on a forty-year planting-to-felling cycle. The steam generated is used for heating water, the stills, and there are plans for it to also heat the offices, and houses.

Distilling also uses a vast amount of water, mainly in condensing. Having a cooling pond allows Nc'nean to recycle all of the water that runs through the condensers: 80 per cent of its volume.

A mix of long and short ferments, clear wort and slow distillation with plenty of reflux helps to produce a fresh, lightly fruity new make that's now been given a little more depth thanks to a lower cut point – and the introduction of another yeast strain.

'We're now using Fermentis as well as Anchor,' says Gordon. 'It brings forward congeners that weren't present in the old recipe. The new cut point is there to capture those flavours.' Yeast trials are continuing with wine, other spirit yeasts, and some used in beer, including the ancient Norse farmhouse strain, Kveik.

We sit in the sun and have a sneak preview of the delicious first release, all gooseberries, grapefruit and yellow plums, with some almond notes (like the meadowsweet that is all around), green bracken and fresh barley. It also makes a great Highball cocktail.

...

A few months later, Amy's sustainability report was released, revealing that the distillery was net zero for emissions, emitting only 26 tons of carbon, which is then offset. I caught up with Annabel to congratulate her. 'You know the funny thing, Dave? We didn't change anything to get there. We simply counted and measured and discovered that we'd been net zero since 2017!

'Part of what we're trying to do with the report is to educate consumers on what sustainable looks like, and try to establish benchmarks that can be used across the industry. There's plenty of statements made without data or definitions, but if you can't measure it, you can't change it.'

The next step is to further reduce the carbon footprint in the distillery's supply chain, which reveals the complex, interrelated nature of the business – should gift boxes be stopped? Can bottles be refilled? How to source recycled glass, reduce transport miles and examine the raw materials? This takes us back to the farmer.

A switch from an English maltings to one in Inverness has helped reduce carbon, and so has reducing the number of farms from a dozen to two. 'It gives us the chance to do single-farm distillations,' says Annabel, 'but the real reason is that it allows us to work with the farmers to reduce their carbon footprint and explore regenerative farming solutions.'

Has it been hard being a pioneer?

She smiles. 'I'd say yes, because generally you are always taking a harder route. I compare it to being the older sibling who has to have all the big fights. But most of ours have worked out.'

Wouldn't it have been easier to have built a distillery on Speyside?

'That's true! But being here is the essence of who we are. Part of the mission is to bring skilled, year-round, stable employment to the community. Bottling on site meant being able to recruit locally again, which has brought us closer to the community and hopefully made them a bit more understanding of the value the distillery can bring.'

Is it lonely? 'While we have whisky neighbours in Ardnamurchan and Tobermory, the difficulty of travel means that you do feel like you are on your own and that sense of walking your own path is very stark when you are that remote and isolated.'

Self-doubt?

'I don't think so. I don't feel that. It is just where we are. From a broad philosophical point of view, that idea of a sense of place here is about wilderness, nature and community.'

Does the location of a distillery in a remote area adds a greater level of social responsibility?

The answer is immediate. 'Yes. Morvern is large, but sparsely populated, and apart from tourism and work on estates and farms, the only two major employers are the sand mine, and us. What I hope we can achieve is to attract a younger generation locally, because things like the sustainability of the local primary school is essential to the viability of the community, and as more houses are used for lets, retirement and second homes, the number of children falls. Hopefully we can stem that flow, if not reverse it.'

It's a very west-coast problem. People like to retire here because it is quiet and beautiful (that Romantic ideal persists). Having a distillery next door shatters that dream, but the young people who live here need employment.

Is there also a greater need for self-reliance?

'That's right, and it creates an attitude of solution-generating, rather than problem-generating, which you can apply to lots of parts of the business. From a practical point of view it also determines how we make the products we make – the botanical spirit being the best example.'

A distillery, especially in a location such as this, causes ripples that go beyond the making of spirit and touch on the viability of communities, schools, a GP practice, transport, forestry and farming. All are central to the thinking of the twenty-first-century distiller.

...

We bid farewell to Amy and Doug the dug, and head towards Ardnamurchan. It's only around 10 kilometres to the north as the crow flies, but one of the joys of Scotland is the fact that no road is ever straight. At least, as passengers, that's what Rosie and I think.

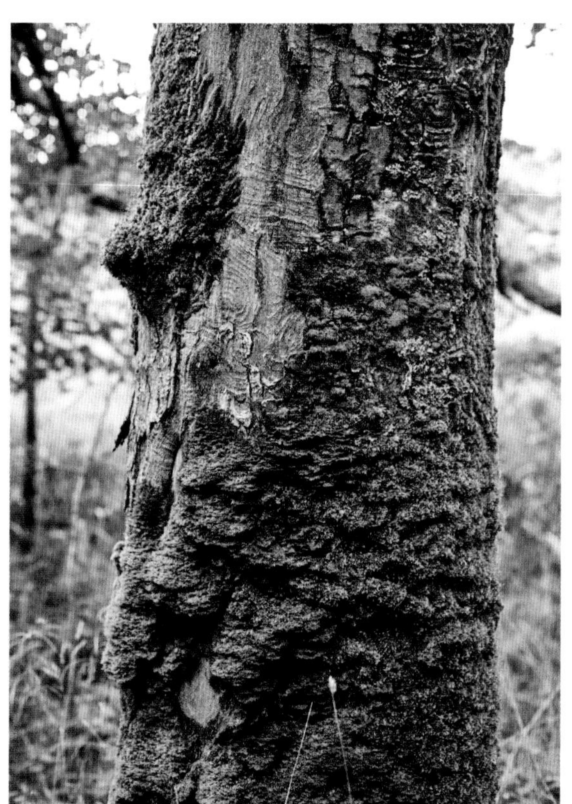

Jo is less sure. To get north, we first go south-east, then north-east, and finally west. 74 kilometres in nearly two hours on a silent, car-free road, hills studded with glacial erratics, one the shape of a diamond, to the head of Loch Sunart and into the woods.

I first came here with my old friend Sami Yassa, who had guided me around California's Muir Woods. That was my chance to show him Scotland's own temperate rainforest. His towering Douglas fir, sequoia and purple light; mine twisted, intertwined, deep green, felted with moss, branches embroidered with lungwort and lichen – 'Suaineart ghorm an daraich' (green Sunart of the oaks).

The poet Gerry Loose spent 18 months living here. His book, *An Oakwoods Almanac*, is a deep immersion in this place.

While it may look like it, this isn't an old-growth forest, but one that was coppiced, the oak used for charcoal, for blast furnaces, and bark for tanning. 'The woodland like all worked landscape, is art and as such, fictive,' writes Loose. 'If I'm expounding on the great book of the woodland, the lives of the trees, their history and economics, then each tree, in its subdividing and recurving limbs, is reciting genetics, performing climate and topography, geology, and its own personal survival so far.'

The road bucks and corkscrews through the trees, blind summit after blind summit. We're meeting up with some of the Ardnamurchan distillery team at Glenborrodale Castle, a former five-star hotel, which has

Left: Festooned with moss
Right: The road to Ardnamurchan

lain empty for years. There's a shortage of accommodation in this part of the world, and Ardnamurchan's MD Alex Bruce (see page 139) has pulled strings. Jo is mildly worried about dress codes and the fact that I'd dropped the information that she was a cook.

We pull up in front of a red sandstone Scottish Baronial pile. Alex, his wife Vikki, two of their daughters, plus sales director Connal Mackenzie and sales executive Graeme Mackay, are unloading cars, swiping at midges.

The castle is suitably faded and grand, filled with gloomy portraits, stuffed heads of Highland cows, large staircases, turrets and as many midges inside as out. A Scottish deerhound wanders around like the ghost of an ancient retainer.

Alex appears. 'I just flushed the toilet and the cistern lid flew off! I need a drink.' We gather in a lounge, complete with a wheezing pump organ, and drink G&Ts. We're joined by Sandy Macdonald (see opposite) and his wife Liz (see page 135), who have a farm further along the lochside. She's bearing a huge platter of lobsters. Liz is also a director of Adelphi (the distillery's parent company), joining not long after Alex bought the firm – almost by mistake. 'I went in to try and buy some whisky, they offered me the job of running the company,' as he puts it. He is one of the nicest men in an industry not short of them.

Adelphi is one of the highest-rated independent bottlers, with an exacting set of standards, rejecting 80 per cent or more of the casks it is offered. 'I think the easiest way to describe the Adelphi style is, "I'd want to have another dram",' says Alex. 'It's got to be nice, easy to drink and exciting. We don't mind where it's from or how old it is. It just has to have that flavour.' Tonight at the lobster feast it's wine, then just the one, or maybe three, afterwards.

...

We rise early. Grey, smirry weather. The sink is full of midges. Alex and I drive to Ardslignish to see Sandy and Liz. Cows in the field. Small farmhouse on the promontory. A sawmill down the hill. The sweet caramel smell of cut timber, piles of sawdust glowing a gentle gold.

Last night, the talk had turned to sailing on the west coast, and the fact that Sandy builds boats. He demurred in true Scottish fashion, insisting they were nothing special and that no-one would be interested in seeing them. Thankfully, he was persuaded otherwise.

'This one is Waxwing,' he says as we enter the first shed. I can haul a sail, and bungle through a tack, but even these eyes can tell the beauty of her lines. 'Larch ribs,' he says, smoothing the hull gently. 'They're all sailboats, 18–20 foot, with traditional rigging.' I'm already calculating how much money is in the bank.

'It's a traditional build, but here's a few things of my own. See, how she has a fine entry and good exit? That makes her fast.' He pats the rail

Sandy Macdonald, farmer, boatbuilder

Distilled sunlight in Sandy's shed

absentmindedly. 'I've sold some, but…' You get the feeling that he doesn't want to let them go. They are part of who he is. He seems to anticipate my thoughts. 'I'm 83. There comes a point when you have got to stop, but I don't want to.'

Each shed contains another boat or two, each one more remarkable than the last. 'You'd really like to see another? Well, this is Lapwing. A rebuild of a boat that was lost with all hands, then found its way home and, as tradition dictates, burned.'

She glows. 'It's like distilled sunlight' says Liz. 'I can tell when he's thinking about a new boat. He starts getting broody.' Amazingly, they are all built by eye. 'I get the idea in my mind and play around,' he explains, as if it were simple. Hand of the maker.

The conversation flits from boats and wood to the changing profile of the area. 'It's altered a lot because of the invasion from the south,' he says. 'I check the estate agents every so often. All it brings up for this part are holiday houses for sale.

'The communities aren't what they were'. He smiles. 'I mean, there's nothing wrong with the English, but they do try to take over… On Knoydart (which is famously road-free), a property developer from Haslemere arrived, sold all the houses to his pals, got rid of the locals. His pals did one summer, but couldn't cope with the winter. They all left, but the prices went up, and the locals couldn't get back in. It's an insidious Clearance.'

And so the arrival of the distillery?

'…was a vast event. There's no employment here, bar forestry, or fish farming. There's no young blood coming into farming because farms are expensive. There should be a Scottish Government plan to train for farming, forestry, handcrafts, boatbuilding, distilling. That's why the distillery is so important. There's 29 locals employed there now.'

Alex chimes in. 'You need traditional industries. You can't survive on tourism. Covid has taught us that. Fishing, farming, forestry and whisky are vital elements in this part of the world.'

We wander back to see Liz's cows. She arrived here in the early 1970s, 'I was a dolly bird from London, hired to work in a bar,' as she puts it. She plays down the fact that the job she left was working as a PR for The Beatles. She calls the cows over. 'They live out on the hill all year. Genuine hill stock are different and only the fit survive.

'Throw anything at them and they'll survive. Folk don't understand about the herb-rich pasture of the hill. The cattle self-medicate, they eat

tormentil, thyme or other herbs, choose the grasses to eat. The old meadows were there as a medicine chest.'

We're looking over the Sound. 'You have to be a realist to live here,' Sandy says. 'It's tough. It always has been, but you can live off what you can grow here. You can be self-sufficient.' He looks around. 'It is being here. The scenery. You can't eat it, but you can enjoy it.' The sense of a couple in a landscape. Not escapees, or seekers of solitude, but embedded in it, knowing its herbs and trees, its tides and history.

...

Alex and I go back to the still. I hesitate to use the term remote, but Ardnamurchan is the most westerly point of Britain, probably known to insomniacs everywhere thanks to the shipping forecast. No railway, few roads. Why the decision to build here? In fact, why on earth even build a distillery?

Independent bottlers rely on stock coming either from brokers, or directly from distillers. The growth in single malt has resulted in the latter building their own brands and limiting the supply of casks, especially those from distilleries that had built up a reputation.

'By 2007, the volume of the third-party stocks was falling, and their prices were rising,' Alex explains. 'We considered filling new make, buying a distillery, or building one. Stupidly, we chose the third option!'

Liz Macdonald with one of her cows

The site was chosen thanks to historical connections to the area from chairman Donald Houston and former director and estate owner Keith Falconer. The thinking then became what sort of distillery this could – or maybe should – be. 'It was how to best fit its location. That's when the whole concept of sustainability and circular economy really started. Ardnamurchan is a small, remote place. It was obvious we should be as symbiotic with the estate as possible.'

The distillery, which started producing in 2014, was the first to install a 100-per-cent biomass woodchip boiler, fed by local, sustainable forestry with supplementary power from a hydro plant in the river. All the draff feeds the estate's cattle. Suddenly the location wasn't a hindrance, but an advantage.

'Food and drink is now Scotland's biggest industry,' says Alex, 'but it relies on its own local, natural resources. I don't agree with taking something out of the food chain. If you're going biomass I don't think you should be burning your draff (which is one option). It should remain as a highly nutritional animal feed.'

Taking this sustainable option also results in a deeper understanding and connection to the supply chain, and opens up seemingly endless possibilities, such as capturing CO_2. 'You don't get a huge amount from a small distillery, but the critical thing was to try and find local demand, because there's no point in doing it unless you help the local economy.

All the distillery's draff feeds the estate's cows

'There's an increase in greenhouses and polytunnels on the peninsula, so we can basically grow our own fruit and veg all year round. Using captured CO_2 for heating might be a possibility. Offsetting emissions is just a sticking plaster.

'The big distillers are doing amazing things with anaerobic digestion, but unless some great scientist comes up with a smaller, efficient model it is just not possible to do on our scale. What you really need is lots of micro schemes, which together become macro. Once a few people have shown that it's possible it becomes more obvious.'

It chimes with the thinking of Tim Ingold, professor of anthropology at Aberdeen University, whose approach asks whether sustainability is not 'how can we carry on doing what we are doing, but with a bit less waste and impact', but rather, 'what kind of world has a place for us and future generations?'

Ingold contends that the current concepts around sustainability are underpinned by an assumption that the 'entire Earth is a standing reserve, and that we need to protect it in the way that a company protects its profits.' What is required, he argues, is to see sustainability from a holistic, rather than human-centric, viewpoint.

Alex's understanding of whisky's interrelated nature has been deepened by the company's adoption of blockchain technology – the first whisky company to do this. The blockchain records and locks in every piece of information to do with the running of the distillery, making the whole process transparent and, from Alex's point of view, allowing greater insight.

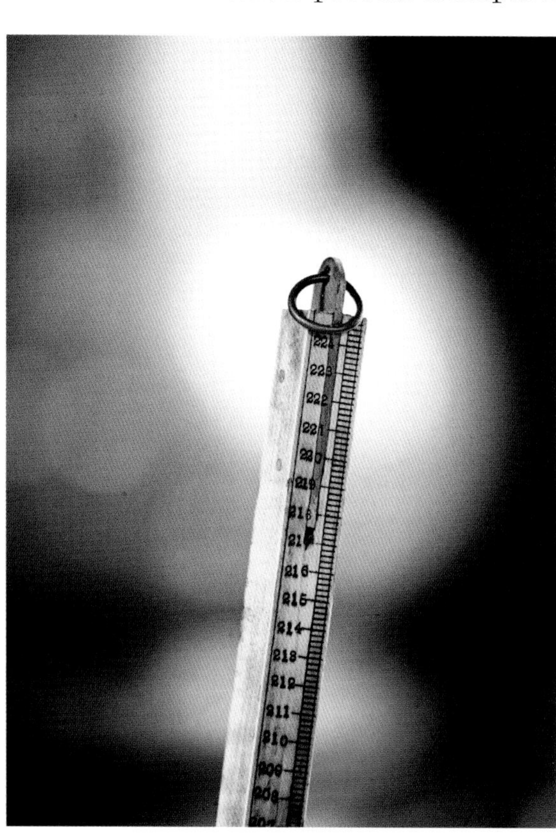

'The more we looked at it, the more arms and legs and fingers and toes it grew. It gives the consumer transparency, while also allowing the producer to monitor the supply chain. Because we already have to register every part of the process with HMRC, we will have everything detailed in the blockchain, from the barley in the field, through the process, into the warehouse.

'That then allows us to look at the casks we have chosen, and see the cool, or hot, or damp, or dry spots in the warehouse and the flavours produced; when we have sampled it, if it has been re-racked, how many times the cask has been filled. Now we can also put our carbon footprint into it as well, allowing us to measure it, and people to see.'

Ardnamurchan's barley comes from the Bruce Farms in Fife. Two styles are made: unpeated and peated. Fermentis and Anchor yeast for the former, Anchor alone for the latter.

Taking the temperature

Very long ferments – the longest over 100 hours – build the fruits, while the cuts are different for each style of new make, which are matured separately, then blended.

The final result is made up of equal parts of 5- to 6-year-old, peated and unpeated whisky, with a roughly 70:30 split between ex-bourbon and ex-sherry casks (varying between batches). Its inaugural release arrived fully formed: a compelling, oily, complex mix of clam juice, sweet leather, orange, baked peach, bonfire and hot oyster shells.

We're in the warehouse now, meeting with Stewart Connor, whose domain this is. Our chat starts with the usual discussion of volumes, sizes, ratios and so on, but soon spins off into history, and once we realize we were at the same Clash gigs in Glasgow, we're off.

Stewart took early retirement from the building trade to move here. He starts on a detailed history of the peninsula, from the Neolithic site at Camus nan Geall, to the medieval Lords of the Isles, the Jacobite years and subsequent Clearances. 'There's a cultural aspect to whisky,' he explains. 'People associate Scotland with this drink, so the history of the place is important.

'The cultural thing drove me to this job. Having a hand in something that's been made for centuries in Scotland, and now helping its continuity is mind-blowing, and it is local. It is from here, so are we. We are breathing the same air.

'Even people on the islands think this place is the back of beyond,' he laughs. 'That's why the distillery is so important. The impact's been massive. All the kids at the school have been given casks for their future benefit when they turn 18. It's created an economy. People stay, visitors come. My partner works with wool, I'm also a weaver, and we get more sales through the distillery shop.'

Climate, air pressure and temperature all drive the interplay of oak, oxygen and spirit. Here, geology also comes into play. There's a rockface immediately behind the distillery, so the first warehouse has its upper floor above ground, while its lower one has the rock at the back and sides. It's given a massive difference in maturation rates – the bottom cool and slow, the top rapid. Two different time machines – the lower showing what happens to flavour if maturation is gentle, the upper a snapshot of the fully mature style.

Connal Mackenzie produces glasses and samples are drawn at random: fresh casks, ex-sherry, refill, peated, unpeated. The quality is exceptional, the characters fascinating. 'We want to make an honest west-coast whisky at an affordable price,' says Alex as we start. 'It is a bolder spirit and it takes on elements of where it is from.

'It's why we've stuck with traditional dunnage warehousing. It will ensure that our own microclimate and proximity to the sea can aid an even and steady maturation. We want to get some salinity in the whisky.'

Ah, the elusive saltiness found in some but by no means all coastal whiskies. No-one has cracked why it exists. Another bung is popped.

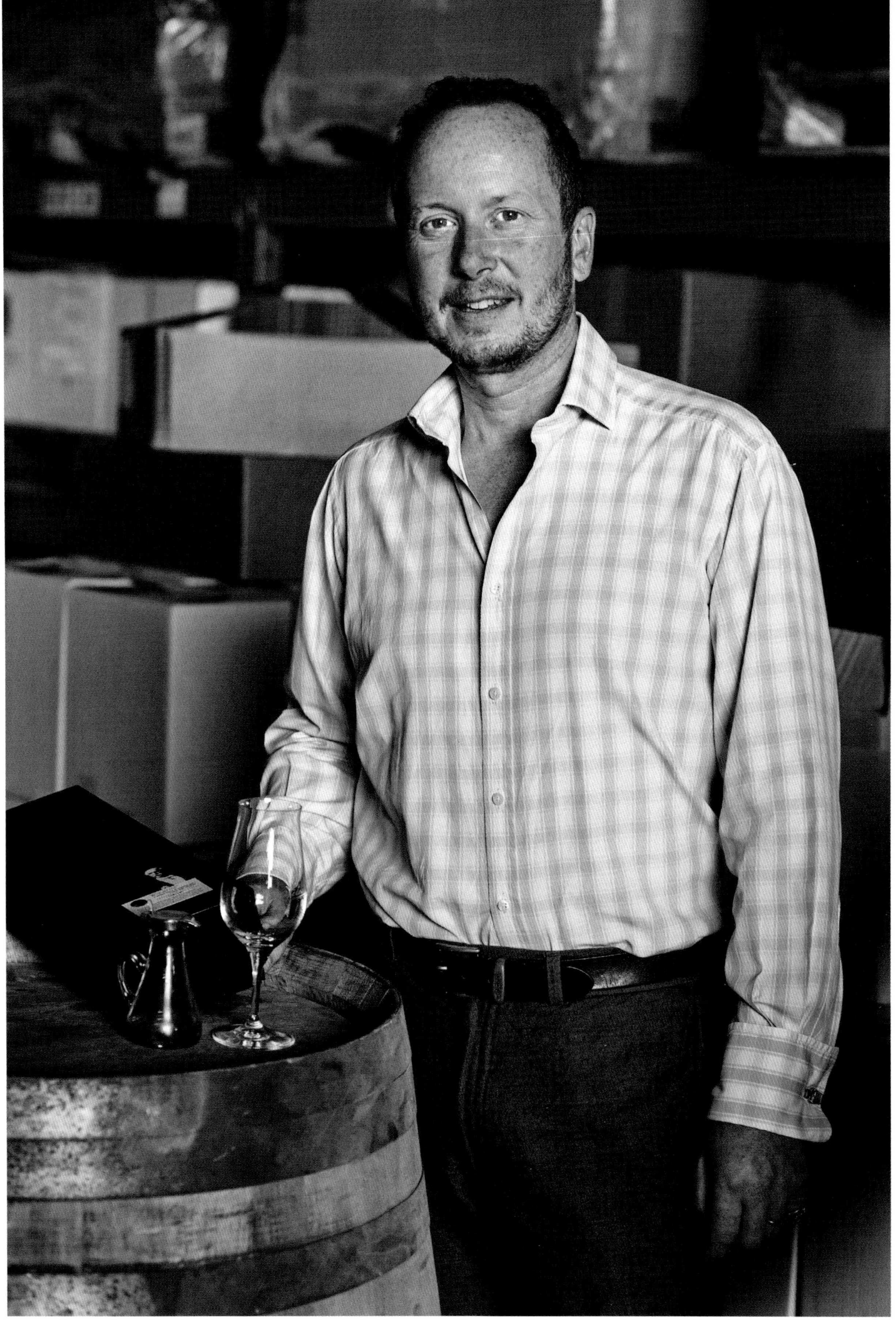

Alex Bruce, visionary whisky-maker

The brininess of the spirit is off the scale, it's like leaping into Loch Sunart. The analytical mind is saying don't be influenced by the fact that you're by the sea, but you can't ignore this saltiness, because it is there.

...

Connal wants to test out his new drone, so we drive up to the water source. The road is high above the river, so we walk gingerly down the steep bank, searching for a route. Alex goes on, disappearing over what seems to be a precipice. We hang back, unsure. 'Can we make it?' we shout to his disappearing head.

'Er...probably,' he calls back, and vanishes. There's no scream, so we follow, sliding down the mossy slope, grabbing birch trees for support. We find him at the foot of the gorge, standing at the river's side, beside a huge waterfall. Cold spray, black rock, a series of deep pools.

'It was worth it,' I tell him.

He grins. 'Why only go so far when you could go all the way?'

Everything about Ardnamurchan is driven by location. I ask Alex the same question I posed to Annabel about whether working here has given them a deeper understanding of place, and whether it's changed any of their initial thoughts.

'Initially we were battling a small minority who didn't want a distillery, so we had to focus on how to do this in a way that wasn't going to upset the neighbours – from architecture, to how we deal with by-products, to transport.

'Having people visiting appeals to some locals because they get business, but it might not appeal to the people who have retired here for the quiet, so it's always been about a sympathetic balancing act.

'One thing, which has become increasingly significant, is the importance of the team. They're now not only experienced in making good whisky, but making good whisky in this place. You can't just pick up the phone to someone around the corner to ask how to fix a biomass boiler, because at the start no-one had one – and anyway there isn't anyone round the corner!

'We were forging our own approach, and the team's grown up around it – and they're local. Gordon Mackenzie used to drive the school bus. He's now production manager and his son's just started.

'The next stage is to push for the next generation and for them to look at this as a local employer with a future career. We'll continue with the cask scheme for the kids, and also get one of the team into the schools to give them first-hand experience of what it's like to work here. Going back to this idea of sense of place – it's the team, and the water source, the climate, the sea, the warehouses and the human influence.'

Back at the castle, I look at a framed geological map of Ardnamurchan. It looks like the multicoloured head of an iguana, with different-coloured rings rippling out from a central eye. The eye is the ice-eroded crater of an ancient volcano, the rings are magma spat out in its eruptions, rock and minerals welling up, distilled, cooled, laid down. Lines of movement.

Tim Ingold thinks in terms of interconnection. His theory is that since everything is in constant motion, at any point where these lines meet they become entangled and form a knot. By separating organisms and placing them in separate individual, enclosed spaces, he argues, we create boundaries. But the world doesn't work like that. Rather than these enclosed spaces, there are moving lines, 'along which life is lived... root of plant, or stream. Each such trail is but one strand in a tissue of trails that together comprise the texture of a lifeworld...a field not of interconnected points, but of interwoven lines...knots in a tissue of knots whose constituent strands, as they become tied up with other strands in other knots, comprise the meshwork. This tangle is the texture of the world...beings do not simply occupy the world, they inhabit it and in so doing, threading their own paths through the meshwork, they contribute to its ever-evolving weave.'

The woods of Sunart are an entangled mesh of root, soil, rock, climate. The whisky-making process is a meshwork. A cluster of people within a place creates the mesh that we call culture. The distillery, whisky, community, geology, fauna, flora, aroma are bound together in these knots, which we can then pull apart and examine.

If sustainability matters – and it does – then it is about biodiversity, not business. To engage with it seriously necessitates that deeper examination of the knotty, and knotted, issues.

It's Vikki's birthday. We're in a castle. No excuse needed to have a grand party. The sideboard is cleared of midge corpses, glasses are polished, candles lit. Jo is in her element in a proper catering kitchen. There's even a shoogly trolley. The deerhound sidles in and casually pisses on the carpet. There's scallops and venison, fine wines, vintage port and drams. As it should be.

It doesn't have to take place in a castle. It could be in a wee pub, or a front room. The point is that it's people coming together, with whisky as the force that pulls them together. We drink the new Ardnamurchan and try to work out what a 'west coast' whisky is.

'To me it's the funk of Springbank, Arran's fruit, Talisker's smoke and Ben Nevis's oils,' says Connal. 'I'd say it has to have saltiness, the beach barbecue and sweetness. I don't know, it just feels like the place, it's a little rough around the edges. The location is tangible.'

Alex takes a sip. 'West coast to me means that weightier, bolder style. We've worked to make this as local as possible, but we're not trying to force change. I don't know which parts are unique to us, or which are because of where we are, but we can't get rid of the salt, put it that way!'

The west coast gives waypoints, possibilities. A sense of place is about belonging, community and wanting to be here. The fact that it is from here is what matters. The fact it also tastes of here is a bonus.

SCOTTISH OAK I

5

I'm standing in the green chapel of the Sunart woods thinking about how oak fits into this holistic view of whisky-making and its deepening understanding of place.

It's not what you expect an oak wood to look like. None of the heavily bossed trunks with expansive canopies that you see in parks, or the regimented, straight lines of a managed forest. This is a dense confusion of warped, thin limbs, writhing from an ancient core, a place of moisture and drip, and mossy hummocks. There is nothing here that is remotely useful for a cooper. At this moment, the idea of using Scottish oak for Scotch whisky seems a mildly deranged notion. Yet...

...

Slowly the trees crept back as the ice started to retreat 12,000 years ago. Juniper, then birch, willow, hazel. Oak was a latecomer. It took 4,000 years before it began its northward trek. Steadily a native forest established itself: the pioneers joined by Scots pine, ash, holly, yew, rowan, alder, aspen, gean [wild cherry], wych elm, crab apple and hawthorn, each species finding niches, coming to understandings with geology, climate and the mycorrhizal mesh.

Oak filled in the bottom and lower slopes of the glens, *Quercus petraea* rooting in less fertile, leached, acidic soils, such as here on the Atlantic coast. *Quercus robur* arrived later, bedding into the heavier, deeper fertile soils. As oak became the dominant deciduous tree they'd hybridize into *Quercus* x *rosacea*.

Oaks support over 2,300 species – birds, mammal, invertebrates, fungi, lichen, of which 326 are wholly dependent on them, and 229 rarely found elsewhere. It was the highest ranked of the seven noble trees of Irish and Scots Gaelic tradition, a symbol of strength, fertility and hospitality. Its Gaelic name – dair (Irish), darach (Scots Gaelic) – is the root of druid, and placenames such as Derry.

Revered though trees were, don't imagine that early Scotland was an arboreal paradise. As Richard Tipping writes in *People and Woods in Scotland*, 'there was probably no "natural" woodland if we think of nature as independent of human beings.' The felling of Scotland's forests started in the Neolithic.

Oak was useful. Its galls (formed around the larva of the gall wasp) were turned into ink; it helped build ships and high-status buildings, furniture, wheels and, of course, casks.

By the seventeenth century, oak forests were being coppiced – the trees cut to near ground level, allowing branches to regrow from the stump, then harvested after 20 years before being cut back again. Its bark was being used for tanning leather, while oak charcoal was used in the expansion of iron works in the Highlands.

One acre of coppiced woodland would provide sufficient charcoal for a ton of pig iron. The most substantial blast furnace, at Bonawe on

Loch Etive, ran from 1753–1876, supporting 600 workers, and would have been supplied by oaks from these woods.

It was a final flaring. The expansion of pastureland throughout the eighteenth and early nineteenth centuries resulted in a significant loss of tree cover. In came cattle, followed by sheep, and then the great deer parks, the tree cover declining with each bite.

Duncan Ban MacIntyre was a 'forester' (aka gamekeeper) and his poem 'Final Farewell to the Bens' (1802) details the devastation:

Yesterday I was on the moor,
and grave reflections haunted me:
that absent were the well-loved friends
who used to roam the waste with me;
since the mountain, which I little thought
would suffer transformation,
has now become a sheep-run,
the world, indeed, has cheated me.

As I gazed on every side of me
I could not but be sorrowful,
for wood and heather have run out,
nor live the men who flourished there;
there's not a deer to hunt there,
there's not a bird or roe there,
and the few that have not died out
have departed from it utterly.

Would early distillers have used Scottish oak casks? Yes, for transportation, but by the nineteenth century, as whisky evolved from an unaged spirit into one that was deliberately matured, the deforestation meant that distillers had to use casks that had arrived on the wharves of Glasgow, Leith or Aberdeen containing sherry, port, wine and rum.

Oak was in decline. The old woods fell silent, un-coppiced, the moss festooning their limbs. Remnants of the forest held on the western fringes and, thanks primarily to its tree-loving landowners, in Perthshire. By 1914, Britain was importing 90 per cent of its timber and only 5 per cent of Scotland was wooded.

The severe lack of domestic timber during World War I saw the establishing of the Forestry Commission in 1919 and a shift away from slow-growing hardwoods such as oak to quick-growing softwoods – primarily Sitka spruce, which, post-1945, became the familiar dense green monoculture. Plant, grow, thin, clear cut, move on, that was the rule.

The hardwoods continued to decline, oaks were ringbarked and poisoned, cleared for grazing. As Worrell and Mackenzie point out in *People and Woods in Scotland*, 'all of these ultimately reduce biodiversity by removing the niches and food plants for a wide range of invertebrates, birds, and mammals...[this] reduction of fauna also reduces seed spreading and maintenance of meadows and wetlands.' Heather took over in the heights, peat bogs spread, isolated trees were left on hard-to-reach sites. Lone pines, fragmented pockets of oak.

Now, however, Scotland's forest cover is increasing, rising from 6 per cent in 1960 to 18 per cent, with a government-edicted increase in native hardwoods. Oak, tentatively, is returning.

...

A few months earlier I'd been standing in another forest in Glen Moriston with Whyte & Mackay's blender, Gregg Glass (see page 191). We were surrounded by juniper, while in front of us a burn fell into a lochan fringed with Scots pine, hazel and oak. This is Dundreggan, the HQ of charity Trees for Life, which is attempting to re-establish the native Scottish woodlands.

Its core mission, the charity's Alex Baxter explained, is to connect the glens of Affric, Shiel, Canach and Moriston, creating a mature forest running from riverbed to montane scrub, creating corridors for wildlife. Two million trees have already been planted, and while Scots pine is the main focus, there are also plantings of aspen, alder, hazel...and oak.

'Oak is an important component in the Caledonian picture,' he said. 'Oaks set the tone of a woodland because they live the longest.' The mixed

planting also allows the mitochondrial network to flourish. 'Pines are happiest with other trees, then in comes pine moth, which brings in red squirrels. It can all happen with minimal human intervention. Hardwoods are also better at locking up carbon because they are so dense.'

A short time here changes the way you look at the landscape. Many of those classically heather-clad hills are the product of logging, high-impact grazing by sheep and the explosion of the deer population since Victorian times. The picturesque glens are a landscape that is out of balance. As Gregg and I drove south, familiar hills looked different, wrong, too bare.

The conversation about Scotland's forestry is changing. Gregg believes that whisky can be part if it. 'It started around 15 years ago when I was working as a tour guide,' he says. 'It was then I began to wonder why we weren't using Scottish oak.' He started visiting local sawmills, collecting bits and pieces, macerating spirit in oak, seeing what effects different chars had. Work then took him to London to work as a whisky-maker at Compass Box, before returning north to be trained up as the successor to Whyte & Mackay's legendary master blender, Richard Paterson.

The visits to sawmills continued. 'What started as, wouldn't it be interesting to use Scottish oak? has mushroomed into, what are the problems that are preventing us from using it? You breathe it in, you smell it and you meet these great people who live for what they are doing. Wouldn't it be great if the whisky industry in general could help them, that it could be mutually beneficial?

'Whisky makers are problem-solvers,' he continues, 'so how could I make it work? I was considering starting my own company, then with my new role we created Whisky Works, the experimental arm within Whyte & Mackay.'

...

We visit Drumore Wood near Killearn, close to Glasgow. A 2,700-acre planted forest, it hadn't been worked since the 1930s until recently. 'Most of the oak from here has been sold for firewood or fenceposts,' forester George Broadhurst explains. 'Anything bigger was milled for boards and beams. It's time-consuming and financially unsustainable. If we're selling for firewood we have to cut, dry, then go out and sell it. The new project is getting timber out to provide an economic and environmental base and maintaining biodiversity.'

He talks me through the different categories of 'sticks' (trunks to us). Whisky-grade is at the top, those rare sticks that are straight, with no branches or clusters of twigs that will cause knots, and no burrs either. Those might be great for woodworking, but not for staves.

'We've started to look at it differently, to maximize the value for everyone, as well as thinking of provenance. Whether it's a frame for a house, or a whisky cask, you can say this oak came from this place, and this person. Premium money for premium timber, that's how we can work together.'

Later that day, Gregg and I go to a farmer who has trees to sell. He leads us down to a wood, showing us the sewage pipe and recounting how virginities were lost on its surface while the trees' roots penetrated the iron, of the glade being a shooting gallery for air rifles and junkies, riddled with pits where unwanted puppies and kittens were thrown. 'But,' he continues, 'the bluebells are lovely in the spring'.

Gregg and I glance at each other, thinking that we must be trapped in some Tartan noir plot. 'How many casks from this?' the farmer asks as we stop by one of the oaks. You can tell that in his mind, the trunk had already been turned into a column of barrels. He was already counting the riches. 'Sorry, none of them are any good,' says Gregg, 'apart from that one. I might get some pieces for the heads from that.' We leave, quickly, towards the appropriately named Fife village of Oakley and Scottish Wood, the independent sawmill that helped Gregg's vision become a reality.

It was started 27 years ago by Jim Birley, when he and his late wife bought 50 acres of woodland to build a house. 'I knew nothing about trees. I'm from Orkney!' he laughs, his blue shorts speckled with sawdust. Scottish Wood is run as a social enterprise, funding local charities and giving employment to the long-term unemployed.

'Scotland has a lot of good oak,' he says. 'The trouble is, it's going out as low value, often as woodchips. That's using quality timber, which could be used for locking in carbon. The European market also likes Scottish oak because it has character, but all the value is added outside of Scotland.' It's the same situation facing the fishing industry, selling its catch directly to continental wholesalers. That night I dream of forests of giant prawns marching over the land.

'We're making inroads, though,' Jim says. 'Now 25 per cent of the oak is staying in the country and it will get better. This project helps. It's creating a full circle. The whole chain was broken.'

This isn't whisky riding in on a white charger as some sort of saviour, but as one element in a wider movement of replanting and rebuilding. Gregg's project links the independent sawmills to cooperages, but also with Forestry Scotland, Trees for Life and landowners. 'It's about establishing a gold standard,' he says. 'From planting, to felling, to milling and cask construction.' It's as much about ecology as the need for trees as a giant crop. It's about changing perceptions.

 Opposite: A rich biodiversity

HEBRIDES

Jo, Rosie and I reach Mallaig and the ferry to Armadale on Skye. If you think of the island as the back of an outstretched left hand, we're at the tip of the thumb, on the Sleat peninsula, the most fertile and sheltered part of Skye and home to Torabhaig, its newest distillery.

For over 180 years this, the largest Hebridean island, was home to a single still: the mighty Talisker, which provided the kickstart for my love of single malt – smoky, slightly salty, a little bit peppery, but also sweet and gentle.

Now it has a neighbour, admittedly far to the south. The idea of a distillery on Sleat came from the late Sir Ian Noble, Gaelic educator and founder of the Sabhal Mòr Ostaig college.

Language was at the heart of Sir Ian's plans for regenerating the local economy, and though he never managed to get his distillery plans off the ground, maybe it was those aims that attracted the Swedish billionaire Dr Frederik Paulsen, whose charitable works include preserving disappearing languages, cultures and crafts. He also happens to own Marussia Beverages.

With its lime-washed walls, waterwheel and pagoda roof, Torabhaig looks as if it has been here on the shore, looking over to Knoydart, for a 100 years. In fact, this 200-year-old farm steading only opened as a distillery in 2017 after a tricky 3-year building and restoration project that trod a tricky path between the demands of Historic Scotland, the architectural vision and the need to have a functional plant within the walls of a listed (and listing) building.

Now there's nine distillers working there, all local, under the direction of Kenny Gray, legendary ex-Diageo manager, and Neil Mathieson, CEO of Marussia's whisky arm, Mossburn Distillers.

'I suppose it's a bunch of mad scientists operating their own place,' Neil told me on my first visit. 'But there's a requirement to be experimental. This isn't about sticking to a formula. Whisky is a living thing.'

Every parameter was examined – trialing the same barley variety as peated and unpeated from different maltings, then varying peating levels, yeast strains, cut points, all on a base template of clear worts and long ferments. 'It's been a massive learning experience, seeing how changes affect the final spirit,' Neil went on. 'It's made us think of why we do what we do when we are making it and how we need to make something that reflects us.'

In 2020, the first bottlings came out – salt-washed rocks and smoke, oily with melon notes and herbs. Concentrated, balanced and an instant hit.

For two weeks every year the distillers are given free rein to make their own spirit (within SWA regulations). Anything goes: barley type, kilning temperatures, peated or not, a choice of eight yeasts, ferment times, cuts, then wood type. 'They run the place,' said Neil. 'What better way to get them to understand what is possible?'

Mallaig… next stop Skye

Raasay

We've left Skye's thumb and are heading to the pinkie. As the road spins round the deeply incised coastline, so you lose sense of direction. The world whirls. Mountains that were on the left are suddenly on the right, particularly one odd, flat-topped hill that pops up in apparently random places.

Its position only becomes fixed when you arrive at the ferry terminal at Sconser (home to a fine wee café, which, appropriately enough, serves rather marvellous scones). It's only 20 minutes across to the island of Raasay, which sits between Skye's east coast and the mainland.

Like its neighbours, Raasay's history has been a troubled one. In 1846, the island was bought by George Rainy, who had made his fortune in the sugar and rum trade in what was British Guiana. In 1833, after emancipation, he received £150,000 compensation for the 'loss' of his 2,793 enslaved workers. That's £12.5 million today.

When ensconced on Raasay, he built a wall separating the fertile two-thirds in the south of the island, where most people lived, from the rocky north, and the islands of Fladda and Rona, forcibly moving the people there, and forbidding them to marry.

The southern pastureland was kept for his own use and a sheep run. Half the population were cleared by the end of the century and continued to bleed away as the island passed from one owner to another.

 Isle of Raasay's distillery glows in the sun

The ferry's ramp grates against the slipway and we drive a few hundred yards towards a unlikely-looking golden cube attached to an old manor house. This is the Isle of Raasay distillery, built in 2017. Managing director and co-founder, Alasdair Day (see page 163), is there to meet us. The house has now been converted into a boutique hotel, where we're staying. Jo and Rosie sit outside looking over the spectacular view of Skye while Alasdair and I sit in the resident's bar and catch up.

He has whisky in his blood. In 1885, his great-grandfather, Richard Day, started work at licensed grocer J&A Davidson in the Borders town of Coldstream. By 1923, trained as a blender, he owned the firm. When Alasdair inherited a ledger containing all of the firm's blend recipes, he started recreating the long-vanished Tweeddale blend in his kitchen. As the brand grew, the notion of a distillery began to form.

'I bought nine casks, because there were nine whiskies in the blend, but to control a brand you have to control supply. One option was buy new fillings, or build a distillery.' His idea was to build it close to Coldstream. Then he met entrepreneur Bill Dobbie.

Bill's best friend from school, the writer and broadcaster Ian Hector Ross, had a Raasay connection through his wife and knew of this abandoned country house hotel. 'When we stood here in May 2014, Bill asked me if I could turn this into a distillery,' says Alisdair. 'I was so busy looking at the view I said yes immediately, then wondered... where's the water?'

Left: Looking over to Skye
Right: Eilean Green, Isle of Raasay distillery

It transpired that Raasay's weird geology had provided a well right beside the house. 'We're sat on permeable Jurassic sandstone, while pretty much everything around it is impermeable,' Alisdair explains. 'The water flows down from Dun Càna (the flat-topped hill we'd seen), then percolates up through this rock. It allows us to use it for our own use and not abstract anything from the local supply.' Unusually, it's used for mashing, cooling, cask reduction and at bottling (everything is matured and bottled on the island).

Water supply sorted, the next question was what should the whisky be like? 'We came up with the signature of lightly peated and dark fruit. As soon as we had that, we could design our process and our wood policy. It wasn't about how to get a whisky that matures early, but how to get complexity and depth at a young age.'

In we go. The mash tun gives clear wort, stainless-steel washbacks with cooling jackets allow for temperature control for the long ferments; there's two yeast types and two styles of spirit (peated and unpeated) are made. The wash still has a cooling jacket, while the spirit has a purifier pipe and a small set of rectifying plates. These can be engaged to add reflux for peated (adding oiliness) or left alone for the unpeated. That's a lot of bells and whistles. 'It's a distillery designed by a blender!' Alasdair says with a smile. 'We can turn things off and on to give me a greater range of flavours to play with.'

Then there's the barley. For three years they trialed different varieties on a plot owned by Andrew Gillies (aka Cuddy; see opposite) and helped by Peter Martin (see page 30), to see what might be able to ripen in Raasay's 'interesting' conditions.

In 2017, Concerto, Tartan, plus bere, Kannas (from Sweden) and Iskria (Iceland) went in, but only the last three ripened. The year after, Iskria went back in along with Swedish variety Anneli, the Norwegian Braga and the old UK standby Golden Promise. The following year, only Braga and Iskria were trialed. More recently there's been trials of Berwickshire-grown bere, and a promising-looking early-ripening Scandinavian variety, Salome, both malted in Fife by Crafty Maltsters.

The island will never be able to grow sufficient barley for all of the distillery's requirements, but the trials show that it is possible at a small scale – and with varieties that suit the specifics of the conditions, which are substantially different to the warmer, drier east coast.

Along with operations director Norman Gillies (Cuddy's son, see page 160), we drive down to the warehouses, where the next layers of complexity are added. 'Everyone uses first-fill, ex-Bourbon, ex-sherry and refill,' says Alasdair. 'It's a formula. We had to be different.' The question is, how far can you push different before it becomes contrived?

The mix for their single malt uses the two types of spirit, aged in three types of cask: ex-Calon Segur Bordeaux red wine, ex-rye casks from Woodford Reserve in Kentucky and Chinquapin oak (*Q. muehlenbergii*).

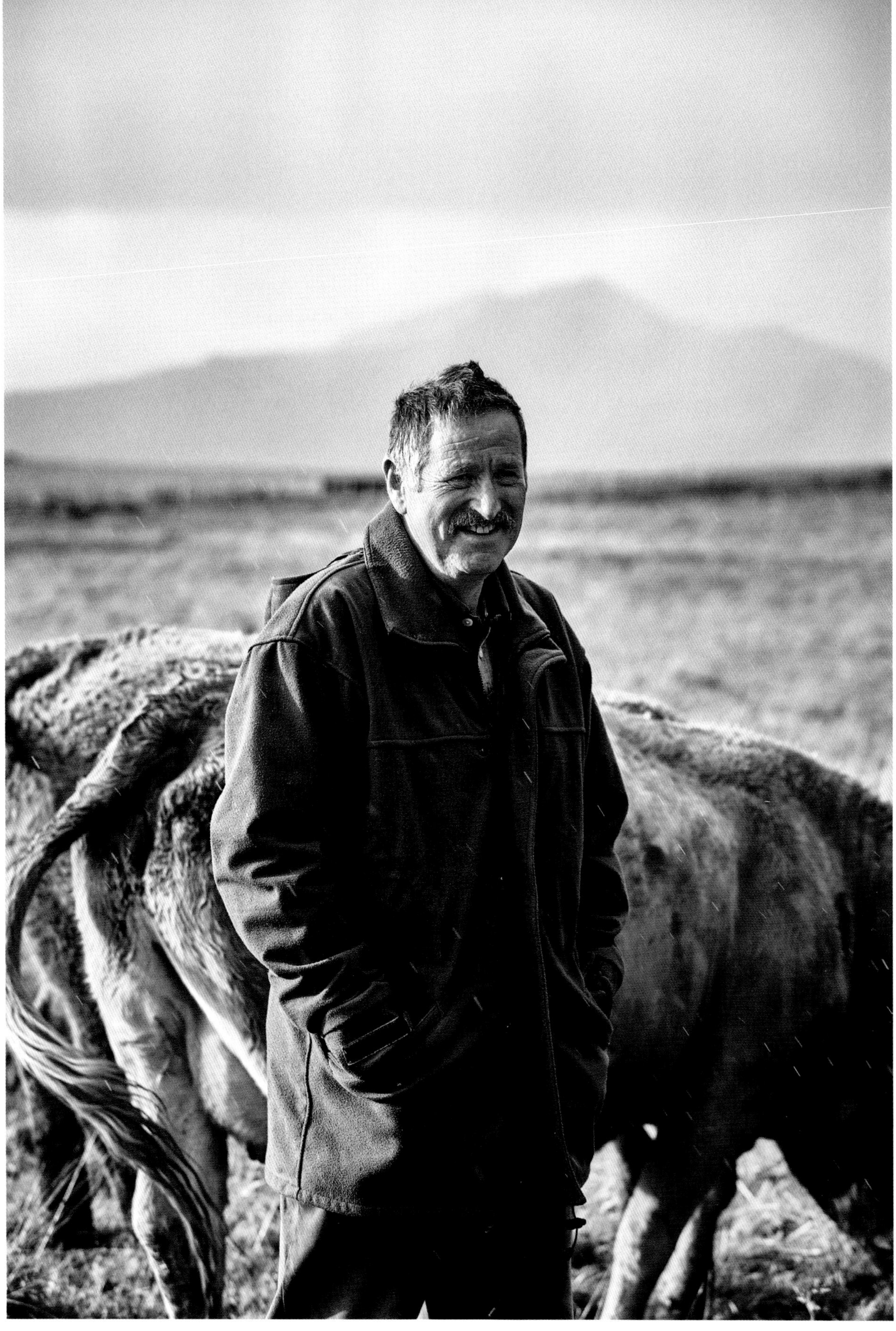

Andrew Gillies, aka Cuddy

Norman Gillies, distillery manager

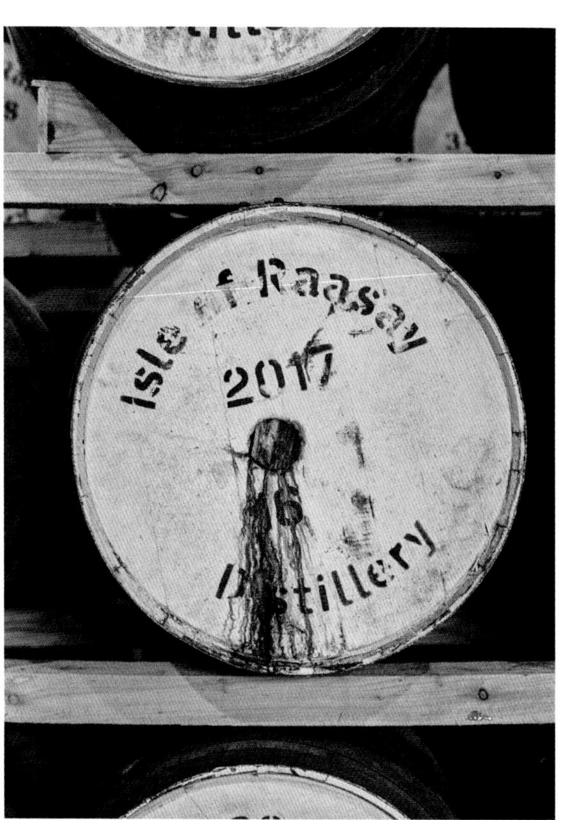

The spirit in the red-wine casks has been allowed time to penetrate through the surface layer of wine, combining subtle oak-derived spice with the cassis-like fruits. The rye adds a Szechuan pepperiness, while the Chinquapin treats the spirit to breakfast in an American diner – all cinnamon toast, maple syrup and, in the peated version, bacon bits.

What of the barley trials? I ask. The casks have never been opened. We pop one, sniff. Look for clues in others' eyes. 'The bere...' I start. Alasdair grins 'It's the bere... It's leading the way.'

It's not Raasay's normal new make. It's different: fresh barley, pear, energy. Even though bere only made up a small portion, its character is dominant. 'Imagine if Raasay-grown barley was part of the mix,' he says. 'That's our signature.'

Was the aim, like Ardnamurchan, to make a west-coast whisky? 'The light peat idea came from Talisker,' he says, 'the dark fruit idea came from 1970s Bowmores, but I wanted to get them in the new make, not just from the wine casks, but the question was always what else can we bring that makes it Raasay? Single malt is at the stage where excellent isn't good enough. We have to be different, as well as high quality.'

The single malt is now out, in two styles. R01 is equal parts peated and unpeated and the six casks, R02 is a little smokier. Both are gentle, layered and elegant.

Although single malt only emerged as a significant category in the 1990s, it is now sufficiently well-established to mean that any new distillery has to find ways to cut through not only all of the established Scotch single malt brands, but the growing number of whiskies from around the world, hence the experiments with barley varieties, yeasts, distillation techniques and casks that you see here, or in most of the other new distilleries.

Another element of that imperative is that a new distillery has the freedom to be able to do this. It's easier to experiment as a new player than as a distillery whose character might have been fixed 200 years before.

Part of discovering what the distillery is also involves understanding the peculiarities of its location.

Raasay is about more than whisky. There's carved Pictish stones, Iron Age forts, a ruined castle, an abandoned iron mine where German prisoners of war were put to work during World War I. It is filled with stories of people and their resilience, best exemplified by Calum's Road

A wide range of different oaks are being used

at the north end of the island, 3.2 kilometres of it, built with only a pick, shovel and wheelbarrow over 15 years by Calum MacLeod to link the end of the road to his home in Arnish in the hope that people would then return to live there. His attempt at resurrection. Jo and Rosie head off into the mist to explore its twists and dips.

I'm heading over to the east coast. Raasay was the birthplace of the most important Gaelic poet of the twentieth century, Sorley MacLean, and the setting for his best-known work, 'Hallaig', a work about a Raasay Clearance township.

'Hallaig' is a memorial to the lost place, repopulated by the township's young, now transformed into trees, in which a deer personifies time. It ends with the poet shooting the deer with 'the bullet of love,' freezing time, allowing the past to be alive and memories to be retained. It is both a lament and an act of defiance.

I've never been to the long-abandoned village, so, Alasdair, marketing manager Eilean Green (see page 155), Norman and Cuddy are walking there, along the road 'under mild moss', as mist blows down

Top: On the road again
Bottom: A deer in the wood of Hallaig

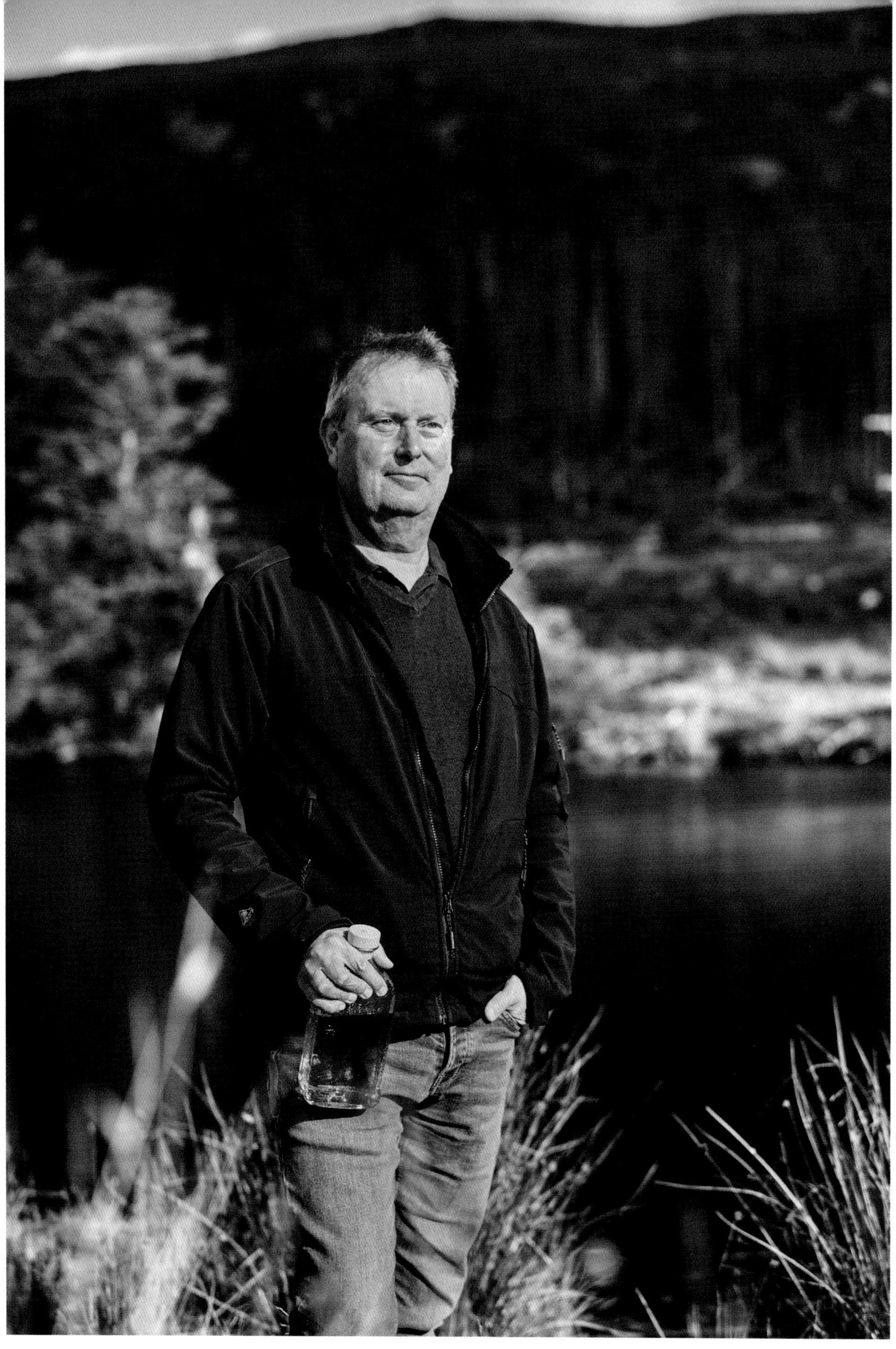

Alasdair Day, co-founder and whisky-maker,
Isle of Raasay distillery

the hill like smoke. By the eerie, stone-walled stables, we enter the woods, lichen holding drops of rain like tears. At the foot of each birch tree is a mound of moss, giving it the look of a graveyard.

and my love is at the Burn of Hallaig,
a birch tree, and she has always been

between Inver and Milk Hollow,
here and there about Baile-chuirn:
she is a birch, a hazel,
a straight slender young rowan.

As we leave the trees, the mist clears from the top of Dun Càna. Cuddy tells us of how one old woman remembered being taken to the top to see a Clearance boat leaving. 'Her brother was a boatman there in Clachan, a MacLeod. She lived long enough to see people coming back again.'

What did your people say of the Clearances?

'We weren't taught any local history at school, there was nothing going back in time to those days.'

This, Eilean explains, was tied to the 1872 Education Act, which banned to teaching of Gaelic, 'and that,' she adds, 'was a way of telling the history they wanted to tell. The history Sorley resurrects is not the sanitized version that glossed over the Highlands.'

Above: The mossy track to Hallaig
Opposite: Moonrise above bracken

Across a dip, the ruins can be spotted. Forty-two families were cleared from Hallaig. 'Probably,' Cuddy reminds us, 'there were more people here than are on the whole island now.'

He points to lines in the heather and bracken, explaining the lazy-bed and run-rig system where mounds of soil and seaweed were raised as beds for crops and vegetables. 'It was good, it was fertile, aye, good land, and everything done by hand. But it was hard a life.' There's silence. The wind's dropped. Two ravens drift over.

'Shall we go on?' Norman shouts from higher up the slope. 'You can see it better from up here.' As we climb, more houses emerge, until we can see the extent of the township. We wander through the ruins, running hands over the rough stones.

I join Norman and Cuddy, who are trying to work out what one house was about. 'Look at how the walls here are built,' says Norman. 'The quality of the building is amazing. That's proper masonry, not piling up stones.' We theorize about where the water would come from, seek in vain for a well, trying to piece together lives and houses.

What would they have grown?

'Oats, kale, maybe even barley.'

What about any distillation?

'Oh, it would have been frowned on,' says Cuddy. 'Donnie MacLeod was shown where there was a wee still up beside the burn at Eyort and there was another one on Rona, but I've never see them. I've wondered about the fire pits you find at Screapadal, but whether that was for baking or whisky I don't know.'

What were your memories of whisky?

'Celebration, or when you were ill. If people came round they'd have a cup of tea and a dram, but other than that I don't recall the bottle coming out. When we were shearing you'd have bottles of beer, but that was because it was hot weather. Whisky, though – it was expensive, a week's wages.'

Eilean's joined us and the talk turns to language. She and Cuddy are both native Gaelic speakers. Were you brought up with it, Cuddy?

'Yes, yes. I was told I didn't have English when I went to school, but when I left the primary I had very little Gaelic. You were discouraged from speaking it, in fact, but I took 'learner's Gaelic' at high school in Portree (Skye) and won two prizes for it. Right enough, I was cheating, I had a head start!'

Can you talk of a place, understand it, without the language? I'd asked the question years previously on Skye to the writer and photographer Cailean MacLean. 'No,' was his reply, and he began to speak about the Gaelic name for the hill opposite and the reason for its naming, the legend behind it, the people involved. It's called by a different name on the OS map. A link lost.

'I've always liked the name of that ridge up there,' says Cuddy. 'In Gaelic it means "the hill of the back of the old cow." See how it looks just like that?' I listen to his talking of placenames and villages, and think of Sorley MacLean's slow incantation of the same words: Hallaig, Inbhir, Baile-Chùirn, Sgreapadal, Bheinn na Lice, Leac, na Feàrnaibh, Suidhisnis. 'Casting a net of names over the cleared landscape so that a territory can be repossessed by its former inhabitants,' as John Murray writes in *Literature of the Gaelic Landscape*. An occult spell of repossession and resurrection, both central to what has happened to Raasay since the distillery has opened.

'It has completely changed what is possible on Raasay,' Norman tells me as we head back. 'When I grew up here, the jobs were the fish farm, the ferry and Raasay House, but there was no career possible.'

Like so many, he left: university, a Masters in engineering, then work offshore, allowing him the time to have a house here. As he puts it, 'you could live here and have a career, but that career couldn't be here.' Repeat that across the Highlands and Islands. The downturn in oil came at the same time as the build was starting. He began as site engineer. Now he runs the place. 'The distillery has meant people have returned, others have come to live. There is a reason to stay, scope to progress.' Now repeat that across the Highlands and Islands.

'The scale of this business compared to the size of the community is enormous. There are 170 people on the island, mostly above retirement age. The average age of the people in the distillery is around 30.'

There are 30 working at the distillery now: making whisky, bottling, giving tours, running the accommodation, doing media work. Its opening ripples out across the island – an increase in visitors means more work, businesses, a new café (ham, cheese and marmalade toasties a must), an increase in bed nights and food at Raasay House. Two of the operators, Ross Gillies and Rosie MacLeod, both engineers, have crowd-funded a local hydro scheme.

'People talk about whisky tourism,' Alasdair adds, 'but they don't think about what that means. We're not just a distillery, we are creating jobs, and being here has brought the community in.' Not just that, it has transformed the island.

Looking back on the way to Calum's Road

Harris

There's always an element of doubt when you arrive at the Loganair departure gate in Glasgow airport. Will the flight go? If it does, will it land? All you can do is trust. Today, the weather in Stornoway is dreadful, so Christina and I just have to sit and wait.

An hour later, there's a weather window. It's only a 30-minute flight, so according to the pilot 'we're making a run for it'. No guarantees. Flying through grey, engines howling, then suddenly a gap in the clouds and there's the Minch, deep indigo ruffled into white. Waters I've sailed, in multiple failed attempts to reach St Kilda.

At Stornoway, the wind is relentless, the rain horizontal. 'Mì-chaìlear', they call it here, which means a stage beyond dreich. It's evident that there will be no outside photography today. Hire car obtained, we head south, discussing potential options, praying for clearing skies, or at least good textures in the clouds, picking out possible shots for the return journey; the expanse of rusty heather flecked with lochans and pools, Balallan's tiny, red-roofed post office, brutalist bus stops.

The border with Harris is unclear, somewhere between the end of the perforated landscape of Lewis and the start of the mountains. Down the winding hill to Tarbert and the Isle of Harris distillery.

...

 A glimpse through the clouds

Christina's staying in the hotel, I'm biding here, in an apartment with a window into the still-house. Memo to self: be fully dressed before opening the curtains. Head distiller Kenny MacLean (see page 172) comes in for a cup of tea and brings us up to speed. With how the idea came from Anderson 'Burr' Bakewell, musicologist, philanthropist and owner of the nearby island of Scarp.

'His original purpose was to create permanent employment,' says Kenny. 'The island had lost half its population in 50 years. What better way than whisky?' With more investors on board, in 2015 it began operations on a purpose-built site next to the ferry terminal.

Harris Gin gave the project an early injection of capital and gave an indication of how important location was going to be: a local spin given by the use of sugar kelp, a stunning bottle reminiscent of sea glass and the fact that everything was bottled and shipped from the island.

The team, all local, none of whom had distilled before, have been guided by Kenny Gray and Gordon Steele from the Scotch Whisky Research Institute. Kenny (MacLean) had recently returned to the island after years down south, working in internet security.

Why whisky?

'I'm an engineer. I knew how to keep the pumps running! For the first five years that's what was needed.'

We head inside. They run a mix of long (72-hour) and longer (120-hour) ferments – the latter partly driven by religious observance, as

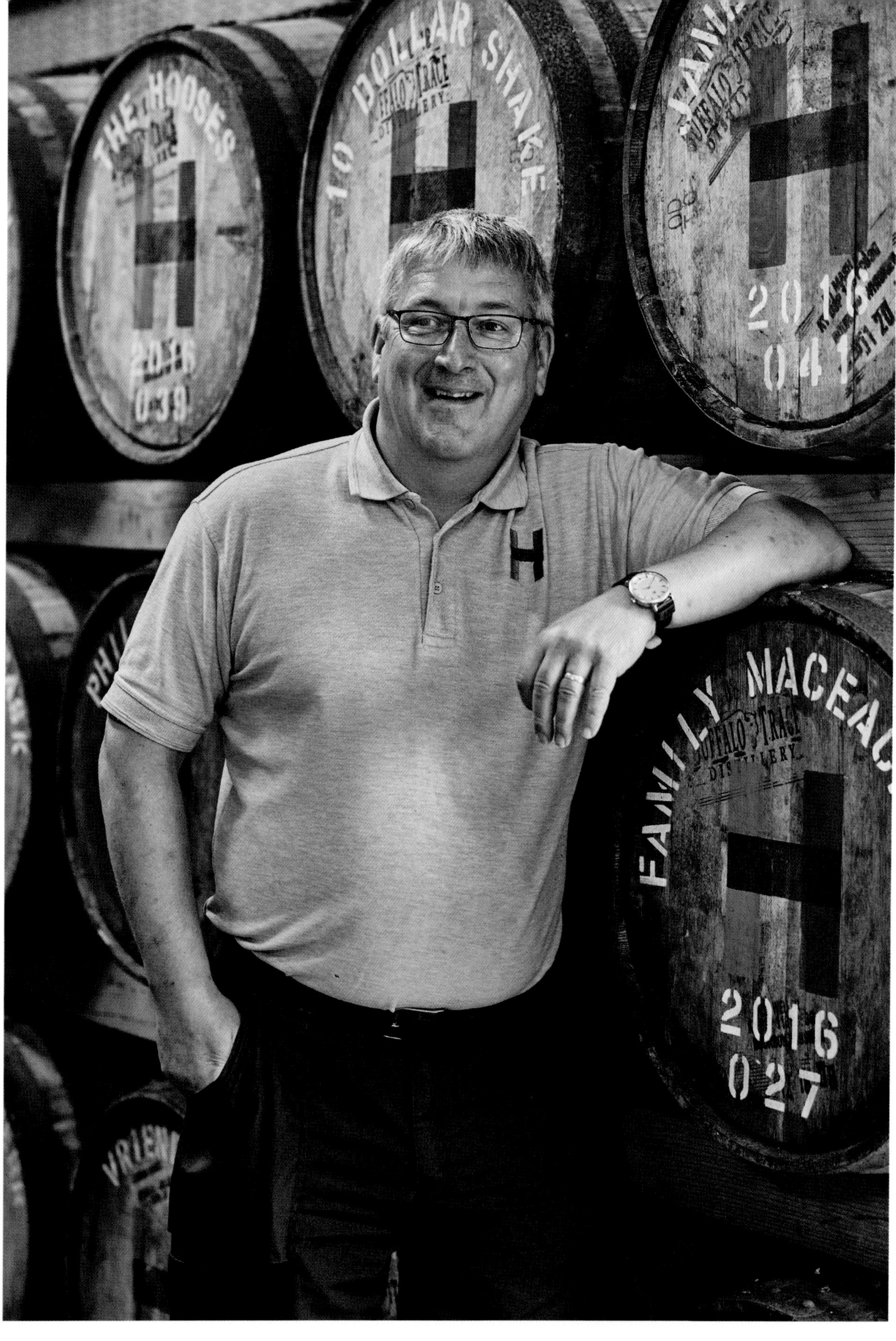

 Kenny MacLean, Isle of Harris distillery

there's no working on a Sunday. Distillation is equally prolonged, with a purifier pipe also at work, adding reflux.

The malt is only lightly peated, 'just to fill the space for peat in the taste, so you don't get a blast of smoke on the nose. The Hearach (as the single malt will be called) represents Harris, and the island is a quiet place. It's the smell of walking through the village when peat fires are burning.'

Neil M. Gunn said woodsmoke was danger, and peat was the smell of home.

'Definitely. A gentle, warm peat fire with the smoke just coming off it. Like wet soot, sweetness, the ashes from the fire, a warm, nice smell.'

We jump in his car and drive to the warehouse. With the wind shaking the roller door and the rain battering the roof, it's like being inside a snare drum. The casks are a mix of American oak, plus some ex-sherry – initially oloroso, but some fino casks have recently been added to give an aromatic lift.

He pulls a sample from an ex-Bourbon: subtle and soft, lychee, apple, mirabelle, dill, a wisp of peat, and a peppery kick – the character is there. We continue to chat about identifying aromas. 'For me, the smell of the gin is the smell of boiling winkles on Sunday morning. It was the only pastime allowed on a Sunday. I don't get all those things you're saying though.'

That's the joy of tasting, though. Our experiences are different, and so therefore are our smell memories. I've never boiled winkles on a Sunday, but I did suck on sweeties in church. The smell from Glasgow's chimneys was coal smoke, not peat. Those are my reference points. Knowing what they mean in a whisky is what matters. Trust your own palate, keep nosing as many things as you can; just don't try to find the aromas that someone else is talking about.

...

That night we settle into the hotel's snug and taste more samples, the talk turning to Harris itself, the island which isn't. 'We're joined to Lewis,' Kenny says, 'but the mountains act as a barrier. In the old days, people wouldn't travel by land there, so there was always more of a sea connection with North Uist [to the south].'

He talks of his childhood in Strond, in the south. 'It was a busy crofting place, there was no reason to leave other than to go to school.

We planted potatoes, grew our own veg, slaughtered our own animals. My first memory is of a trailer taking the horse away and bringing the tractor. That was 1971. As a child it was a wonderful place. As a parent with ambitions for your children it was probably a very difficult place.'

So the young people left?

'Maybe there's a small-island mentality of looking out and thinking it's all better out there. I certainly did. Now we are all realizing how important community is.'

Burr's idea was to have a 'social distillery' for the long-term benefit of the community. 'We don't make any big decisions without thinking what impact it will have. Plenty of people have asked for us to ship the draff off the mainland, or burn it for electricity, but we have a contract with the local farmers – and the holding of cattle has increased.

'In the 1970s and 80s, there was a feeling that this was a backwater, you were second class. Now there's a totally different vibe about it, pride in what we do and where we are. It is important to get this right for Harris.'

...

The next day we're joined by Mike Donald, who returned to the island after years in Glasgow. He's now the distillery's storyteller (a better and more accurate term for PR).

He's taking us south to Northton to meet Bill Lawson (see opposite), genealogist and author of 50 books. Shirt the colour of the deep sea, he sits next to a wall of books, speaking as precisely as only a historian can. Weighing the words, testing the argument, questioning the question.

He arrived here from Ayrshire 55 years ago. 'I was fascinated by the sense of community, the history and the families, but also frightened about how many of the stories were held by old people. Today, I can think of three people here who are what you can call tradition bearers, and they're all in their eighties or nineties. So, I left my job, moved here and decided to concentrate on doing what I wanted.'

Part of the work was rebalancing the history?

'We've had centuries of teaching people that local knowledge was rubbish, and what mattered was the kings of England. People came to believe it.'

Plus the steady loss of people?

'Either you fund industry, or emigration. They've tried a few times to find industries for the islands, but they were never particularly successful.' There's a wry laugh. He speaks of the short-lived kelp boom of Napoleonic times, then Lord Leverhulme's failed ideas for a modern fishery industry, the whaling station and the notion of selling whale meat sausages to the Belgian Congo, the herring boom and the more recent travails of the tweed mills. 'The problem is people move in for the boom, and don't want to stay when the bust comes.'

Bill Lawson, Hebridean griot

So the distillery?

'It's created employment. That's the important thing. We're not keeping young people here. The aims are good after a long period of complete neglect.'

Was whisky-making in the island's blood?

'I'm still on a steep learning curve with that,' says Mike. 'One of the islands off the west coast, Pabbay, is where whisky-making happened. When it was cleared, that knowledge went. How many people knew how to make it? Was it just one family?

'This is an oral culture and the fragility of this culture is an issue that runs alongside depopulation. All it take is one generation for it to be lost – look at Gaelic.'

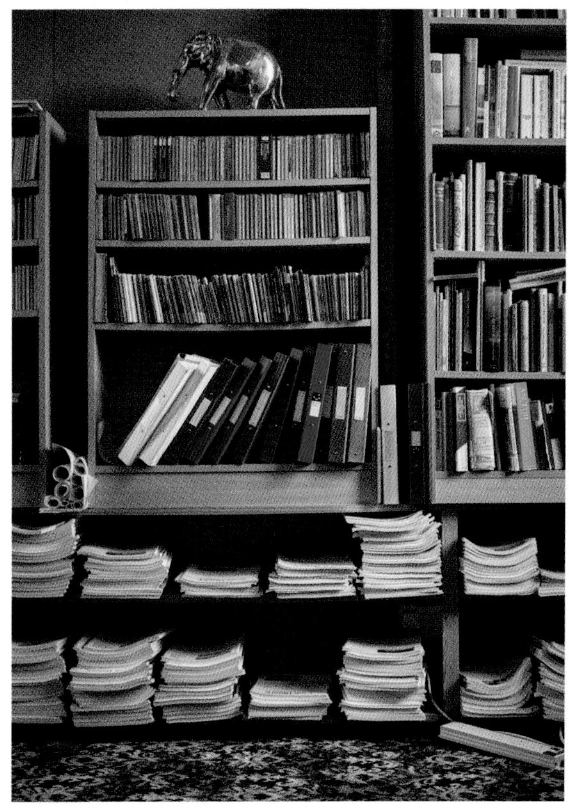

Can Harris survive, even prosper, on whisky and tweed? Not without housing. 'It's one thing to create jobs for young people,' says Mike, 'but where are they going to stay? Why should you stay if you are never going to get a house? As a young person you're priced out of the market quickly. There's crofting land with 2 or 3 acres going for £250,000.

'The moment you start losing young people is when you start losing language, music, stories and culture.

'We have 35 full-time, year-round jobs and a handful of seasonal ones. That's a massive number on an island this size, but the challenge is that Harris is incredibly popular with people wanting to secure an island retreat. Tourism is a double-edged sword.' The same story has been repeated by every distiller I've spoken to in the west and islands.

'There has to be a lot of joined-up thinking between businesses like us, the local trusts, the Crofting Federation and the council to try and rein in the market, otherwise we'll end up as a playground for the wealthy.'

'Come through,' says Bill, leading us into an office lined with shelves, filled with box files and buff folders. He opens one. 'It all started with this,' he says, with that gentle faraway smile. 'I traced my wife's family tree. It was meant to be a one-off. Now...' he grins and gestures. 'These are the family trees of every household in the Western Isles for the past 200 years. When I last had the temerity to count, there were 33,500.'

Whole islands reside here. Names and genealogies, places and ownerships, exile and drift, the product of sifting archives and migration logs, and speaking to those who remembered.

'There still a lot more to do,' he says. 'I am horribly conscious of the stuff that's in my head, and so many of the people I spoke to have all gone.'

The lost are found, the threads pulled back, communities are rewoven. It's a selfless, utterly compassionate deed. It isn't simply a mammoth task of cataloguing, but preserving the past, giving people their history back. It's Sorley MacLean's bullet of love in action. I'm fighting back tears, thinking of how delicate this web is, and of his dedication, this griot of the Hebrides.

...

Mike leaves us at Luskentyre on the west coast. Christina and I walk over the soft machair to the sea; tiny flowers underfoot, knitted together by marram grass growing from white shell sand. The light is ever changing, turquoise and aquamarine, periwinkle and blue jade. A storm rolls in, the hills to the left are black, those on the right bright gold and green. It changes every second, the elements passing through you, becoming part of you.

We stand in the needling rain, laughing as more clouds blur in, knowing that in a few minutes the sun will return and all will be tropical again. Christina kicks off her shoes and races into the sea, camera aloft.

Seilebost, Harris

The poet Ian Stephen got it right when he wrote of Harris:

Then there are the katabatic bursts of breeze
against the grain of decent predictions
bringing destroying brightness

to brush down deep
below the several surfaces
of the Sound of Taransay.
Constant as change.

We wander back over the sand to meet up with Mike and Donald John Mackay (see opposite), who might be the most famous weaver in the world. One day in 2003 he got an email from America asking for some samples of his tweeds. Requests followed for 2 metres, then 10, then 40. 'It was these people called Nike,' he says. 'They wanted it for shoes. I hadn't a clue who they were. Then they asked for 950 metres, then called back to apologize. They'd meant 9,500!' The story has by now taken on the trappings of an Ealing comedy. 'Every mill was turning out the yarn. There were poor old men in their eighties brought out of retirement to fulfil that order.'

After Nike, Clarks, then Savile Row. One day some other folks appeared. 'They didn't say anything, but I knew they were foreign. They asked if I could do 1,000 metres of a purple tweed. Then they said they were from Chanel.'

He's totally unfazed by all of the fuss, and speaks of dining with the Queen (he now has an MBE) as if they were sitting in the Tarbert café.

The story is even more remarkable when you understand that to be called Harris Tweed, the fabric must be woven by one person in their own shed in Harris (or Lewis). 'Have you ever seen inside a shed?' he bellows. 'No? Right, come on let me show you.'

Made of corrugated iron, it sits next to his bungalow. We somehow all squeeze in and he sits on the seat behind the loom. There's bolts of tweed, the smell of lanolin, oil and paraffin, a dusty sweetness.

His father was a crofter and weaver. 'We grew up with it. I suppose it started more or less as a survival product, to keep people warm, then it became a bit of a currency. You could pay your rent, perhaps your groceries as well. He'd have to make three tweeds a week. If the crofting took him away, he'd have to work into the small hours. No electricity, just a Tilley lamp hissing away in your ear. Many's a time me and my brother spent the night at the loom just to get that third tweed ready. Then go straight to school.'

His auntie set him up here in around 1968 with an old second-hand loom. It was just as the fashion for Harris Tweed was in decline. He shrugs. 'There always will be peaks and troughs. That's the nature of the game.' If only all of Harris' 'saviours' had the same attitude.

Donald John Mackay, weaver

So how has it changed?

'Well...I'm sure that most of what my dad was doing was for clothing, and it would have been earthy colours and thicker tweed. When he was coming to the end of his weaving lighter tweeds were coming in. He hated them!

'Now we're making it for any number of end uses. The colourways are different as well. Brighter. And there's more young people. When the Nike thing came in, the number of weavers were down to double figures. Now there's 200 or more and young folk working in the mill, in design.

'It allows people to stay on the island. To live here you need work and the tweed affords them that. It's like the distillery. Any youngster who goes there I can guarantee will be there until they retire. No-one's going to survive without the youngsters. We're the history part of it now.'

Away you go Donald John, you've plenty to give.

'Ach well man, I'll bluff my way through!'

As Christina works, he talks me through the process. How 'a tweed' is a 55-metre length, the warp thread running the length acting as the foundation. 'I go to the mill and pick the colour I want, then prepare the warp. That takes a day to prepare, winding it onto the beam, then tying each thread, 696 of them, then I fit the bobbins for it and the weft – that runs side to side.'

He begins to pedal – these old Hattersley mills are basically bikes attached to a loom. The shuttle flies, he's immediately into the rhythm.

Shuttle and loom

'Listen to that...Oh, to me it is music, better than any jazz or anything.'

What of the patterns?

'They're all mine. I just look out the window and see the colours, or go walking, look at the sea or the heather at different times of the year then try to incorporate that into the tweed. We go out every day, and it always changes.

'The colours represent here. In days of old you could tell where people came from because of the tweeds they wore, because the dyes mirrored the landscape.'

...

There is a weave here, of grasses and thread, people and place, but underpinning every conversation here and on the west coast has been the knowledge of how easy it is for it to unravel.

The need is not just to halt the loss, but rebuild and reappraise, which spins us back to Patrick Geddes. His philosophy was based around an ongoing interaction between work, place and folk, and the ways in which this triad intertwined. It's a holistic view, sensitive to landscape and economic possibilities, applicable to urban or rural settings.

Seven decades after Geddes, this thinking became known as bioregionalism. The title of a book, *Dwellers In The Land*, by Kirkpatrick Sale, one of its main proponents, pretty much sums it up.

Some of Donald John's tweeds

A bioregion is 'a place defined by its life forms, its topography and its biota rather than by human dictates,' Sale writes. 'Region governed by nature, not legislature...' Vitally, a bioregion reflects the way in which the environment and people interact and create an individually distinct (but not parochial) culture.

With increasing awareness of all that lies behind the need for sustainability – from barley to water to energy – and how a distillery can benefit a community, a bioregional approach to whisky begins to make some sense.

'To know the spirit of a place is to realize that you are part of a part, and that the whole is made up of parts, each of which is a whole,' writes Gary Snyder in *The Place, The Region, The Commons*. 'You start with the part you are whole in.' That, to me, sums up the approach of many of the new Scottish distilleries.

A whisky bioregion isn't defined by a nineteenth-century tax line or political boundary, but by the distiller asking, 'why here?', a process which makes you look deeper and more intently at what is around you.

That, in turn, opens up new possibilities for location-specific and appropriate cereal varieties, rediscovering landraces, digging deep into history, asking: what is special about this place? Topography, climate, cereal choices, varieties, peat, help to provide flavour possibilities, which are also triggered by cultural conditions such as history, palate and approach. The individual distillery is the terroir. The bioregion is the context. Work, folk, place.

'"Place" itself can be conceptualized as the synthesis of nature and culture,' writes ethnologist Mairi McFadyen. 'The natural environment influences the way we create our culture, while our culture, in turn, affects how people read and relate to the environment. The environment both shapes us as we, in turn, shape the environment.'

Looking bioregionally opens up a valid connection to land, location and community, offering local solutions to farming, environmental issues and housing, because living in the place gives you an understanding of what is possible. In Geddes' own words, we must 'think global, act local.'

It isn't one size fits all. A Hebridean distillery needs Hebridean understanding and a Hebridean solution, just as a Borders one requires something appropriate to that location. Fife, Speyside or Glasgow will be different again.

The shift from blends to malt has also meant a paradigm shift in thinking, which has led to the idea of place coming into sharper focus, because of the need for the distillery to talk about itself and its provenance. The 'why here?' becomes more relevant.

As a new distillery you let the place come to you and you become part of the place because it has been there a lot longer than you have. It is not just about experimenting, but also about rebuilding. It is allowing the place to speak and then living and working within it.

As Donald John says, 'it's out there. Out of the window.'

...

We'd somehow forgotten to eat the day before – bar an extremely cheesy late-night pizza in the pub – so the final day was dedicated to exploration and food. We head down the east coast on the Golden Road, so called because it cost so much to blast through the rock that it might as well have been made of it.

It's a dramatic contrast to the stunning beaches of the west. A place of exposed knuckles of rock and peat banks. When the west was cleared for sheep, this is where people were moved to, for the fishing or kelping. A place of bays and barely tenable anchorages, rusted roofs and houses perched on rocks. It's a remarkable, almost lunar landscape, but imagine trying to make this land work.

As Christina shoots, I pick up a fist-sized lump of rock, gritty, zebra-striped, kibbled with crystals. Lewisian gneiss is 3,000 million years old, so ancient it contains no fossils, just the sparkles of those early minerals. I hold the roughness of unimaginable time in my hand, a rendering of liquefied rock from the earth's heart, warped and buckled over eons.

As tectonic plates shifted, these rocks were heaved out of the planet's belly to its surface to cool. Gneiss is the planet's bedrock, obdurate, impermeable. It flares red on geological maps, which is appropriate enough, as it holds water in boggy, oxygen-starved conditions,

The Golden Road, Harris

building up peat that, billions of years later, gives fuel whose smell means home, drifting away like the blue shower, now passing over the Shiant Islands out on the Minch.

We drive to Rodel and Sam's Seafood Shack and stand patiently in a southwesterly gale for seaweed roast potatoes, fish-finger sandwiches and mackerel. Hungry. Don't judge us.

I think of Cuddy and those discussions about the excision of history, the suppression of language, of Bill's tradition bearers and his files of those who have left, but also about the way that distilleries are helping to revive communities, of the links with weaving and traditional crafts, of Donald John's knots and all the others, meshing grass to sand, people to place.

Whisky's roots bind it to a community by giving it a focal point while working from a tradition. The potential is there, but cannot be achieved without housing. Whisky cannot solve all of these problems on its own. It's not the panacea, but it is one of the new warp threads.

There's a sense of a new Hebridean movement: distilleries working together, a new whisky trail, a festival. Lewis has Abhainn Dearg, while new distilleries are planned for Benbecula, Barra and Tiree.

In *The Other Side of Sorrow*, James Hunter writes of how the future of the Highland economy shouldn't be based around the region being a cross between a national park and an open-air folk museum. The key is connectivity, environmental and social rehabilitation, and economic investment. There is plenty of talk (rightly) about rewilding, but repopulating is just as important. Bioregions are about biodiversity, and that includes people.

Distilleries in these remote places are more than production plants. They are inextricably linked to the social needs of their community, and with that – as these new distillers all agree – comes a moral dimension. Whisky-making becomes a co-operative occupation that benefits a community. As it used to be.

We head back to Stornoway, the rain falling in katabatic sheets of static so loud that we yell with glee. There are rainbows over Loch Seaforth.

 Opposite: Machair, Luskentyre, Harris

SCOTTISH OAK II

7

I'm at Fettercairn distillery in Aberdeenshire. In front of me, a huge table is littered with numbered glasses. Nothing like a blind tasting to get the mind working. All that I knew was that somewhere within the selection, Whyte & Mackay's blender, Gregg Glass (see opposite), had included samples from the Scottish oak project (see page 146–7).

A couple of hours later, the big reveal shows that every possibility appears to have been considered – oak chips at different toasting levels, casks with Scottish oak heads, others made entirely from the wood, different toasting levels, some filled with new make, others re-casked.

The most remarkable came from the cross-sections he'd taken from the same tree at five different stages of its life, from sapwood to 120-year-old wood, which had been placed in the base of a bell jar, then filled with new make.

The flavours moved from pineapple (sapwood) to musk (10 years), then butterscotch (40 years) and black fruits (80 years). Then, counterintuitively, at 120 years the pure fruits returned. A life of a tree through flavour.

Could a Scottish-oak signature be discerned? Maybe the dark fruitiness, the honeyed element, coffee and the low levels of vanillin. Enough to suggest there's something at work. I remembered that earlier chat with Andrew Russell at Speyside Cooperage (see page 101).

'There's been great claims about terroir in barley, but there's terroir in trees as well,' he'd said. 'Which side of the slope, how much sun they get, the soil. We see the differences between oak from Appalachians, the Ozarks, Spain, Hungary. Why wouldn't that be the same here?'

The distillery sits next to the 8,500-hectare Fasque estate. A few minutes later, Gregg and I are standing in the midst of 13,000 oak saplings, which he and the Fasque team have planted on a 3-hectare plot. A new distillery forest, just one small part of the 720 hectares of mixed woodlands that are planned for the estate.

Fasque also owns Christie-Elite, Scotland's largest forestry nursery, which raises ten million saplings a year, while the estate also has two sawmills, one of which processes bespoke timber – including oak for Gregg's casks.

'It's increasing the diversity of the estate,' says operations director John Harrison, 'and also reintegrating it into the community. All of this brings back local jobs and old-style craftsmanship.'

Once air-dried, the oak will head to Speyside Cooperage as part of the stocks of Scottish oak that Andrew Russell is building up. Though Scotland can hardly compete with Missouri in terms of volume, Andrew has a simple reason for using it – 'because it's Scottish!'

'Any whisky aged in Scottish oak will be sought after because of the provenance. Scottish barley, distilled here, then aged in a cask from a tree grown and coopered here. That would be remarkable.'

What started with Gregg asking 'why not?' has ended up as 'why we have to', because this is bigger than just a tree for a whisky cask.

Gregg Glass planting oak saplings

It's about locking in carbon and improving biodiversity; it's sustainable and regenerative. It links foresters and estate owners to sawmills, cooperages and distilleries, creates local employment, and gives training.

It's also long term. Gregg and I, fingers crossed, will see the Fettercairn forest thinned in 25 years, but neither of us will be around when the trees are felled.

...

'This is what I love about Scottish oak,' says cabinetmaker and designer John Galvin (see opposite), smoothing his hand over a plank. 'It's got these amazing thick figures, patterns, cracks and natural defects that are a reflection of the environment in which they've grown.

'American oak is linear. Every tree is straight and clean. It's great for casks, but Scottish timber...see how gnarly it is? This little cat's paw?' He points to a tiny cluster of dark dots. 'You'd never get that with American. It's clean, boring.'

I first met John at the launch of the 1964 Black Bowmore, for which he'd designed the case, and Brodie Nairn the bottle. The two finest craftsmen in their fields have become the go-to for any whisky firm sensible enough to realize that their high-end releases deserve the best. He's not only highly skilled, and the fastest talker in the world, but also a fine drinking companion.

Born in County Cork, he came to Glasgow to study at the College of Building and Printing and set up John Galvin Design in 2007, making bespoke furniture. The way he tells it, his success was good fortune, but you don't just get an exhibition in the Saatchi Gallery, an award from RIBA, a Wallpaper* exhibition in Milan and a commission to make a case for Highland Park 50-year-old in the space of six weeks unless you're doing something right.

'I didn't know anything about working for whisky, but knew that the original design they'd had wasn't right,' he says with a grin. The result was a silky, rippling, blond-oak case that wrapped itself around a bottle encased in tendrils of silver designed by Scottish jeweller Maeve Gillies.

More commissions followed: Glenlivet 50-year-old, Dalmore L'Anima and Constellation, Macallan and Bowmore. The studio expanded. What was a two-man operation (him and business partner Derek Wilson) is now 21 strong, covering three units in a Clydebank industrial estate.

The expertise has expanded from wood into leatherwork, metalwork and precious metals. 'If you have the basis of high-end craftsmanship in one medium, plus the drive and desire to learn, you can apply it across other mediums,' he says, 'but you have to be dedicated. We're pushing the bar all the time.'

The culmination of this, so far, was the one-off cabinet-bar that he designed to hold a five-strong archive collection of Black Bowmore, which combined hand-patinated copper, brass from the distillery's old spirit safe, charred and carved oak, wood from old washbacks and the five glass pillars that Brodie had shown us in Tain. Less a cabinet, in fact, more a functional sculpture. The £400,000 it raised at auction went to to the distiller's Legacy project, which supports the Islay community.

Luxury is often seen as being synonymous with ostentation. John's work however is subtle, complex – there are clear links with a Japanese aesthetic always at work. 'I could cover things in gold and shit like that, but there's no thought in that,' he laughs. 'True luxury is understated, not in your face. The more you look at our work the more detail you see, and anyway, it's the liquid that's the hero. You need that balance to hold the jewel in the middle. You protect and showcase.

'There's a lot of synergy between high-end craftsmanship and how whisky is produced,' he goes on. 'In both, it takes a long time to know your medium inside. Time is key. It frustrates me that people don't realize that we don't pull this out of thin air. I want a piece to have soul. He picks up another piece of oak. 'See here? That's where two branches have been. That compression is where the tree is flexing, it gives an amazing grain. It will suit one element in a piece, but not another. You need to be able to look at the block and see the end result. You can go down the factory-made route, but it will be soulless.'

Spend even a few minutes in his company and you know that he's only happy when he has delved as deep as he can into process, design, creation and story. Each piece is more than just a beautiful case for a rare liquid. As he says, 'don't give me some half-arsed story. I need truth and depth in something.'

A case in point is a project for a 54-year-old release from Highland Park, whose case was inspired by the strata of Yesnaby's cliffs. 'The piece is about the genesis of the island; the whisky sitting like lava cloaked by a cabinet with the wood, textured like strata cooling into rock. The story of the whisky, the provenance of the materials, that's what we are trying to get across.' It would, sadly, be the final project devised by Highland Park's brand director Jason Craig, the man who gave John his first break in whisky, and a longstanding friend of mine who died just as this book was being completed. The stunning 54-year-old is a tribute to Jason's joyous love of whisky, Orkney and craft.

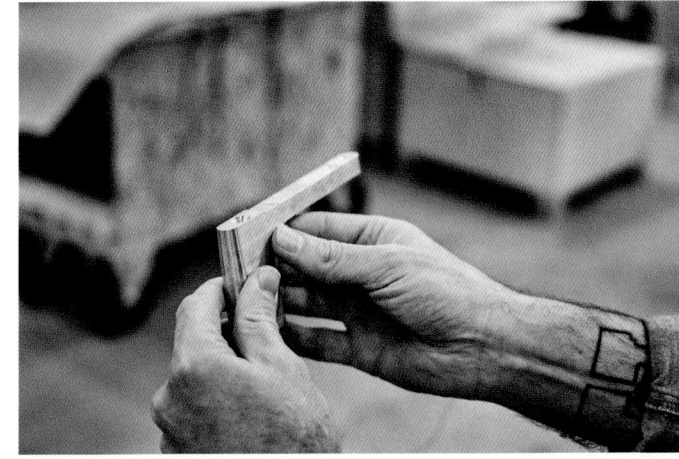

It strikes me that in the various conversations I've had, that all the people working closely with wood have deep connection with, and understanding of, time. This, I think, is one of John's signatures, his awareness of elemental forces at work in rock, water, metal, wood and liquid, and how they then combine.

His understanding of whisky goes beyond product, and he can therefore place it in context of its location, story and reflective of the skills of the people from its community.

This last element extends to the workshop, which sits a few hundred yards from where the old John Brown's shipyard was – the place where the *Lusitania*, HMS *Hood*, *Queen Mary*, *Queen Elizabeth* and *QE2* were all built.

'Think of what was built in this area over the last 150 years,' he says. 'All the best cabinetmakers, the best metalworkers. All gone. Destroyed. There's no opportunities for kids here. If that doesn't give me incentive enough to walk in here and recreate that in some way, well...

'All we make, we invest back to create jobs for younger craftsmen. It's given hope.' It's almost as if he's tapping into the inherited muscle memory of the grandchildren of those former craftsmen. What could seem like a jarring juxtaposition of luxury within urban devastation now makes sense.

'Was that OK?' he asks as we get ready to leave. He hadn't stopped speaking for two hours. 'It's the first interview I've ever done when I didn't have to ask a question,' I reply.

Left: John Galvin, bringing skills back to Clydebank
Right: Attention to detail is key

CASH BOOK No. 19.
CASH BOOK No. 18.
CASH BOOK No. 17.
CASH BOOK No. 16.
CASH BOOK No. 15.
CASH BOOK No. 14.

BLENDS & PERFUME

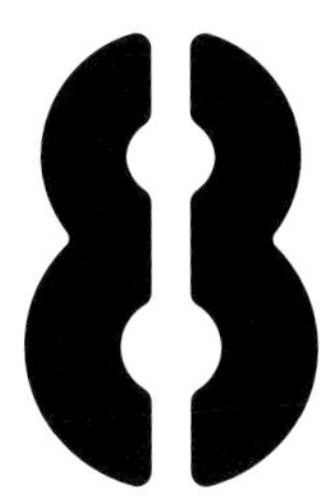

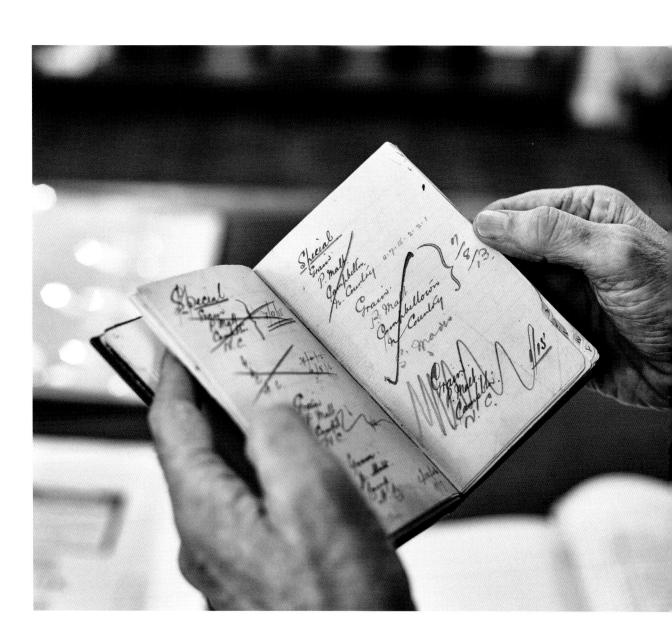

I was born in a city of fogs. Thick ones, blotting out the houses opposite, smothering steeples and cancelling the Clyde. The evening skies were full of starlings clustering onto soot-blackened buildings. A world of aromas as well: the tarry miasma of the subway, cigarettes, my granny's baking, chalk dusters, cut grass, vinegar, mince, roses...and the Black & White whisky my dad drank.

When we went to visit the family in Perth, I'd meet my cousins at Dewar's Corner and we'd hang out at the Bell's Sports Centre. My uncles there drank Famous Grouse because it, too, was a Perth blend. Whisky was everywhere.

I began drinking in pubs where water spigots and bottles of lemonade were always on the bar to dilute the drams that all of the men drank. Whisky, blended, was one of the strands that held Glasgow together. Socially, for good and ill, but also economically.

Since the mid-nineteenth century, it had arrived by train from the north, up river from the west. It would be blended, then sent out to the world, a country's calling card.

If eighteenth-century Improvements had changed the look of Scotland's landscape, then its subsequent image was finessed by writers, and one in particular: Sir Walter Scott.

The author of 25 novels, countless poems and works of non-fiction, Scott was the most popular novelist in the world at the start of the nineteenth century. His work built on that of Ossian to create a new national mythos. It was he who choreographed the great PR stunt of King George IV's visit to Edinburgh in 1822, when all (including the King) were festooned in tartan, and the monarch drank illicit whisky from the glens.

So tempting was Scott's vision that in 1852, seeking solitude and quiet, Queen Victoria and Prince Albert bought a castle in Deeside. They dressed in Highland gear, stalked stags, landed salmon and helped trigger the start of mass tourism. Though Scotland was by now an urban, industrialized country, its image was of untouched, heather-girt hills, stags at bay, lonely lochs, misty mountains...and space. A theatre set with costumed actors. Scott-land.

Whisky latched on to this. Although single malts were sold in the nineteenth century, it was blends – that mix of malts and higher-strength, lighter grain whiskies – that were to make Scotch a global spirit. Blends gave consistency, volume, could be made to suit drinkers' palates, and be created (initially by grocers familiar with blending teas, coffees and rums) in signature house styles.

The early blenders utilized Scotland's signifiers to their advantage. Most of the labels and advertising sported scenes from Scott and Burns, Highland cows, sheep and faithful hounds. There were kilted soldiers and pipers, smugglers, landscapes, ruined castles, hunting scenes and other country pursuits. Whisky, wrapped in a plaid of late-Victorian clichés, sold the world Scotch-land. On one hand you could say this is where it all went wrong, but were it not for this, Scotch wouldn't be where it is today.

...

My first job was at Stepps, Black & White's modern bottling plant on the outskirts of the city, where I placed cases of whisky onto pallets destined for, it seemed, every country. I drank as well. Bottles snaffled from the line, stashed in cisterns in the toilets, everyone hammered by lunchtime. Whisky was a constant, like the docks and shipyards. And then, somehow, it wasn't.

Is there a correlation between whisky's domestic decline and that of Scotland's industrial base? Whisky belonged to the now-silent slipways and cold steel mills, and that Victorian idea of 'Scotland' that I couldn't identify with.

Until, that is, when on the staff of a weekly drinks journal in 1988, I was sent to Glasgow to write its annual whisky category report. I found a world of hefty drams before lunch and no work afterwards. Although distilleries were closing and volumes were crashing, the glasses in those directors's dining rooms were brimming. 'Don't worry, son,' I was told. 'As soon as they turn 35, those young folks will stop drinking vodka.' They didn't.

My new job got me behind the scenes, into blending labs and the people who made whisky: John Ramsay and Alan Reid at Highland Distillers, Colin Scott (Chivas), Richard Paterson (Whyte & Mackay), Robert Hicks (Teacher's) and, on one momentous day, the kingpin: Diageo's head of distillation and spirit supply, Turnbull Hutton.

He was one of the last of a generation who had worked their way up from the shop floor, whisky's equivalent of Bill Shankly or Alex Ferguson: working class, irascible, huge-hearted, loyal.

On our first meeting, I'd asked him what his job entailed. 'Well... the numpties in sales and marketing tell me how much whisky they think they'll sell – which I know they won't,' he'd growled. 'The guys at the distilleries tell me how much they can make. I'm the c**t in the middle, trying to sort the whole fucking mess out.'

He was the most important man in Scotch, and is now recognized for being the one who helped steer whisky through the worst of the bad times of the 1980s. He, and many others, opened up a different world of whisky to me.

Editors demanded pieces about single malts, but blends and the incredible skill of those blenders fascinated me. How was it that the style that accounted for 98 per cent of the whisky sold in the world was so looked down on? To most of the world, blends represented Scotland. To Scotland, they didn't. Little has changed.

...

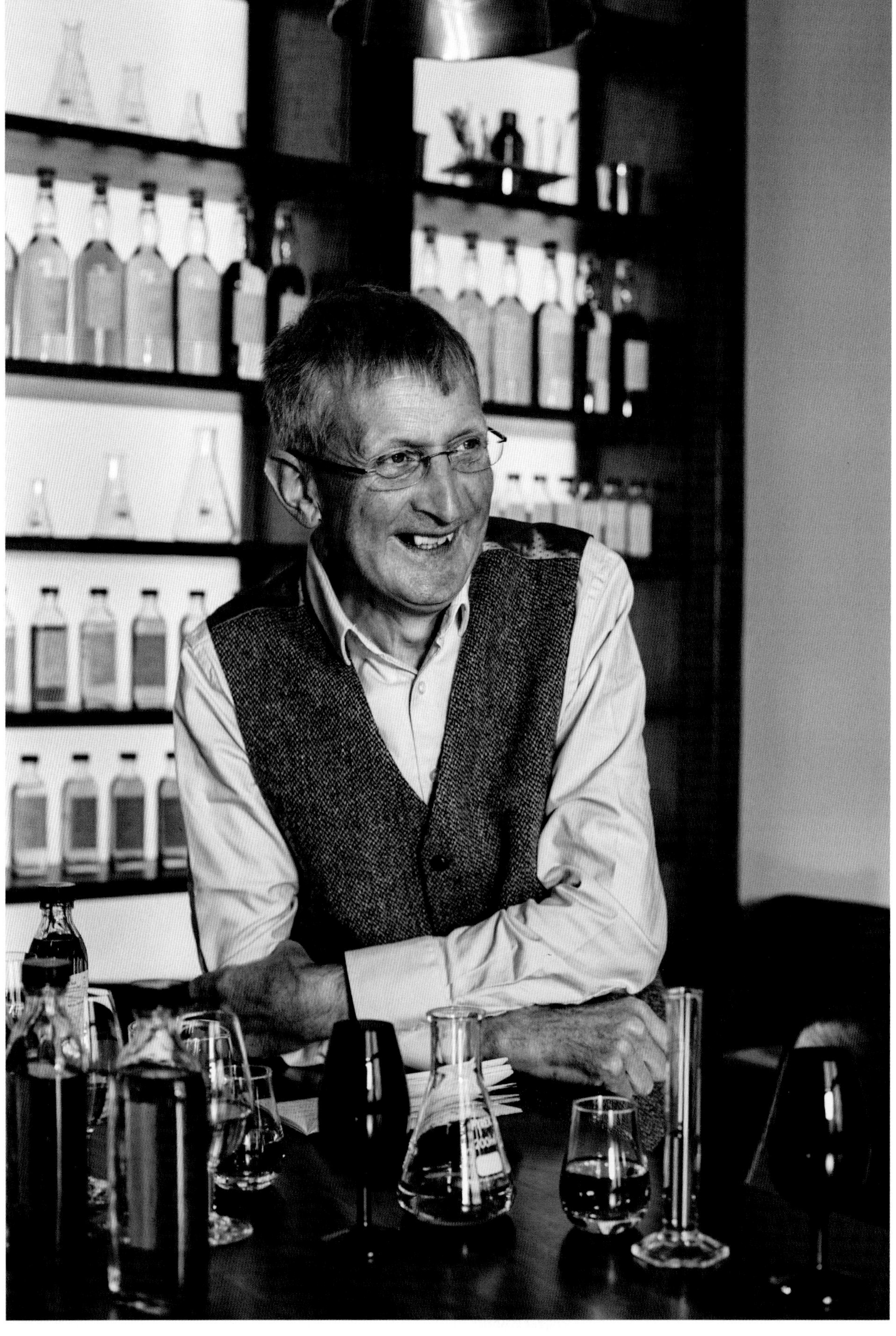

Dr Jim Beveridge, former master blender at Johnnie Walker

Christina picks me up in Glasgow's George Square. We're heading north to Menstrie, close to Stirling, and to Diageo's blending labs.

We're here to meet Jim Beveridge (see opposite) and Emma Walker (see page 203). At the time, Jim (since retired) was master blender for the world's biggest-selling Scotch whisky, Johnnie Walker, and headed up a 12-strong blending team, which included Emma, who is now master blender.

I've known Jim for 20-odd years, and our many chats have wandered around how to change the perception of blends, flavour, language, creativity. I've got used to the prolonged silences as he ponders a question, before answering in an oblique manner, which takes the idea off in another – and more interesting – direction.

People relate to provenance, so single malts work. Blends are stateless, global brands. Is place important to blends and if so, did it come from those early days when the grocers utilized local whiskies? Walker based on west-coast whiskies; Chivas drawing from Speyside; Dewars and Grouse from the Highlands?

'Take J&B,' says Jim. 'That was a flavour-led decision [light, fresh, ideal for the post-Prohibition palate in the States], which took them to Speyside. The Walker style took them west because they were in the west.' There's a long pause. 'It's a thought worth pursuing, because the same applies with Usher [Edinburgh], or Chivas [Aberdeen]. Flavours influenced by where blenders were.' Another pause. He's working this out. Emma and I know to wait.

'A lot of what we do is continuing the tradition of flavour that we inherit. Despite all the pressures from the outside world, our job is to navigate through those changes and still produce that whisky. It's only when we innovate do we get to do something that you could say is us.'

How irritated do you get by people saying Scotch isn't innovative?

Emma sighs, then smiles slightly wearily. 'I think you can be innovative in the ways you use the flavours, using the tradition, but moving it into different spaces. Getting feedback from consumers, brand ambassadors, bartenders to get an idea of what could be happening in the future. There's a lot more of that going on than is possibly understood. It helps to be part of that loop.'

Is it more difficult when you're dealing with a supertanker like Johnnie Walker?

'There is huge momentum behind what exists,' says Jim, 'so, yes, it's difficult to turn that supertanker around. On the other hand, if Walker wants to innovate it can direct all that energy into innovation. In the last ten years there's been a lot of that.'

'That's the fun part of working next to the archive,' says Emma. 'Going back to the old logbooks and recipes, and seeing the innovation there. When doing any innovation project we'll go through the archive looking for inspirations, things that will trigger an idea. Inspiration comes from lots of different areas.'

Can a blend exhibit a sense of place?

'When you asked that, I thought of the places where they were first made,' says Jim. 'Kilmarnock, Shieldhall, Stepps, Markinch, Leith, South Queensferry, Perth. There was a sense of place with all of those blends.

'I learned my sense of place when I started working here [in 1979], in the research station just across the road. Everything I do will refer back to this place, and that period, for that's the first time when the products, the distilleries, the warehousing, the blending all came together in the work we were doing. The sense of place is relevant.'

Emma nods. 'This is where we bring the different parts of Scotland together. Each distillery has its own sense of place, which has come through nurture and nature, where it's been made, and the people who have made it. A blend is a distillation of Scotland. Its shape comes from the different places and layers we bring together here.'

Jim's still mulling it over. 'The research station was where I first experienced a diversity of flavour I never thought existed. That was the world I entered, the pure science, so it was a unique perspective.

'I began to expand that understanding, going to the distilleries and getting to know the places that made these flavours, and how it was a combination of the people, how they designed the distillery and how they operated it. It was people- and place-led.

'The blender is behind each bottle. The expectation is that whatever you nose and taste will be connected to that place. When I nose that Glendullan,' he points at the sample in front of him. 'In my mind I go to Glendullan and think about that place, then all the other distilleries and places, and how to take all of these bits and make products from them.'

Why isn't this appreciated? I ask. His answer is simple... and surprising.

'There's this definition about blended Scotch whisky that I think is really...annoying. Actually, it annoys me intensely. "Blended Scotch" on the label means it is a mix of malt and grain whisky, and within that context blending is a pejorative term; it's mixing magic stuff with cheap stuff. It should just be called "Scotch whisky", maybe with a back label saying "a blend of malt and grain".

'The mixing of things together to make something that is greater than the sum of its parts is just magic. It's a huge place to be, and huge fun, and without question it is the best way to express Scotch whisky.

'The best thing you can do with malt is...' he stops and laughs. 'No! I'm not using those terms! The best you can do is bring the light ones, the sweet ones, the heavy ones together to make something special. That is what blending is about.

'That word "blended" should mean the skill of blending. Maybe then people would say, "This is a blend? Great! It's going have lots of different flavours. It's better than a single malt, it's a blend!"'

...

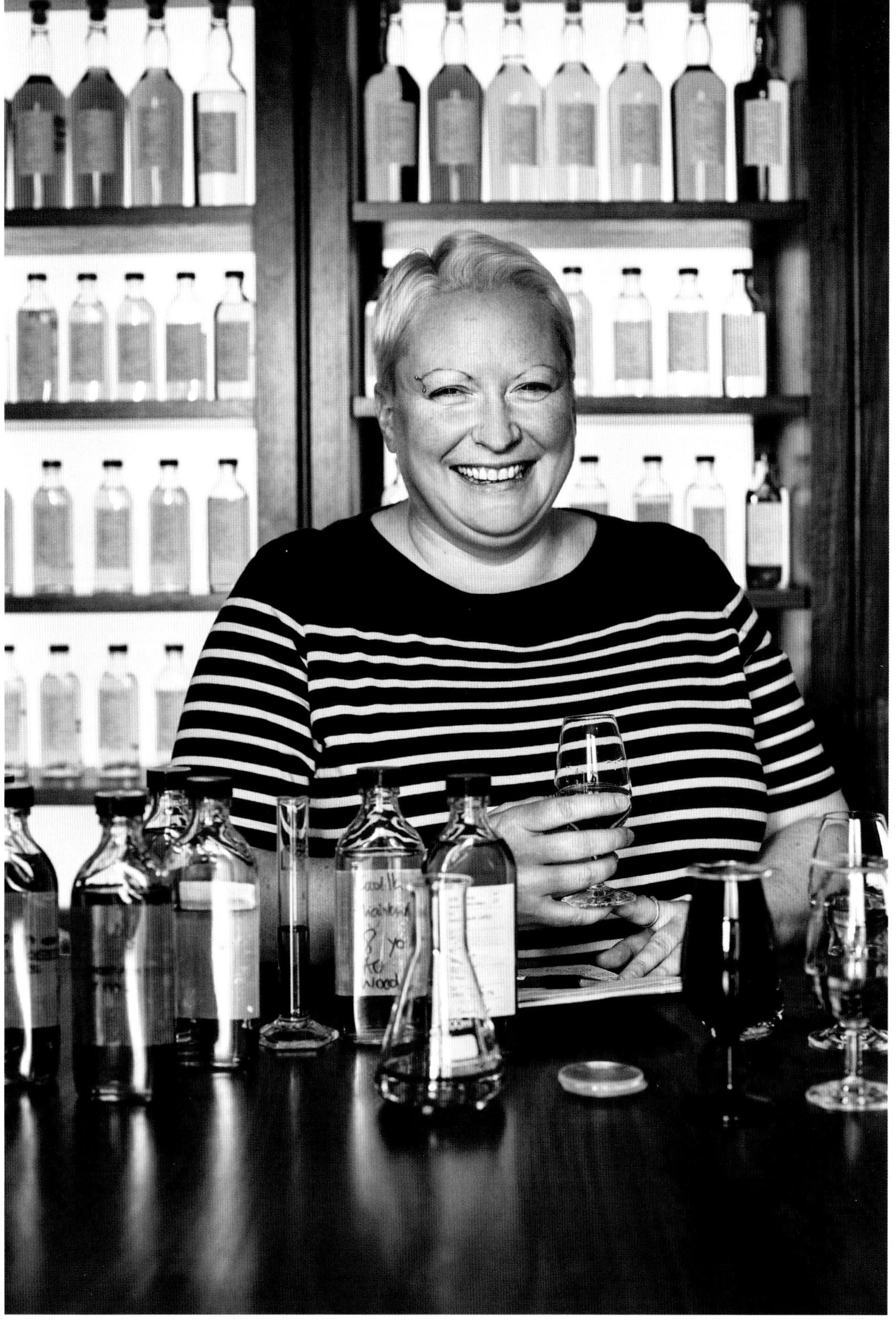

Emma Walker, master blender at Johnnie Walker

 Hydrometers

 Imogen Russon-Taylor, perfumer, Kingdom Scotland

Back in the car, we head south to Edinburgh's Royal Botanic Gardens to meet up with Imogen Russon-Taylor (see opposite). I'd first met her when she was head of PR at Glenmorangie. We'd lost touch when she left to bring up her family. Then, one night, my friend Annabel sprayed some perfume on me. It smelled of smoke and leather, moss and the mineral notes of sea spray. 'Imogen's new business,' she said. 'She's called it Kingdom Scotland.'

Ensconced in the sunlit gardens, Imogen rattles through her life story. Born in Manchester to Scottish-Irish academics, summer holidays in Ardnamurchan, a degree in physical geography in Edinburgh, study at the Sorbonne, PR work on beauty, wine and whisky, and now this, Scotland's first-ever fragrance house.

Why perfume? 'I had a very glam grandmother who always wore scent, heavy 1980s ones like Poison. We had a big garden, and from a really young age I was just exposed to scent. Then, because I was working in beauty and whisky simultaneously, I could see how these two aromatic worlds were colliding. I saw drinks in a different way.'

You could say the same about her scents. She brings out the first, Portal, her encapsulation of a Caledonian forest. Green, pine sap, oak moss, forest floor. I'm back in those twisting Atlantic woods. The longer it sits, the deeper it seems to pull you in.

The next, Botanica, was a commission by the gardens to commemorate its 350th anniversary. Heady, rain-sodden blossoms, exotic, hothouses and green border. Albaura is the opposite: crisp, fresh, and is inspired by the Scottish Edwardian polar explorer and botanist Isabel Wylie Hutchison. 'It smells white,' I say. 'Like blue sky after the snow has fallen,' she counters.

Then comes the one Annabel had spritzed on me, the deep, resonant, complex Metamorphic. All of them evoke time and place, stir surprising emotions.

It's Metamorphic that intrigues me the most. She speaks of living close to Arthur's Seat (where James Hutton, the eighteenth-century father of modern geology, first gazed into deep time), her travels and degree. I get that, but making that leap into making a perfume that encapsulates the idea of a rock?

'It's probably weird, but I think isn't it obvious?' she says with a huge laugh. 'Maybe it's because I think in scent. Metamorphic is the most complex rock, created under intense heat and pressure.' I babble something about Lewisian gneiss. 'That's what it is! That's why there's a nod to whisky with the smoke – it's the rocks of the west coast.'

Jim had spoken of how successful innovations were consumer-led rather than production-led, which he said was 'the sum of the lowest common denominator, because they are driven by cost'. Is it the same here?

'It's similar to whisky,' she says. 'When you want to buy something special, you have to engage your brain and make an intelligent choice by

discovering the story behind the product. People are looking for something that's different, and authentic.'

That, in turn, means being able to articulate your feelings about the perfume, and language can be a problem. 'When you start nosing as a novice it's intimidating because you don't have the language that others appear to.

'The more sophisticated a culture becomes, the less language it has for scent. We have forgotten our sense of smell, but it is innate in us all, and enhances our life experience. You navigate the world by your sense of smell.' Not for the first time, she could be talking about whisky.

It's a topic that Jim, his colleague Maureen Robinson and I have talked over for decades. Crack the issue of language, give people confidence and the tools to navigate what can seem a baffling, intimidating world, and you have them for life.

If language is one element, so is changing the thinking about what a perfume (or blend) is. This new approach to perfume came crashing into my life at an exhibition of contemporary scents at Somerset House, which took the idea of perfume into new, wilder areas: truck stops, unmade beds, back streets, a logging camp.

The scents on show were pushing an immensely lucrative, but safe, luxury market in a radical direction, bound up in the belief that perfume had to change its frame of reference and be experiential. They told stories. Imogen's perfumes belong in this world.

Imogen's perfumes are inspired by geology

They are also marked out by their intensity. 'That's because, for me, Scotland has a sense of drama in landscape, history and the people,' she says. 'Everything is dramatic, so I thought the fragrances have to be as well. They wouldn't be Scottish otherwise!'

These are personal creations. It must be nerve-wracking at times. 'I suppose when you're on your own you get quite nervous. It's like any art, in that you are giving a bit of yourself, which can be nerve-wracking and exposing, but thank goodness it resonates with others.'

But, she adds quickly, she isn't on her own. 'I am a curator, a perfume designer, but I'm not a perfumer. I wanted to go through that classical training, but it's 18 years plus and I didn't have that time, so I work with different perfumers.

'I find it disingenuous to sit here and say I am the maker. The chain of ingredients is complex, they come from all over the world and there's a huge number of people involved.'

It matches precisely what Jim and Emma had said. When Jim was awarded an OBE, he immediately deflected the congratulations, saying the award wasn't for him, but the team. 'Anything I say about blending is about the team,' he'd said soon after. 'Any success for Walker is a team effort.'

The parallels between the two worlds are obvious and many: distillation, combining different ingredients, accords, internal balances, aroma, complexity. When I think of Imogen's approach I can imagine any whisky blender saying the same things. There are links with the boundary-pushing work done by blending houses Compass Box and, more recently, Woven in Leith. Looking at whisky blending through a different lens – experiences, feelings, emotions. Making it human. Making it, I realise, like these new perfumes.

A few weeks later, I see Emma at the opening of the Johnnie Walker Experience in Edinburgh's Princes Street, an eight-floor, £185-million investment that takes people on a flavour journey through whisky. It's fun, unorthodox and places people at the heart of its story.

It struck me, Highball in hand in the rooftop bar, that it was a sign of blended whisky coming home, that the days of the stateless international brand might be coming to an end. This was Scottish.

ISLAY

The further west from Glasgow we go, the wetter it becomes. A smirr in Loch Lomond becomes dreich in Inveraray, a downpour in Lochgilphead and a gale by the time we get to Tarbert. The ferry's delayed, so we drive on to try and get some photos of twisty roads, but only find an ancient milepost and some wet sheep.

We eventually set sail, weaving out of the West Loch. Innumerable blues and greys, the clouds ruckled like a child's bedsheet. The island of Gigha, with a line of silver underneath, seems to float in the air. Slowly, Islay emerges from the mist.

An older man is leading a group of 20-something Oxbridge students. They talk loudly of 'perfidious' Russians 'and Turks' one adds. It's like sitting in on a failed battle plan for the Crimean War. When some drawled racism is added, Christina decides it's best for her to go on deck. A slightly tattered St Andrews flag wraps itself around the pole.

'I can't see Lagavulin. That big rock's in the way,' one of the students moans. I'm tempted to say that the 'rock' is Dunyvaig Castle, seat of the Lords of the Isles, and that it predates the distillery by 700 years, but what would they care for context?

We drive on familiar roads to the Ballygrant Inn, with its remarkable selection of whiskies, our home for the stay. Smoke from the maltings, old peat banks, Bridgend's woods, the fields golden with barley.

This is a complex island. Imagine Islay like a hunchbacked wizard, the southern Rhinns his chin, Loch Gorm his eye and Ardnave the top

Left: Heading out to Islay
Right: Milepost, near Tarbert, Loch Fyne
Opposite: Back on Islay

of his hat. On a geological map, his beard is henna-dyed with gneiss and metagabbro, his eye sockets bruised by the purple of phyllite, his eyebrows are menacing zig zags of acid green dolerite.

His robes, which fan out to the east, are a golden field of quartzite, and blue limestone. On the south coast, parallel green streaks of amphilolite and hornblende fray the hem of his cloak.

The rock says whether to plant or graze, dig or build. It says where barley can be grown, how rivers run, where the springs are. It drains water or holds it in peat bogs, helping to create the character of its smoke that scents its malts, and the location of its distilleries.

Fertile, and close to Glasgow, Islay was less damaged by the Clearances, thanks to the gradualist approach to Improvements taken by its lairds, the Campbell family – particularly Walter and his grandson Walter Frederick – who introduced mixed crops, encouraged legal distilling and diversified the economy.

Proximity to the mainland made Islay's whisky a staple element in blends, giving them a touch of smoke. Reliance on that trade, however, had its drawbacks. A little smoke goes a long way and any time the blended market crashed, distilleries closed. The fallout of the crash of the 1980s, saw Port Ellen, Ardbeg and Bruichladdich close and the rest go on to short-term working.

Islay was saved by single malt. The smokiness of (most of) its whiskies gave them a singular and easily identifiable signature, a character that new drinkers were able to name. They were 'smoky', 'peaty', 'wild', 'medicinal', they reminded people of beach bonfires, barbecue sauce or dead guillemot (the last one ©Charles MacLean). Name an aroma and you speak with confidence. Have confidence and you are hooked.

...

Whisky-making is regularly referred to as an 'industry'. We view distilleries as masterpieces of engineering, and are equally fascinated and baffled by the science. It is a valid approach, yet who speaks of wine in the same way? Whisky, too, is an agricultural product and Islay is an agricultural island.

For millennia, its wealth has come from cows. When the island's creamery closed in 2000, the dairy herd was culled. Some farmers switched back to beef, but many also looked to diversify. Whisky was booming. Was there a way to link the two?

The morning after, we head west. 'Where is it?' asks Christina as we head along the bumpy single-track road. I point to a white blob on a side of an outcrop, Loch Gorm in front, the Atlantic just over the rise. There's an anvil-shaped gilded patch hanging on the edge. It could well be the most westerly barley field in Scotland.

It is just one of the 100 acres that farmer Andrew Jones (see page 217) has planted with cereals for Bruichladdich (mostly barley, but also some rye). It is part of a project that has changed the look of Islay's landscape, a demonstration of the need to diversify. In 2009, Andrew was one of the first to take up the new challenge. There are now 22 growers and 1,000 acres under barley.

We pull into the farmyard as he drives in on the tractor. Black-haired, young (or younger than you expect a farmer to be, at least), with an ever-present smile. 'Come away in. Tea?' We settle in the farmhouse to catch up.

'Did you like the sunflowers?' he asks. We'd noticed them growing alongside the steep farm track. 'It was time to give something back, so there's sunflowers and a pollen mix for the butterflies and bees. It won't stop the geese eating the barley, but it's good for the wee birds.'

He's also sowing green crops after harvest to add nutrition to the soil, then grazing sheep before the barley seed goes in, as well as spreading the straw dung from wintering cattle on the sandier fields, thereby cutting down on fertilizer. 'We're trying to be greener,' he says taking a gulp of tea, 'but it's not always easy. We're learning every year.'

Islay is marginal for barley growing. Maybe there's no surprise that no barley had been grown for whisky production for over a century and, as Andrew points out as he outlines the impact of climate change, things aren't getting easier.

'There's definitely a change to the weather. Winter is longer, so spring's later, the summers are hotter, and autumn is unpredictable.

You can't judge it. The joys of farming! It's harder to get the barley in as the weather window is smaller. The return is good, but yes it comes with its challenges.' All of this is said with a smile. Just an honest assessment of working in these times.

What's the incentive, then?

'I'm looking to the future,' he says. 'The average age of farmers on the west coast is 61 and I'm at the age where I want this to be growing through my farming life and into the next generation. I have a part to play.'

How much of this is driven by whisky?

'We'd still be growing barley for feed, we'd still be on same route of trying to improve where we can with cover crops, but because Bruichladdich gives us a good return, we can grow barley at scale, and we'll take on more risk with them being involved, rather than if we were growing it for ourselves.'

I also get the feeling that he just likes a challenge. Take rye. Used in small quantities for Scotch whisky in the nineteenth centuries it had disappeared in the twentieth. Then, in 2017, independently of each other, four distilleries contacted me. 'Can you keep a secret?' they all asked. 'We're going to make Scottish rye. Don't tell anyone.' I didn't. One of them was Bruichladdich and the rye was grown by Andrew.

'Why? Because of my youth and stupidity! I'd become the go-to if Bruichladdich wanted to try something different. Allan Logan (Bruichladdich's production director) asked what I knew about growing it. I said 'nothing'. Next thing I was trialing it. Rye's not easy, but as we learn we'll get better.

'Right enough, if you went by the textbook you wouldn't grow malting barley here either!' He grins. 'They said you couldn't do it. It was the same with winter crops, the same with the rye. Oh, the stick I got was unbelievable! If they say you can't do something you're even more determined to bloody prove them wrong.'

One of the phrases you hear most frequently on Islay is, 'ach, it'll be fine'. Things work out somehow, no matter what the obstacles. Tie that to inbuilt Hebridean resilience and pragmatism and you begin to understand why barley's being grown here again.

There is no moral necessity to do it, but it's a way to spread risk and get a return. If it doesn't pay, however, the farmers will stop growing it. On the face of it, Islay-grown barley gives distillers like Bruichladdich and Kilchoman a handy marketing edge. The latter even bought the farm on which it sits to control its supply for its '100% Islay' release.

We go outside, Andrew pointing out the fields, explaining the soil and the hard, relentless work involved in farming. 'Why do I do it?' he asks. Looks around 'because...' Smiles. The most westerly field on Islay. The Atlantic Ocean. Choughs flung around in the wind. Barley is meant to be here.

Andrew Jones, Coull Farm

Half an hour later, we're in another field, this time above the Museum of Islay Life in Port Charlotte. 'Can you hold some barley?' Christina asks. James Brown (see opposite) pulls up a fistful by the roots. Grins. In his other mighty fist is his shepherd's crook. Carved into the horn is the word 'Octomore'. It's the name of his farm, that of a (long-gone) distillery situated there, and of Bruichladdich's most heavily peated expression. Anything marked 'Octomore .3' is made from James' barley exclusively.

He also owns the spring the distillery uses for diluting its whiskies to bottling strength. It also used to be the Port Charlotte supply. When the village went onto the mains, James would fill containers with the spring water and carry them to the old folks, who swore it had health-giving properties.

'I approached Bruichladdich,' he says. 'I said, if you make all this fuss about water why don't you sell a bottle of the best spring water with your whisky?' What started with six barrels, now requires transit tanks. 'The more it went on, the more I got tied in, and the more I was enjoying it. It's changed my life.'

The many layers of James Brown. Water supplier, farmer of Highland cattle, sheep and barley; also in his time special constable for Port Charlotte, lighthouse keeper, piper, rugby player, whisky collector and storyteller who holds court over the odd highly social dram (of Octomore, naturally) in his eyrie as he gazes across the ever-changing light on the loch.

Port Charlotte lighthouse

James Brown of Octomore

Allan Logan, production director at Bruichladdich

He looks at the stook he's ripped up. 'Until Bruichladdich came along we weren't interested in whisky. It was a drink, it was the draff. Now? It's changed. It's our barley, it's the water...it's people like you Dave, asking me questions.' He attempts to glower. Fails.

I know him well enough to anticipate the moans about how hard growing the barley is, the low yields, the high costs, but I also know he'd not have it any other way.

'You work with what you've got,' he says. 'The fields are good, it's the weather that's the problem, but,' he looks around, 'farming's a gamble all the time. We're used to living on the edge. It shows the resilience of Islay farmers that not one of them went bust when the creamery went. We're used to surviving here.'

Things have changed since the Brown family moved to Octomore in 1961. 'There was no electricity,' he recalls. 'We had running water, but it was all paraffin lamps. Mother, father and the three of us in one bedroom. We just managed until the estate put a new roof on the house and the electricity came in.'

Now, there's the farm buildings, some holiday rentals and a studio for his daughter, the jewellery designer Sarah Brown. It must be a good feeling.

'Yes, there is something special and it's not only that I actually like the whisky! Think of it. The water from this well goes around the world. The fact you can drink Octomore whisky made with barley from Octomore...' He beams. 'Its changed my life completely, particularly the water. The barley's a nightmare, though!'

...

Back along the road we go to Bruichladdich to hook up with Allan Logan (see opposite). He started, aged 19, in the warehouses, then moved into distilling. 'I always wanted to make whisky,' he says. 'All my friends flew the nest. Nobody was interested in staying on Islay and working in whisky. I was one of the exceptions.'

Nine years in, he was given the role of running the whole, increasingly complex, site: whisky- and gin-making, a bottling line, liaison with farmers and maltsters. He's the right man for the job. Allan exudes calm. His is the voice who asks the practical questions, turns ideas around, patiently examines them from different angles.

Bruichladdich was an outlier in Islay terms – unpeated due to the requirements of its owner, Whyte & Mackay. After being on short-term working in the 1980s, it closed in 1994 but reopened in 2001 under new ownership, embarking immediately on a reinvention of what a distillery could be – the bottling line, multiple releases, three different styles.

It placed itself on the margins, wearing its maverick status with a certain manic swagger. Now owned by Rémy-Cointreau, there is a more reasoned focus, which, increasingly, is on the land and sustainability. Allan personifies this evolution.

Your job is...complex.

'I know! Some days you feel you are far removed from the whisky-making process, but it's about the wider issues. If we were just distilling in the typical way our jobs would be totally different, we'd be analyzing yields and costs per litre. Those things are relevant and interesting, but what makes our job more exciting is that we're working for something bigger.

'We're paving the way for the future, building that supply chain from farmers where we understand what varieties they're growing and the challenges of climate they face. That gives us more of a connection with the ingredients.'

Speak with him, or Anthony Wills at Kilchoman, for five minutes and that notion that Islay barley is there for PR quickly disappears.

'It's made me see things differently,' he says. 'We have far more appreciation of the whole chain, from breeding to genetics and farming. If you can be more involved you have more influence on what you're making, rather than just ordering so many tons of malt. 'There's also a weight of responsibility. For our 21 farmers it is a big part of their revenue. We understand that we have to share some of that risk and build trust. The turning point was when, in 2009, we invested in drying and storage. That's when you saw combines being bought.'

It has to make sense for the farmer?

'Totally,' he says. 'It's the farmer first. Working with them you get more out of the relationship, rather than just a contract.'

The next addition to Allan's workload is the trialing of hydrogen combustion technology as part of its aim to decarbonize its production process by 2025. There's also the not-insignificant building of an on-site maltings – making it the fourth on the island with one. When you consider that there are only four others in the rest of Scotland, it gives an indication of how the island looks slightly differently at things. Anyway, back to Allan.

'It's not only going to create opportunities for the distillery, but it's investing in the future of growing barley here, allowing it to be viable for the farmers. If we are making commitments it encourages them to do the same.

'It also made sense. Half of the barley we buy is from Islay. At the moment it has to go off the island to be malted, so the carbon footprint doesn't make sense. It will also allow us to process smaller batches, which opens up new possibilities.'

Is 50 per cent the maximum you can go?

'It comes back to vision for the next 40–100 years,' he says. 'If we keep trying to increase the volumes of barley grown, the farmers will decrease livestock numbers. That might sound appealing, but we know in terms of sustainability we need livestock in the mix.'

when he and his father had taken the cows off the fields in 1999, half of the wildlife also disappeared. 'You need the mix,' he'd said. 'We have a lot of rare species of flowers, there's different insects, birds. We regularly have up to 500 peewits and it's because we have cattle and sheep. Livestock and barley go together.'

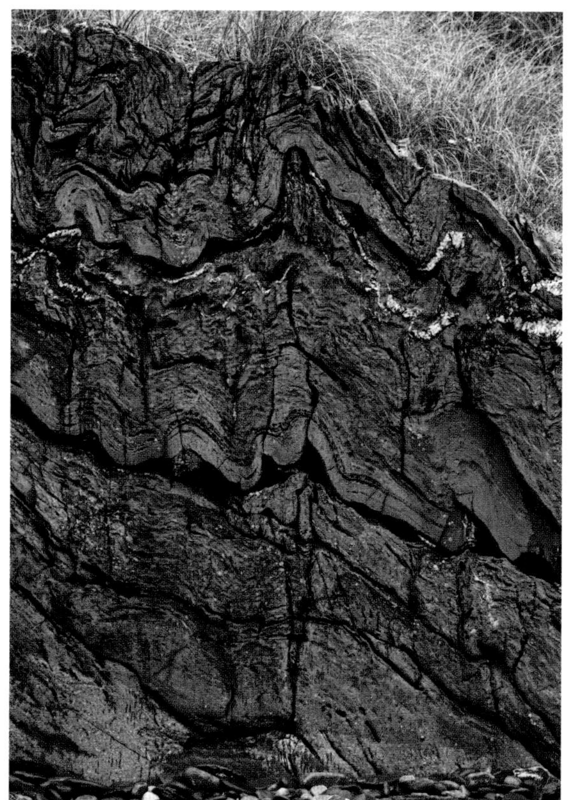

There's just time to end the day on one of my favourite beaches, Saligo on the west coast. Over the machair, through the dunes to where the Atlantic is running ice blue. The space.

Christina, as is her wont, finds a precarious rock in the sea to balance on. I head towards the strange rock formations higher up the beach. Folded and twisted greywacke, frozen waves of time and, among the rock's drapery, a niche with what looks like a figure inside.

What does living in a place like this do to the mind? The huge skies and relentless sea makes you aware of being on the edge of something enormous, yet you're simultaneously aware of the tiniest of details – a flower, a pebble, a fleeting aroma.

It reminds me of a film of the poet Norman MacCaig in which he (dram probably taken) tried to describe the landscape of Assynt to his slightly sceptical interviewer.

'It's a miniature landscape,' said MacCaig.

'You call this miniature?' responded his interlocutor, looking at the mountains and sea. 'Yes,' said Norman. 'If you walk 200 yards, it's new. I love this landscape, and ask myself why? Bursting into wild generalities, maybe for me the rolling stuff, the low stuff is the generality of humankind out of which comes the odd, separate, individuals, but they are rooted together by what is underneath them.'

...

The next morning we're back at the distillery. For all of its innovations, most of the distillery's equipment dates from the late nineteenth century. Take the mill, for instance, which remains belt-driven and, as we say in Scotland, shoogly. Like much of the plant, it was restored with care by the late Duncan MacGillivray, an engineering wizard.

The open-topped, cast-iron mashtun with a 'rake and plough'

mechanism for mixing the grist and water is one of the few remaining in Scotland. We arrive as they're mashing in.

A sweet aroma like biscuits dipped in tea comes first, accompanied by a rumbling noise, then the steaming mix of ground barley and hot water jets in. Motes of barley dust hang in the sunlight. The sweet wort created will go into one of the six wooden washbacks for a long fermentation, and then distilled in stills, which at first glance seem to be encased in pitted black leather. Everything is controlled by hand and eye.

Adam Hannett (see page 226) is taking us round. Like Allan, he is an Ileach (native of Islay) but unlike his colleague, he left the island to go to university, then dropped out and returned.

'My dad said I should get a job with the distillery,' he says. 'His reckoning was at least I'd get a bottle of whisky.' In 2004, he started as a tour guide and had his first meeting with the boss, legendary distiller Jim McEwan, who, like Duncan and Simon Coughlin (now CEO of Rémy-Cointreau's international single-malt whisky division), were part of the 2001 takeover team. 'After speaking with Jim for ten minutes, I was hooked.' Fifteen years later, he's taken over from him as head distiller. 'Jim always wanted to give people chances. I had this love for whisky, even cleaning out the mashtun at 3am I felt was a privilege.

'Without me realizing it, he was passing things on to me, without any formal training. Then one day he came in, said "right boys", to Allan and me, "do you want to take over?" We both said "sure".

Left: Catching the flour
Right: The old-style mashtun at Bruichladdich
Opposite: Darkened by time

Nº 2
12,275 Litres
1975

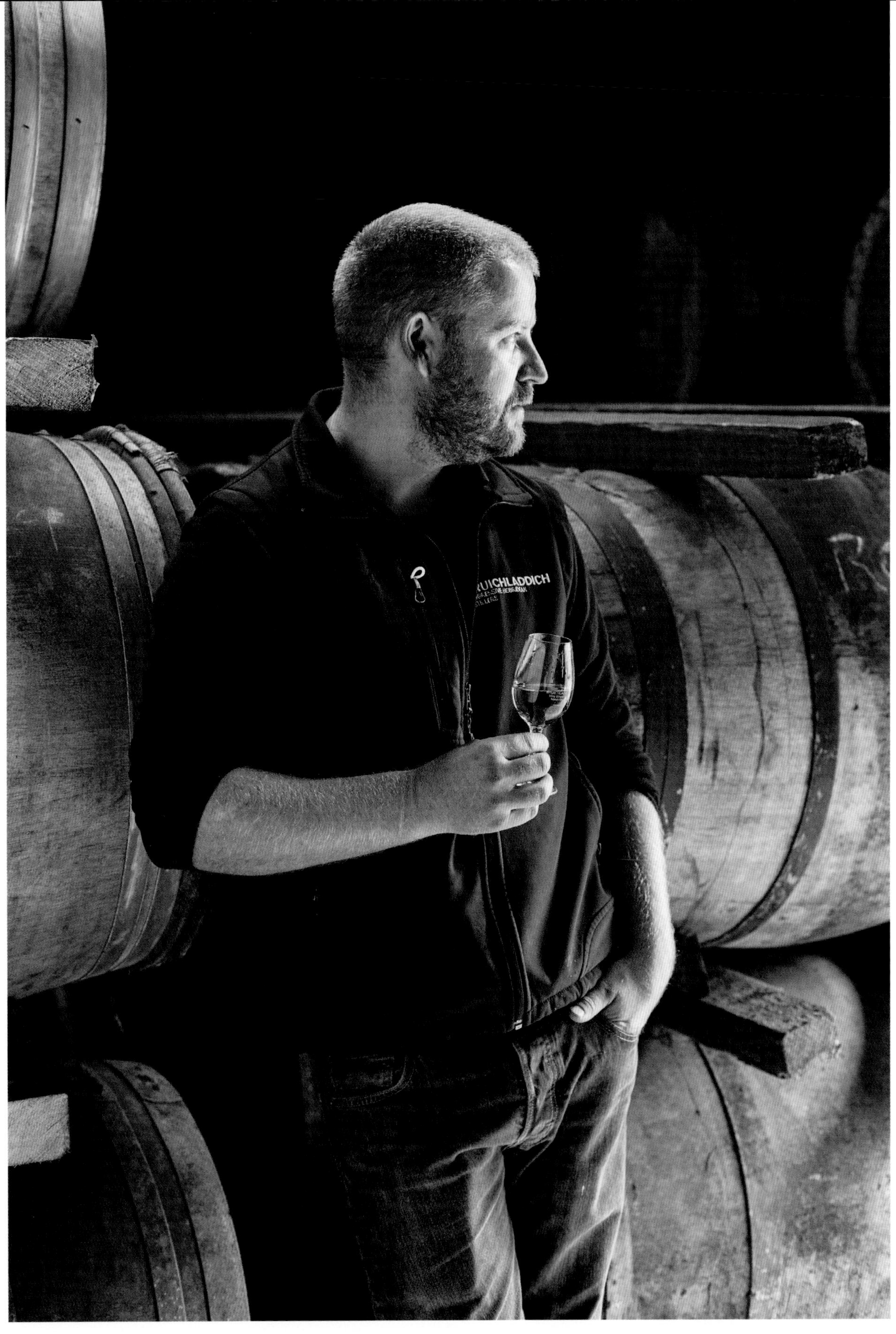

Adam Hannett, Bruichladdich's whisky-maker

'It was a pretty intense few months, learning the secrets. He said: "don't forget where you come from, who you are. Be your own man, do your own thing and you'll be fine." No pressure, then.

'I didn't want to come in and change everything. That's not what this distillery is about.' He pauses. 'It is about expressing the way we do things – the patience, the long ferments, the slow distillation, what we fill into.'

Like Allan, he's helped that transition to the new B Corp-certified Bruichladdich, which is now the largest private employer on Islay. It's evolved.

'In 2001, there was a need for things to be shaken up, and that's still in our DNA, but it has to stand for something. Make our rules then break them, that's the Bruichladdich way, isn't it?'

How conscious are you of the past?

'More and more, especially since we started to release some of the older vintages, the 1988s in particular. Bruichladdich works in second-fill casks if you give it time. The previous owners didn't have what we have and filled into crap casks, because that's all they had, but the spirit that went in was beautiful. You also want to honour the people who worked here in the old days: Budgie, Neil MacTaggart, Duncan, and be true to that past. It's not all about razzamatazz, it should always be about the sense of those people who are rooted in it. Making sure you don't forget that that connection with the past.'

Perspectives shift. In those early days, the need for cashflow meant, sensibly, that releases tended to be of young whiskies. Now, with greater financial security, Adam is laying down casks to be used in three decades' time, 'in that old, uncomplicated Bruichladdich style'.

It doesn't seem necessary to ask him what it means to make whisky in this place, but I ask anyway. He smiles quietly.

'One of the best things about lockdown was packing up a picnic and taking the kids to the beach. We'd just watch the kids run on the beach just...running...It was then that I got the sense of being in this place, being connected to it, drinking it in. This job is telling that story by distilling it; being part of the whole, understanding this connection to place.'

Can you distil it?

'I want to! But it is hard.' He pauses. 'It is more of an honesty thing, Dave. It's asking "what is an Islay whisky?" How can we be good to the community, how can we give people opportunities?

'The choice made by the directors when we reopened was to invest and do more for the folk on the island. It's important. Because we live here you have that option to do that, to do good for people.

'For me, it's having the pride of making whisky on the island and making it with Islay barley. Seeing the barley in the field and knowing that we will distil it; it's knowing the efforts the farmers go to, understanding them. Making that connection.'

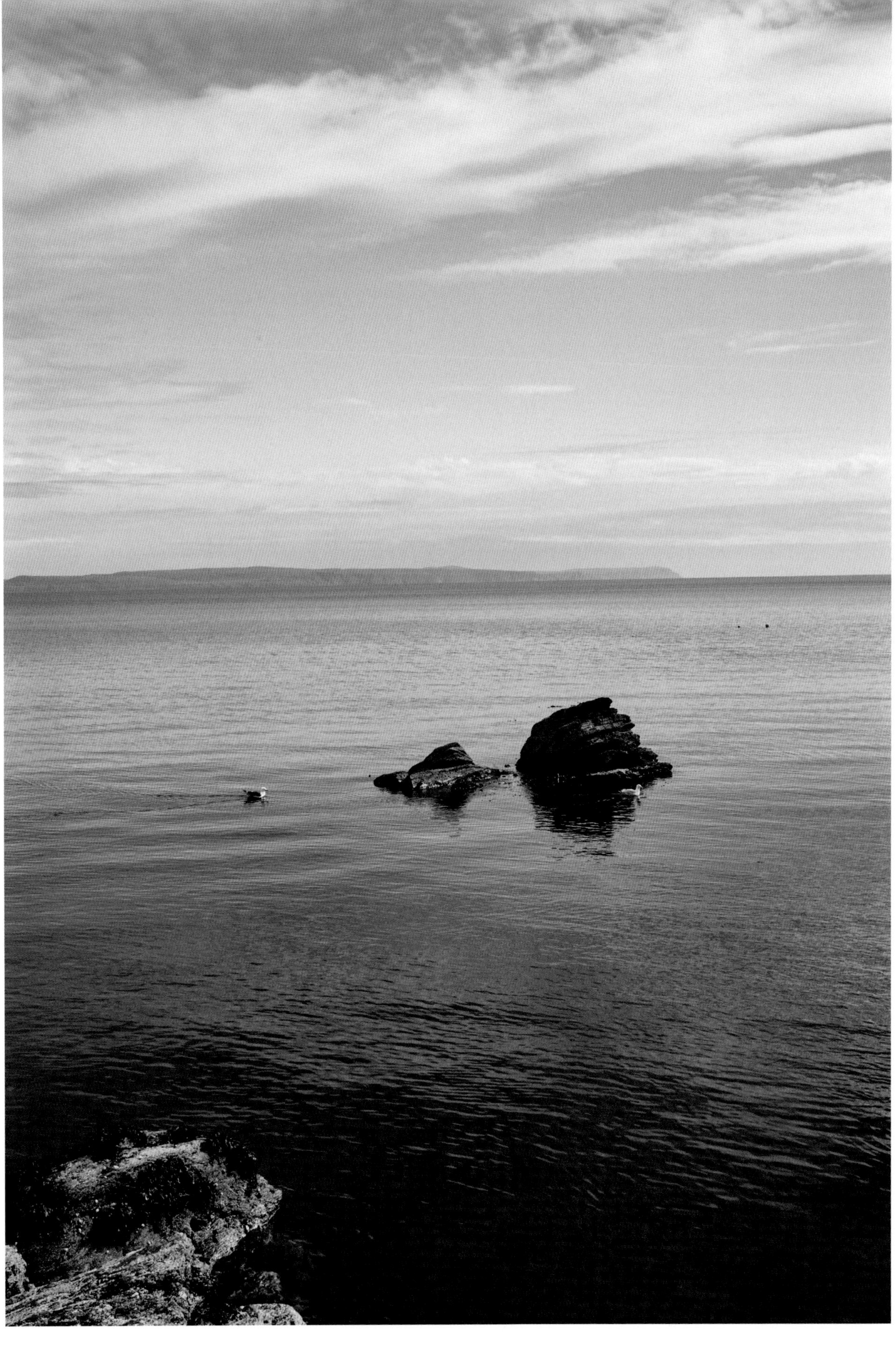

The first time the phrase 'whisky is about people' was said to me was in my first meeting with Jim McEwan. He worked at Bowmore then, but any time spent with him there or around the world was always about the bigger picture.

He'd drive me around Islay, slamming on the brakes so we could leap out to smell flowers and seaweed; he'd dump me in pubs and tell me which of the old guys I should speak to, getting me under the skin of this thing called whisky.

That line about people is often rolled out by marketing departments without any understanding of what it means. When I think of an Islay distillery I think of the people first, not the whisky: Jim, Duncan, Bowmore's Eddie McAffer and Ginger Willie; Lagavulin's Iain McArthur, Mike Nicolson and Donald Renwick; John Campbell and Iain Henderson at Laphroaig; Jackie Thompson and Mickey Heads of Ardbeg; John MacLellan at Bunnahabhain and Kilchoman, the Wills of Kilchoman; Billy Stitchell at Caol Ila; Georgie Crawford and Niall Colthart. Speak to any of them and they all speak of the island first, why it is special. It's in the blood, it gets under your skin.

'Adam and I don't just do the whisky thing,' Allan had said as he stood in the field for his portrait. 'We're both local lads. We care about the island. We're more about doing what's right for the distillery, the island, the community.'

...

We head south to Port Ellen for lunch, through the peat moss. Many times I've stood here, as a tutor on Diageo's Malts Advocates course. Lagavulin's Iain McArthur, warehouseman, crofter, wit and one-time star of the TV show *Parks & Recreation*. He'd be showing folks how to cut peat, why you take off the top layer and place it on the ground behind you (to allow the roots to knit and the bank to grow again). Why the top peat with all the rootlets was good for the smoke you need for whisky, and how the dense, coal-like bottom peat was used in houses for heat.

We'd be out there, a bunch of incompetents, a soundtrack of curlews and skylarks, irritated by midges and laughing at Iain's jokes. It was a tiny insight into an old, retained rhythm.

Peat helps define Islay's drams, partly because Islay's peat is different in composition. Although peat predominantly comprises sphagnum moss, the higher lignin in mainland peat produces a woodsmoke-like aroma, whereas Islay's peat moves things towards

Bruichladdich pier

the marine. Food scientist Harold McGee also posits that some of that marine character is down to bromophenols, created by bromine-laden rain carried from the ocean falling on to sphagnum moss.

If there is an Islay peat character, each distillery then stamps its own signature on it: Laphroaig's iodine, Ardbeg's soot, Lagavulin's Lapsang Souchong and bog myrtle, Bowmore's bonfire, Caol Ila's salt-washed rocks. I wonder how it will change Bruichladdich's Port Charlotte and Octomore when the maltings start.

Standing here, the peat moss seems like an endless resource, but there are significant issues around sustainability.

Covering approximately 18,000 square kilometres of Scotland, peatlands are an important carbon sink. Although, as Andrew Painting writes in his book *Regeneration*, pine trees are 15–25 per cent quicker in absorbing carbon, the trees will die or be felled. Peat bogs are ultimately more efficient at locking in carbon – until the peatlands are damaged.

It's been estimated that 80 per cent of the UK's peatlands are degraded, some irreparably so thanks to erosion and muirburn – where grouse moors are set on fire to regenerate heather (actually killing off all vegetation bar heather, which is then more flammable). 'Pristine peat bogs will capture around 0.9 per cent tonnes of CO_2 equivalent per hectare, per year,' writes Painting, 'but a hectare of damaged peat will emit between 1 and 23.8 tonnes of CO_2 equivalent depending on how much it is eroding. 'Restoring at least 50 per cent of upland peat and 25 per cent of lowland peat would reduce peatland emissions by 5 megatons of CO_2 equivalent by 2050.'

Although the whisky industry only removes annually between one and three per cent of the peat extracted in the UK, it has to be involved in the peatlands restoration project. In 2017, Diageo funded the restoration of 280 hectares on Islay, while Edrington is partnering with RSPB on Hobbister in Orkney. Suntory Holdings and Beam Suntory (owners of, among others, Laphroaig and Bowmore) has launched its Peatland Water Sanctuary™, a £3 million investment in the restoration and conservation of 1,300 hectares of peatlands by 2030.

'Sustainability is the right thing to do,' says Adam, as we meet up with him and Allan later. 'It is more expensive to buy a ton of Islay barley than a ton of organic barley. We could go 100 per cent organic and tick that sustainability box, but you can't greenwash things like that. What matters is what's happening here on the island, with our farmers.

'Growing barley is underpinning the agriculture of Islay. Do we wait until there is only enough soil on the island for ten more harvests, or do we start putting in more change now? Sustainability is about looking outside these gates and realizing that we have a big responsibility.'

...

Opposite: Islay's peat has a different composition to that of the mainland, resulting in different phenols

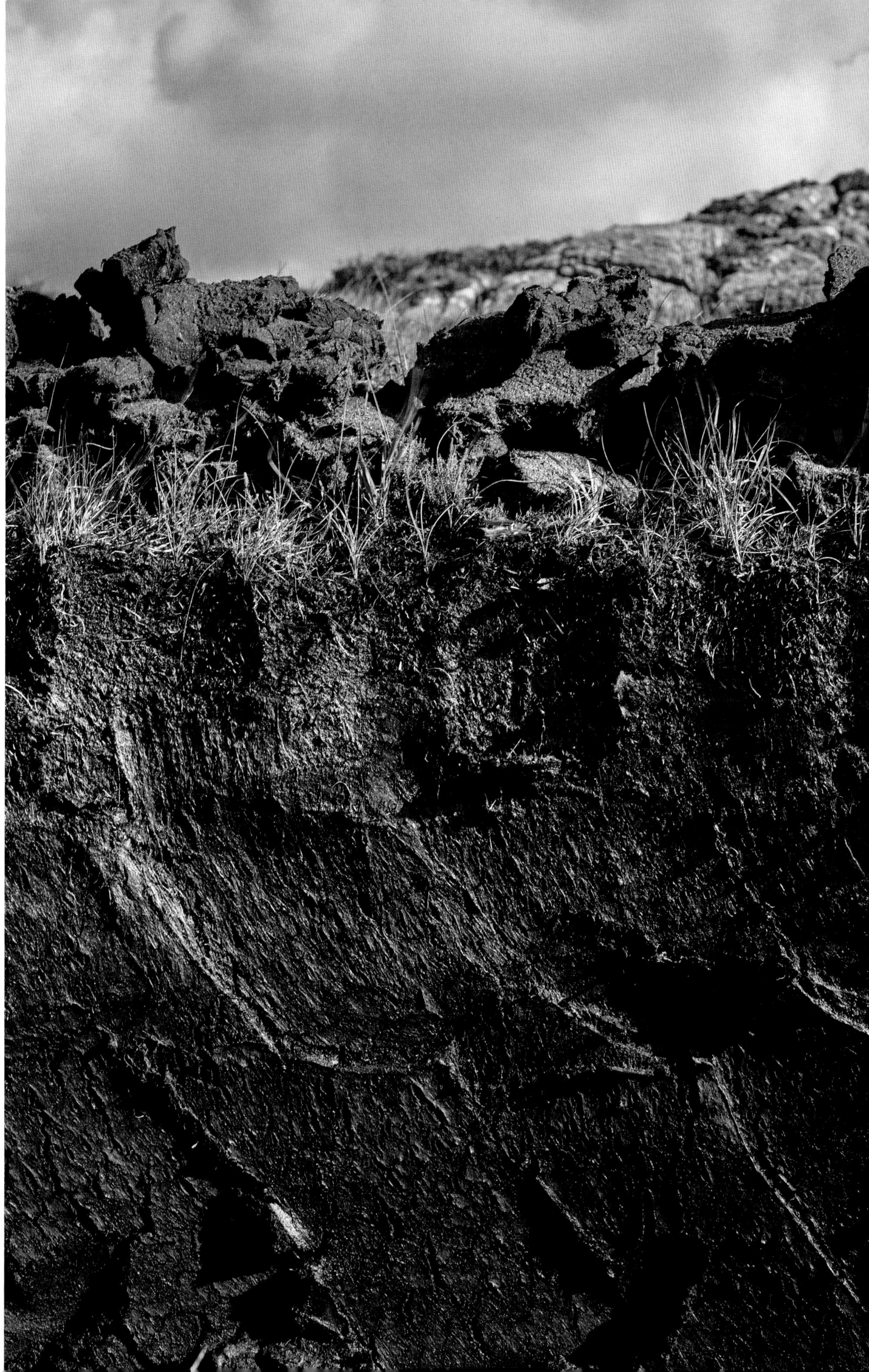

It's not the first time that the three of us have talked about this. In 2018, the distillery bought the croft next door. The question then was what to do with it. They invited a group of people: colleagues from their sister distilleries Westland in Seattle and Hautes Glaces in the French Alps; scientists from cereal research body the James Hutton Institute; Bairds Maltings; Peter Martin; biodynamic farmer Richard Gantlett; Islay farmers including Andrew; Jack Algiere from the pioneering Stone Barns in New York State; Professor Steve Jones from Washington State's Bread Lab...and me. Over two days we listened and discussed issues around sustainability, farming and distilling and what possible solutions could be tried. Retying the knots.

Westland is already further down this path, planting local Garryana oak, exploring local peat, and working with the Bread Lab to trial old forgotten varieties and new crosses – growing for flavour.

This touches on the idea being explored by the Raasay team (see page 158) – that if you're on the extreme west, with weather being flung at you, the same varieties that prosper on the drier, sunnier east coast might not work as well.

'Different varieties might be the key,' Andrew had said yesterday. 'It's going to have to come from trials in places like this. People also have to take the risk, but there also has to be a bit of joined-up thinking. The distillery needs to get what it wants, we need to see what varieties work the best.'

The risk factor was what played most heavily on Allan's mind. 'The most logical thing marketing wise would have been to grow barley on the croft and have a home-estate release, but we want to use the land for more purposeful ventures.

'What if we broke it up to look at soil health, barley varieties and other cereals, different cover crops, and rotation programmes to improve soil fertility and reduce inputs?

'We realized that we were asking the farmers to take all the risk in researching barley on Islay. We should be taking that risk and do the research on our own land, then share it with our partners who, hopefully, will adopt the same methods, which will benefit them and the whole island.'

He leans forward. 'If we find we can grow wheat, would we distil it, or mill it for flour and create an opportunity for a local bakery? Islay would have grown vegetables, but all of that's gone because they are competing against supermarkets. Could we find ways to re-establish local produce, local supply chains and import less food? Regenerative thinking.

'If we want to have a positive impact on the environment then we have to administer change. It isn't easy, but we're used to working against the tides.'

Not all of the ideas might come to fruition, but what the discussions demonstrated was the need for a holistic view of what whisky's role could (and should) be in a world which must become more sustainable.

If, and it is a big if, some of this works on Islay, what could it mean for the Hebrides and the west coast, not just for whisky, but agriculture? How then to adapt for the rest of the country?

What can grow here, how best to grow it, how does it benefit the community, what can be learned from the heritage, what can be introduced? All of the ideas that have been slowly amassing throughout this journey from Orkney to Islay are finally cohering. Whisky isn't just a liquid in a bottle, it is part of a whole. It sounds simple.

'In the old days, distilleries were a closed shop,' James Brown had said as we sat in his eyrie drinking Octomore. 'They were who they were, and we were just farmers. Good looking like! That's all changed.'

Bruichladdich played the terroir card pretty heavily, but its pivot to regenerative farming seems to have more in common with a bioregional approach.

'Initially we were trying to prove that barley grown on the west coast would be different to barley grown anywhere else, so there was an element of provenance,' says Adam. 'The strategy was to keep the releases young to see differences in vintage and location, but to be honest I think it's not always about that.

'Does it matter if it has a different flavour, or does it matter where that barley came from and that we have a deeper connection? If there is a difference at new make that's great, but for me the provenance is always more important.'

Octomore or Coull barley might be slightly different at new-make stage, but what really matters is that this whisky came from barley grown by James Brown, or Andrew Jones on their farms, that Kilchoman's '100%' Islay is from the farm itself. Not Islay barley because of marketing, or maybe even flavour, but because it is the right thing to do.

Once home, I compare the three new Octomores: the mix of earthy peat, honey and herbs in 12.1; the sweetly fruity depth given by ex-Sauternes casks lifting the smoke into a campfire setting in 12.2; then James' Octomore 12.3 sitting between them, with darker fruits, more animalic robust smoke and concentration.

A Port Charlotte made from Islay barley has the fragrance of burning sage and cedar incense mixed with red fruits. In the final glass, a 2011 bere barley grown by Petr Martin on Orkney. It's fresh, like lemon barley water, powdered almond, a hint of green fern, peaches, a hint of salinity. Our trip started on Orkney when the bere was still green. Now, on Islay, the harvest's coming in. Circles completed.

...

On the last day, Christina and I head east towards the mighty Caol Ila, which is readying itself for a new visitor centre, and the refurbished Bunnahabhain. Above the latter sits Islay's newest operational distillery (at time of writing), Ardnahoe. Islay is booming, thanks to whisky.

Port Ellen is reopening (with an 'experimental' still-house), Farkin is being built, Bowmore is returning to its legendary tropical-fruit style of the 1960s and '70s.

We follow a green track down the hill past old, once-coppiced woods, to a bothy on the beach. The rise and pulse of the seaweed, the brindled hills of Jura like the flanks of a deer. On top of one of its raised beaches is a lochan like an infinity pool. Gannets punch holes in the water. To the north is Colonsay and the hills of Mull.

How, then, to read Islay? It depends on your context. There's maps of soil, geology, archaeology; there's a farmer's map, a hiker's map. There's a goose map, an eagle map and a deer map; there's a swallow map and a dolphin map.

There's a map of wind with different meanings to fisherman, farmer and the guys malting barley who gauge its strength to judge how the fire will draw and how smoky that batch will be. The air has meaning.

There's a sound map, of birdsong, the incessant playground chatter of sparrows, the clattering of flag iris, the scrape of corncrake, the shriek of barn owl, the sound of laughter and songs, of shiels in the malt barns and the hiss of steam in the still houses, the knocking of gauging hammer against cask end and, behind it all, the incessant sound of the sea.

Aroma, place and whisky become interlinked: that honeyed, almond aroma by Kilchiaran Bay is Bruichladdich; the crab creels at Port Askaig are Caol Ila; you get oyster brine and machair sand in Kilchoman; herbal woodland notes in Bunnahabhain; Ardbeg's minerality and hot roads, Laphroaig's moss, and dried seaweed; Lagavulin's bog myrtle and rock pools and Bowmore's mix of flowers and salt; and through them all, Islay's smoke.

Islay cannot be fixed, nor can any of the other places we've visited. When we wear whisky goggles we only look at distilleries and curse when a castle's in the way. Can it be seen holistically? I look at the water. The tide is turning.

Secret beach, Sound of Islay; Jura's Paps

Epilogue

> *Human existence... unfolds not in places but along paths. Where inhabitants meet, trails are intertwined... Every entwining is a knot, and the more that lifelines are entwined, the greater density of the knot. Places, then, are like knots, and the threads from which they are tied are lines of wayfaring.*
> — Tim Ingold, *Being Alive*

The field is being steadily eaten by the combine. The end of another year here in the Howe of the Mearns (the fertile plain between the Grampians and the North Sea) and across Scotland. Next year, after malting, this crop will be heading a couple of miles down the road to Fettercairn distillery. Though this might seem logical, it is an exception to the norm. Being able to name the farm (or farms) used for a whisky is a rare occurrence.

This journey into place has also been about finding those lines that Ingold speaks of: those that tie people to place, bind communities together, as well as the lines of supply and realizing how many have become broken. The search for, and rediscovery of, place within whisky is also about retying those knots.

The fact that this barley will be going to its local distillery is thanks to Whyte & Mackay's Grow Scotland initiative, which aims to link farmers and maltings, in order to source locally for each of its distilleries. Fettercairn is now directly partnering with 180 local farmers.

Trying to establish those direct links is not simple, as Ian Palmer, MD of Fife's InchDairnie, points out. With a stated aim of provenance, flavour and low carbon footprint, he has experienced the problems of the commoditized barley market.

'In the past, when distillers simply wanted the same malted barley all year, the whole supply chain worked well,' he says. 'All the farmers grew the same varieties, which could be blended together at the maltings. It was set up to give homogeneity.

'The result was that maltings reduced in number and became larger, but the consequence was a disconnect with the farmer. Now, if you want to work from a specific farm or field, the current supply chain cannot cope. In my view, the whole supply chain – seed developer, farmer, grain merchant, maltster and distiller – need to be part of the conversation. If not, it will not work. The one-size-fits-all approach has had its day.'

Farmers are also restricted to only using barley varieties on the official recommended list, chosen to suit a system whose aim is to maximize tons per acre and litres of alcohol per ton. A farmer could grow a non-approved variety, but it couldn't be malted because of the way in which the system is set up.

It's a model that has been challenged by Washington State's Bread Lab. The mission of Steve Jones and his team is to make 'good, delicious

food accessible at a reasonable price point'. They have a bank of 40,000 grains (wheat, barley, buckwheat, beans) and trial between 5,000 and 10,000 new ones each year.

As Steve told me, 'We develop wheat and barley that works best for farmer first, and then we have the lab to define its best use – it could be bread, beer or whiskey, but it has to work for the farmer.

'The wheat commodity has reduced the wheat in the world to two varieties, red or white, feeding an industrialized system making bread with zero nutrition. The wheats being developed around the world aren't best for the farmers, but best for the industry.'

The parallels with barley are striking. It too is drawing from a narrow genetic base, there's the same drive for yield and efficiencies, while low prices to the farmer increase the need for higher yields, meaning more inputs, resulting in degraded soil. A vicious circle.

These factors lie behind the creation of the International Barley Hub (IBH) located at the James Hutton Institute (JHI) in Dundee. 'We grow spring barley drawn from this narrow genetic pool, all of which is harvested at the same time,' says Professor James Brosnan, director of the Scotch Whisky Research Institute. 'That's a lot of eggs in one basket. One of our projects at the IBH is trying to broaden the genetic diversity and spread the risk.'

This also involves breeding varieties that avoid GMO, can cope with changes in weather and require lower inputs. When nitrogen fertilizers

Re-examining sustainability starts with resources: barley (left), peat (right)

react with microbes in the soil, high levels of nitrous oxide are produced. It is 265 times more effective at trapping heat in the atmosphere than carbon dioxide.

I think back to all of the conversations about finding varieties to suit conditions, to grow for flavour, to rebuild links with farmers. The system seems stacked against such important moves. Not only in the fields, but in the ability to process small batches. Maltings are not set up to do this.

This was the dilemma faced by Alison Milne and her husband Daniel who farm 750 acres in Auchtermuchty, Fife. Their solution? A small-scale maltings called Crafty Maltsters. 'Scottish barley is world-leading,' she says, 'but there was a mismatch in small-scale distilling's desire for provenance of barley, and the inability to support it.

'There's a reason we're focused on yield, there is a reason we're forced to use fertilizers and chemicals – it's because the supply chain has forced us in that direction, but we want to grow varieties that are best suited for our farm, that give the best flavour. We wanted to challenge the idea that barley is a commodity, and that the variety doesn't matter in terms of flavour.'

Crafty Maltsters now works with the JHI, growing bere sourced on Orkney, and the heritage varieties Scotch Common and Scotch Annat, which are distilled by the Thompson brothers at Dornoch. They have also malted Scandinavian variety Salome for Raasay.

'It's rebuilding a fractured supply chain and creating that place beyond commodity for those distillers who are looking for some sort of differentiation in flavour, and provenance. Telling the story about the people and the place behind the barley.'

'Alison is on to a winner,' says Palmer, 'but our requirements are too large to be able to use her. There needs to be this parallel supply chain for mid-sized distillers who are wanting to break free from this homogenized system. The logical conclusion is more local maltings.'

There is a more fundamental need for this. As sustainability becomes the driving force for the industry, cereals will have to be grown locally to help reduce carbon footprint.

The sustainability issue also incorporates peat. With the banning of horticultural peat extraction in 2024, the focus will suddenly be on whisky. I chatted with peatland scientist Dr Mike Billett, author of forthcoming book *The Story of Peat and Whisky*.

'The goal of the whisky industry must be to embrace the sustainable use of peat,' he says. 'And that doesn't mean planting trees. It means investing in a programme of peatland restoration that captures on an annual basis at least the same amount, ideally more, carbon from the atmosphere than extraction and combustion releases.'

He feels it could happen. 'Scotland is one of the world leaders in the science of peatland restoration. We now know that, depending on the site, it is entirely feasible to return a degraded peatland to a functioning ecosystem within 10–20 years. So, the rewards are enormous. If the

 Opposite: Peat restoration is vital

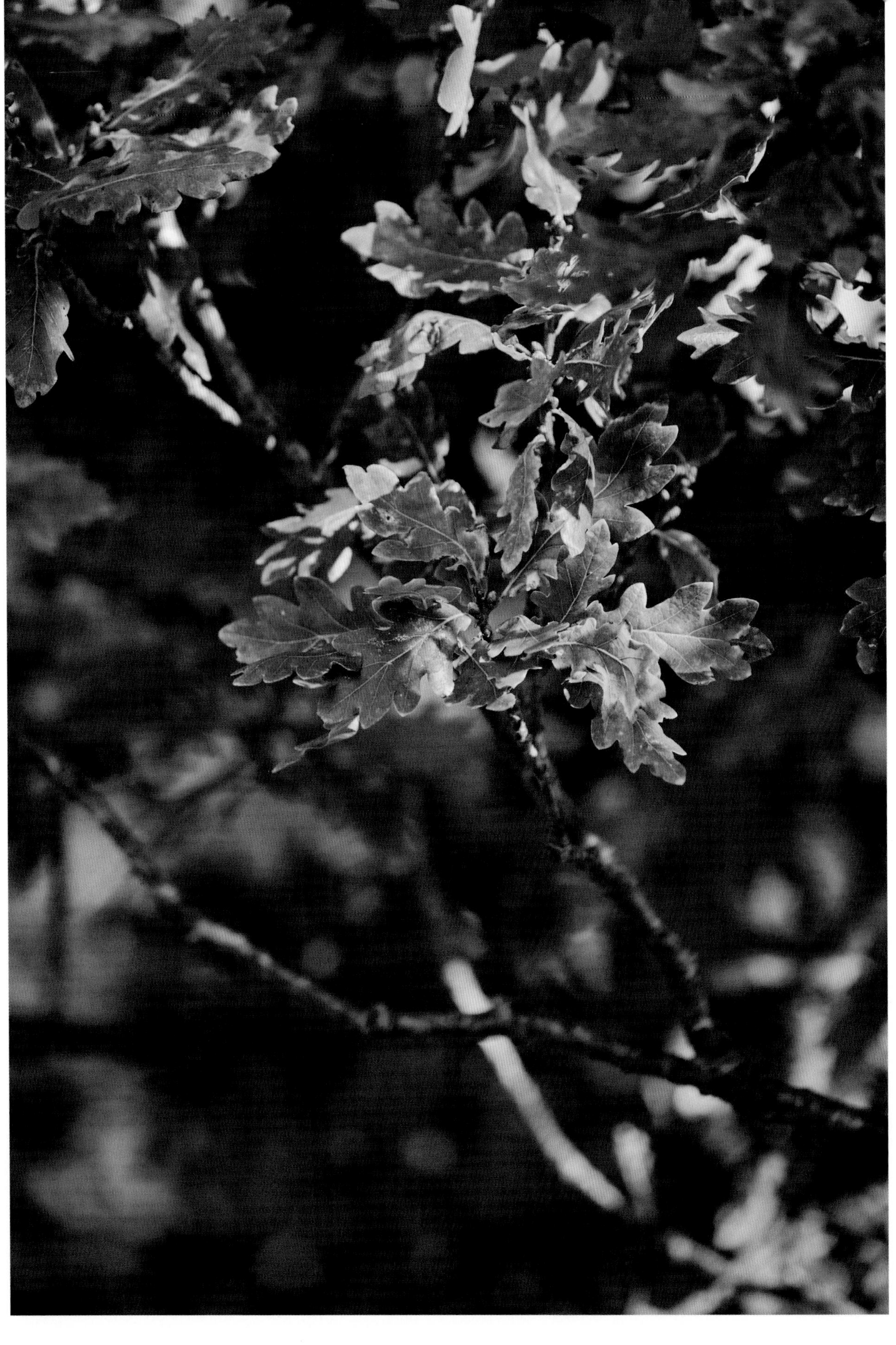

Replanting native woodlands is part of the larger picture for whisky

industry acts now, it will be in a much stronger position in the future.' The increased moral and social responsibility to community and planet is all allied to place.

We've met some of the distillers engaging with this already, but it is also worth mentioning the farm distilleries Arbikie and Daftmill, and the experimental approach being taken by Edinburgh's Holyrood.

There is a tendency to presume that these concepts are exclusive to new distilleries, but the model for much of this is Campbeltown's Springbank, which until recently most 'modern' distillers considered to be hopelessly antediluvian in its equipment and approach. It is the only distillery in Scotland to malt, distil, age and bottle on the same site, and should be seen as the model for this new wave, from Alex Bruce's search for the so-called west-coast style, to the producion of multiple distillates from one plant, the increase in self-sufficiency, the use of local barley and, most of all, the understanding of the role a distillery plays within a community. In Campbeltown's case, this means providing employment and security in a town where jobs are at a premium. Springbank was sustainable before the word was coined.

The Wee Toon is undergoing a revival. As well as the resurgent Glen Scotia, the owners of Isle of Raasay are building a new distillery at nearby Machrihanish, which will exclusively use locally grown barley. Other distilleries are also planned.

This journey set out to explore the links between people, whisky and place. It has ended with an understanding of how complex the web of culture, craft, climate, geology, history, farming, distillation and land is. None of these factors can be removed from this liquid called Scotch whisky. It is a global spirit, but the solutions to take it forward are surely local.

Making whisky in the Anthropocene age will be different, and difficult. Knots will have to be retied. Distillers need to work with foresters, farmers, maltsters and conservationists. It will mean reappraising history, rediscovering forgotten links, finding new solutions and looking beyond 'brand Scotch', and even 'brand Scotland'.

'Some people have strange ideas that they live by money,' wrote Patrick Geddes. 'They think energy is generated by the circulation of coins, whereas the world is mainly a vast leaf-colony...We live not by the jingling of our coins, but by the fullness of our harvests...By leaves we live.'

Place is more than just a marketing tool: it is a visceral link with land, community, the past and the present, an active engagement with all the conditions that brought whisky to life.

Glossary

alembic another term for a pot still

awns the fine, hair-like bristles on barley stems

bannock (Scottish) a basic form of round unleavened bread, often enriched with butter or milk

barm the froth that forms on top of fermented liquid such as beer, and which can be used as a leavening agent

bere an ancient form (landrace) of barley

boil ball a bulbous protrusion at the base of the neck of a still, which increases *reflux*

bonxie (Scottish) a large seabird, also known as the great skua

bothies (Scottish) basic buildings, often used as the site of illicit stills

browst (Scottish) a brewing of ale, tea or spirit

burn a large stream or small river

chime the small lip at the top of a cask

Clearances the forced evictions of people who lived in the Highlands and western islands of Scotland during the eighteenth and nineteenth centuries

cleg (Scottish) a horsefly

condenser the attachment on a still where alcohol vapour is turned back into liquid (spirit)

cut point a crucial point in the distillation process, at which different parts of the distillate are separated out in order to capture certain elements and eliminate others

congeners chemical compounds formed during the fermentation process that give distinctive characteristics to alcoholic drinks

draff the residue of spent grains in the *mash tun*, which can then be used as animal feed

dreich (Scottish) dreary weather

dunnage warehouse traditional stone-walled, earth-floored building used for maturing whisky

esters chemical compounds created when alcohols and acids interact. They provide fruity aromas

feints aka 'tails'. The third and final part of the second distillation, containing characters unwanted in the final spirit

feints receiver a vessel in which *feints* are collected

foreshots aka 'heads'. The first part of the second distillation. It is diverted into a tank, mixed with *feints* and *low wines*, then redistilled

glaur (Scottish) mud or mire

griot (West African) a person responsible for passing on oral history in the form of storytelling, music and poetry

grist milled malted barley. Mixed with hot water in the *mash tun* to produce sweet *wort*

guddle (Scottish) a muddle or confusion

haar (Scottish) a cold sea mist or fog

howff (Scottish) a pub

katabatic a fierce downslope wind made of dense cold air

lie pipe (or, also, lyne arm) the part of a still that joins the neck to the *condenser*

lochan (Scottish) a small loch

low wine the product of the first distillation in the making of malt whisky

machair (Gaelic) sandy, fertile grassland found on the western shores of the Hebrides

malt floor the space where steeped barley is spread out and left to germinate

mash tun a large vessel in which grain is mixed with water to release its sugars

midden pile or mound an ancient dump of organic waste

new make the clear spirit that comes out of the still. By law, the term 'Scotch whisky' can only be used after the new make has been aged in oak casks for three years

peat hag ground from which peat has been cut

pibroch/piobaireachd (Scottish/Gaelic) a solo musical composition for bagpipes, based on variations on a theme

puncheon a specific type of cask with a capacity of 500 litres

reflux the redistillation of vapour within the still. The higher the rate of reflux, the lighter the spirit will be

shebeen (Scottish) a place where alcohol is sold illegally

shiel a maltman's shovel

shielings (Scottish) simple huts in high pastureland; the high summer grazing

shoogly (Scottish) wobbly

skailk (Gaelic) a blow to the head; first dram of the day, often taken in bed

smirr (Scottish) fine but penetrating rain

spirit safe a locked container through which distillate flows. It is here the distiller can measure strength and separate the middle cut from the *foreshots* and *feints*

strath (Scottish) a broad, flat river valley

stook (Scottish) a stack of cut grain stalks that have been stood on end to keep their grain ends off the ground

stott (Scottish) to bounce or stagger

stromatolite layered microbial mats of limestone sediment formed by algae and bacteria that helped to increase the amount of oxygen in Earth's atmosphere

washback a large vessel in which yeast is added to the *wort* to start fermentation

worm tub the traditional form of *condenser*, consisting of a coiled copper pipe immersed in cold water

wort the sweet liquid drained from the base of the *mash tun*

Notes

p.14 – 'The common conception of evolution…': Snyder, Gary, *The Practice of the Wild: Essays*, San Francisco: North Point Press, 1990
p.53 – 'My love the dun fellow' [1650]: from An Ciaran Mabach, 'On His Exile In Edinburgh', in Black, Ronald (ed.), *An Lasair: Anthology of 18th Century Scottish Gaelic Verse*, Edinburgh: Birlinn, 2001
p.53 – 'It is in general in the hands of poor illiterate farmers…': Keith, George Skene, *State of Facts, Relative to the Scotch Distillery*, Aberdeen: A. Brown, 1798
p.54 – 'was also a smuggler…': Sage, Donald, *Memorabilia Domestica*, Wick: W. Rae, 1899
p.55 – 'the most extraordinary example…': Hunter, James, *Set Adrift upon the World: The Sutherland Clearances*, Edinburgh: Birlinn, 2015
pp.55–6 – 'the people [were] brought…': *Papers on Sutherland Estate Management, 1802–1816* (ed. by R.J. Adam), Edinburgh: printed for the Scottish Historical Society by T. & A. Constable, 1972
p.56 – 'nursed the people…': *Papers on Sutherland*, 1972
p.66 – 'inexplicable scent of honey…': Gunn, Neil M., *Highland River*, Edinburgh: Canongate, 1996 [1937]
p.66 – 'Keep silent and still…', Gunn, Neil M., 'The Flash', in *Landscape to Light* (compiled by Alistair McLeery and Dairmid Gunn), Dunbeath: Whittles, 2009

p.66 – 'I do not know…': Gunn, Neil M., *The Atom of Delight*, Edinburgh: Polygon, 1986
p.68 – 'called it by the English name of Gordonbush…': https://www.ainmean-aite.scot/placename/gordonbush/, accessed 17 March 2022
p.71 – 'Community can be defined...': Quoted in Stephen, Walter M. (ed), *Think Global, Act Local: The Life and Legacy of Patrick Geddes,* Edinburgh: Luath Press, 2018
p.71 – 'entirely packed and crammed…': *Papers on Sutherland*, 1972
p.76 – 'We spent time trying to accompany it…': https://www.youtube.com/watch?v=UlvHpjxmuAw, accessed 17 March 2022
p.81 – 'rugged individuality': Gunn, Neil M., *Whisky and Scotland: A Practical and Spiritual Survey*, London: Souvenir Press, 1988 [1935]
p.85 – 'the mode of living…': Sinclair, John, *The Statistical Account of Scotland, volume XVII*, Edinburgh: Creech, 1796
p.105 – 'the wards of Buckie, Elgin City North…': 'The Scotch Whisky Regulations 2009' https://www.legislation.gov.uk/uksi/2009/2890/regulation/10/made, accessed 17 March 2022
p.115 – 'The land is often perceived through a prism of animism…: Murray, John, *Literature of the Gaelic Landscape: Song, Poem, Tale*, Dunbeath: Whittles, 2017
p.115 – 'delightful on a spring day…': Mac Mhaighstir Alisdair, Alasdair, 'The Royal Bottle Song' [18th century], quoted in Wittig, Kurt, *The Scottish Tradition In Literature*, Edinburgh, London: Oliver & Boyd, 1958
p.115 – 'thigging…gets a fill…': from MacIntyre, Duncan Ban, 'Oran do Chaora' (Song to a Ewe), in Black (ed.), 2001
p.117 – 'The passion caused…': Burke, Edmund, *A Philosophical Enquiry…*, Oxford: Oxford University Press, 2015
p.121 – 'The Highlands which…': Hunter, James, *On the Other Side of Sorrow: Nature and People in the Scottish Highlands,* Edinburgh: Mainstream, 1995
p.125 – 'the human mother…': Gunn, Neil M., *Butcher's Broom*, London: Souvenir Press, 1987 [1934]
p.129 – 'The woodland like…': Loose, Gerry, *An Oakwoods Almanac*, Bristol: Shearsman Books, 2015
p.137 – 'how can we carry on…': Ingold, Tim, *Being Alive: Essays on Movement, Knowledge and Description*, London: Routledge, 2011
p.141 – 'along which life is lived…This tangle is…': Ibid.
p.144 – 'there was probably…': Smout T.C. (ed.), *People and Woods in Scotland: A History*, Edinburgh: Edinburgh University Press, 2003
p.145 – 'Yesterday I was on the moor…': MacIntyre, Duncan Ban, 'Final Farewell To The Bens' (1802), in Black (ed.), 2001
pp.145–6 – 'all of these ultimately reduce…': Smout, T.C. (ed.), 2003
p.164 – 'and my love is at the burn…': MacLean, Sorley, *From Wood to Ridge*, Manchester: Carcanet/Edinburgh: Birlinn, 1999. Reprinted by kind permission of Carcanet Press, Manchester, UK.
p.167 – 'Casting a net…': Murray, *Literature*, 2017
p.178 – 'Then there are the katabatic…': Stephen, Ian, 'Seilebost', from *Maritime: New and Selected Poems*, Salford: Saraband, 2016. © Ian Stephen 2016, published by Saraband.
pp.181–2 – '[A bioregion is] a place…': Sale, Kirkpatrick, *Dwellers In The Land: The Bioregional Vision*, Athens: Georgia University Press, 2000
p.182 – 'To know the spirit…': Snyder, 1990
p.182 – '"Place" itself can be…': McFadyen, Mairi, 'The Cultural-Ecological Imagination of Patrick Geddes (1854–1932), www.mairimcfadyen.scot/blog/2015/8/2/patrick-geddes, accessed 11 March 2022

p.182 – 'think global, act local': Boardman, Philip, *The Worlds of Patrick Geddes: Biologist, Town Planner, Re-Educator, Peace-Warrior*, London: Routledge and Kegan Paul, 1978
p.230 – 'Pristine peat bogs...': Painting, Andrew, *Regeneration: The Rescue of a Wild Land*, Edinburgh: Birlinn, 2021
p.238 – 'Human existence…': Ingold, 2011
p.245 – 'Some people have strange ideas…': Quoted in Stephen (ed.), 2018

Further Reading

Barnhill, David Landis (ed.), *At Home on the Earth: Becoming Native to Our Place*, Berkeley, London: University of California Press, 1999
Black, Ronald (ed.), *An Lasair: Anthology of 18th Century Scottish Gaelic Verse*, Edinburgh: Birlinn, 2001
Card, Nick, Edmonds, Mark, and Mitchell, Anne (eds), *The Ness of Brodgar: As It Stands*, Kirkwall: The Orcadian, 2021
Collinson, Francis, *The Life and Times of William Grant*, Dufftown: William Grant & Sons, 1979
Davidson, Peter, *Distance and Memory*, Manchester: Carcanet, 2013
Devine, T.M., *The Scottish Clearances: A History of the Dispossessed, 1500–1900*, London: Penguin Books, 2018
Fowler, John, *Landscapes and Lives: The Scottish Forest Through the Ages*, Edinburgh: Canongate, 2002
Gairn, Louisa, *Ecology and Modern Scottish Literature*, Edinburgh: Edinburgh University Press, 2008
German, Kieran and Adamson, Gregor, 'Distilling in The Cabrach c.1800–1850: The Illicit Origins of the Scotch Whisky Industry', *Journal of Scottish Historical Studies*, vol. 39, no. 2, November 2019, pp.146–65
Leask, Nigel, *Stepping Westward: Writing the Highland Tour c.1720–1830*, Oxford: Oxford University Press, 2020
Lynch, Tom, Glotfelty, Cheryll and Armbruster, Karla (eds), *The Bioregional Imagination: Literature, Ecology and Place*, Athens: University of Georgia Press, 2012
MacCaig, Norman, *Between Mountain and Sea: Poems from Assynt* (ed. by Roderick Watson), Edinburgh: Polygon, 2018
Macdonald, Murdo, *Patrick Geddes's Intellectual Origins*, Edinburgh: Edinburgh University Press, 2020
MacGill-Eain, Somhairly [MacLean, Sorley], *Ris a'Bhrutaich: The Criticism and Prose Writings of Sorley MacLean*, Stornoway: Acair, 1985
MacKenzie, Garry, *Ben Dorain, A Conversation with a Mountain*, Belfast: The Irish Pages Press, 2021
Purves, Graeme, 'Scottish Environmentalism – The Contribution of Patrick Geddes', https://graemepurves.wordpress.com/2014/03/08/scottish-environmentalism-the-contribution-of-patrick-geddes/, 8 May 2014, accessed 10 March 2022
'Frank Mears – A Pioneer of Scottish Planning', https://graemepurves.wordpress.com//?s=frank+mears+pioneer&search=Go, 20 October 2014, accessed 10 March 2022
Smout, T.C., *Exploring Environmental History: Selected Essays*, Edinburgh: Edinburgh University Press, 2011
Webster, David, *A Guide to the Geology of Islay: An Introduction to Islay's Geological Past with 12 Illustrative Walking Excursions*, Glasgow: Ringwood Publishing, 2015

Thanks

First, to Christina, the perfect partner in crime. You got this crazy idea immediately, and captured it in ways I could not have imagined. Your vision has made this book the beautiful volume it is.

Starting from the north, my thanks to all who made us so welcome on Orkney: John Strachan, Charlotte Harrison, Jason Craig, Peter Martin, John Wishart and Nick Card. To the be-tweeded Brora boys: Andy Flatt, Stewart Bowman, Ewan Gunn and Kevin Innes. Long may the gunk grow. Also to Sid's Spice for saving two hungry souls. To Phil Thompson, Jacob Crisp and Euan Christie, Brodie Nairn and Nicky Burns and the staff at Dornoch Links Hotel.

Our trip to Dufftown was given extraordinary new levels of information, wine and laughs thanks to the ministrations of Kirsten Grant Meikle, Vicki Rimmell, Andy Fairgrieve, Dennis McBain, Ian Mac and Grant Gordon. Andrew at Speyside Cooperage has been a fount of knowledge. To Alan Winchester for his unparalleled knowledge and excellent company, and George Grant for being himself.

In the west, thanks to Amy Stammers (and Doug), Annabel Thomas, and Gordon Wood at Nc'nean, while Alex and Vikki Bruce, Connal Mackenzie, Graeme Mackay, Stewart Connor and Sandy and Liz Macdonald (and the deerhound) made our stay at the castle both relaxed, remarkable and suitably surreal.

In the Hebrides, thanks to Neil Mathieson and the Torabhaig team. Alasdair Day, Norman Gillies, Eilean Green and Cuddy all went out of their way to show true hospitality. It has been an honour to be able to see Raasay grow. The Hearachs helped to pull many threads together. Thanks Mike Donald (and Mara), Simon Erlanger, Kenny MacLean, Bill Lawson, Donald John Mackay and Sam's Seafood Shack.

Jim Beveridge and Emma Walker were, as ever, generous with time and intellect, while Imogen Russon-Taylor deserves massive success for her singular vision.

To Gregg Glass, Kieran Healey-Rider, Trees for Life and Stewart Walker; and John Galvin, for not only an astonishing insight into his craft, but his love of great craic.

On Islay, Christy MacFarlane, Allan Logan, Adam Hannett, James Brown and Andrew Jones; while David and Ewan Graham at the Ballygrant Inn kept us both fed and, equally importantly, well-watered.

Mike Billett gave invaluable insights into peat. Ian Palmer, Alison Milne and Professor James Brosnan gave their time to share thoughts on farming and barley, while Professor Steve Jones is an inspiration and a friend. One day we will mill together and bake well-fired rolls.

The Malt Room, Pot Still and Last Word all supplied restorative drams at exactly the right times. Ailana Kamelmacher and Tarita Mullings from The Story exhibited supreme patience and perseverance when all seemed lost, while Cal-Mac and Loganair got us there and back safely.

Thanks too to human sounding boards John Scott, Douglas and Hazel Lipton, Annabel Meikle, Tom Williams, Fionnán O'Connor; and Dawn Davies and the Luncheon Club for sage advice freely given.

To Adam Park for having the mad idea for *The Amber Light*, which helped to cohere some of these ideas, and for being a great walking companion.

Some of these ideas were generated from the Liquid Antiquarian YouTube channel, which my dear friend Arthur Motley persuaded me to co-host. It's been a delight. Thanks also to Professor Niall Mackenzie, Jo McKerchar and Iain Russell for helping to add to and temper our amateur enthusiasms.

At Octopus: Denise Bates, Faye Robson, Juliette Norsworthy, Megan Brown and Matt Grindon. And at Praline: Max Casey. This is a team effort, and what a team they are. It is a delight to work with them all and I so appreciate their trust in me over the years, especially Denise, who is leaving for a new challenge. Best of luck!

To Jo and Rosie, who have not only yet again put up with the madness of book writing, but have also been with me on some of the actual journey. I love you both.

From Christina

Thank you to Dave for bringing me along on this adventure, yelling in the pouring rain with me, chasing elusive pockets of sun and championing me and my work, you have become a firm friend. My thanks, also, to everyone we photographed.

To Chetiawardwinner for introducing me to the world of whisky in the first place. Hen, for always supporting me and talking all the sense. Ann Lou, my cheerleader. Simon, for being the easiest person to work with and for making these images sing. Dad, turns out photography is a valid career choice; thank you for that first camera. The Mother ship, who had an unwavering belief in me and whom I wish could see this and more.

To my husband Neil for pushing me, making me think bigger and holding the fort while I gallivanted across Scotland in search of stories and drams. I love you.

Last, but by no means least, my incredible daughter Alba: you are and continue to be my greatest inspiration. And yes, soon you can come to work with Mama.

Dave Broom has written 13 books, including *The World Atlas of Whisky*, now in its second edition. He has won many awards, including two Glenfiddich prizes and, in 2013, the prestigious IWSC Communicator of the Year Award. In 2015, he won The Spirited Award for Best Cocktail & Spirits writer, and, in 2018, *The Way of Whisky* won an André Simon prize. In 2020 he was awarded Best Drinks Writer at the Fortnum & Mason awards.

He has been a contributing editor to *Whisky Magazine*, scotchwhisky.com and *Malt Advocate*. In 2020 he started his own website thewhiskymanual.uk. He has made two films, 'Cuba In A Bottle' and 'The Amber Light'. The latter, an examination on whisky and Scottish culture, won Best Programme at the 2020 Fortnum & Mason awards.

Over his three-plus decades in the field, Dave has built up a considerable international following with regular training / educational visits to Japan, France, Holland, Scandinavia, Germany, Africa and North America. He is actively involved in whisky education and also acts as a consultant to major distillers on tasting techniques as well as training professionals and the public. Dave has also worked with Suntory in developing a language of tasting that communicates Japanese concepts to English speaking audiences.

Dave's previous books also include *Whisky: The Manual*, *Gin: The Manual*, *Rum: The Manual* and *The Way of Whisky*.